Francesca Biancani is Adjunct Professor of History and Institutions of the Modern Middle East in the Faculty of Political Science of Bologna University. She is also Postdoctoral Fellow at the French Institute for Oriental Archeology (IFAO) and the Centre d'études et de documentation économiques, juridiques et sociales (CEDEJ) in Cairo.

'Francesca Biancani exhibits a knowledge of Egyptian history that begins in the eighteenth century and extends to the uprising of the Free Officers, thereby indicating her grasp not only of Egyptian history but also of a new development in the history of Egypt, namely, the appearance of prostitution, i.e. sex work, as the portal of modernity. Biancani should also be commended for the use of the archives and their contribution to the volume. Readers of the book will be rewarded with a finely written and researched historical volume. Non-specialists of Egyptian history will find much to engage with as well.'

Mary Ann Fay, Associate Professor of History,
Morgan State University; author of *Unveiling the Harem:
Elite Women and the Paradox of Seclusion in Eighteenth-Century Cairo*

'Sex Work in Colonial Egypt is engaging, informative and offers readers a glimpse into the lives of women whose experiences have largely been unaccounted for in historical literature. There is a great deal to learn here about the structure of colonial rule in Egypt, and British and Egyptian constructions of race and racial hierarchies; the book demonstrates exactly how both local and colonial anxieties were inscribed on the bodies of Cairo's sex workers.'

Lisa Pollard, Professor Emerita, University of North Carolina
Wilmington; author of *Nurturing the Nation: The Family Politics of
Modernizing, Colonizing and Liberating Egypt, 1805–1923*

SEX WORK IN COLONIAL EGYPT

Women, Modernity and the Global Economy

FRANCESCA BIANCANI

I.B. TAURIS

LONDON · NEW YORK

Published in 2018 by
I.B.Tauris & Co. Ltd
London • New York
www.ibtauris.com

Library of Middle East History 72

ISBN: 978 1 78831 103 8
eISBN: 978 1 78672 483 0
ePDF: 978 1 78673 483 9

A full CIP record for this book is available from the British Library
A full CIP record is available from the Library of Congress

Library of Congress Catalog Card Number: available

Typeset in Garamond Three by OKS Prepress Services, Chennai, India
Printed and bound by CPI Group (UK) Ltd, Croydon, CR0 4YY

To the memory of my beloved father Gianni Biancani, and to Giovanni and Martino, a concentrate of giggling joy and hope.

CONTENTS

LIST OF ILLUSTRATIONS

Figures

Table

ACKNOWLEDGEMENTS

I am very pleased to acknowledge and express my deepest gratitude to those who helped me in many ways during the years I spent working on this project, which slowly morphed from my doctoral dissertation into a book.

First of all I thank my former PhD supervisor, Professor John Chalcraft, for demolishing my original doctoral project in the most gracious and tactful way possible, during our very first supervision meeting. In spite of an initial fit of desperation, I have to thank him for challenging me to think about my project creatively and indicating some points for reflection, from which I developed the core of the present book, almost ten years ago. He believed in the project, encouraged me through the various stages of writing, carefully reading, editing and offering insightful critiques on a number of previous drafts of the manuscript. His analytical acumen and intellectual rigor constituted, and still are today, a powerful inspiration for me. I would like to extend my thanks to my advisor, Dr Sharad Chari, and to Professor Marilyn Booth and Dr Nelida Fuccaro for taking the time to read and thoughtfully comment on several chapters of this work, and in general for their encouragement and kindness. Of course, neither of them should be blamed for any inconsistencies or errors the reader may find in the text, as I am to be considered solely responsible for any shortcoming.

My research was made possible thanks to the generous financial help from a number of institutions I would like to take the chance to acknowledge here: the London School of Economics, the University of London Central Research Fund and the Gibb Memorial Trust.

The project benefited from feedback received at a number of international conferences and workshops, especially at the Middle East Studies Association meetings in 2007, 2009 and 2013, and at the BRISMES in 2014. Particularly important and enriching were the conversations and feedback received during a workshop at the Advanced Studies Institute of the Hebrew University held in Jerusalem in 2012, entitled *The Middle East and the First Wave of Globalization*, and the fruitful participation in the research project *Selling Sex in Global Cities* at the International Institute of Social History of Amsterdam in 2013. Likewise, I had the chance to profit enormously from a collaboration experience with Slovenian colleagues at the Slovenian Migration Institute, about the historical case of the *aleksandrinstvo*.

Archival research for this project has been conducted at various institutions and across three countries: the UK, Egypt and Italy. Moreover, digital documents have been obtained from the Australian War Memorial in Canberra, Australia. In England, I would like to thank the staff of the National Archives in Kew for their help. Generous assistance has been offered also by the staff of the former Women's Library at the Metropolitan University in London. I am indebted to Professor Joel Beinin who welcomed me as fellow at the Institute of Middle Eastern Studies of the American University in Cairo, and who provided institutional support during my field work in Egypt in 2007. I also take the opportunity to express my deepest gratitude to Dr Khaled Fahmy, who endorsed my application to the National Archives in Cairo, making the whole process as quick and smooth as possible. I am grateful for the assistance I received from the staff of the National Archives, especially by Madame Nadia and Madame Nagwa.

Further thanks go to the staff of the Archivio Centrale di Stato in Rome. I owe a particular debt to the keepers of the Historical Archives of the Ministry of Foreign Affairs in Rome, for helping me locate a whole collection of long-forgotten and virtually untapped consular records. As the sources I wanted to consult were not located in the main storeroom, but lay literally abandoned in a nearby annex, inducing the delivery staff to produce the materials I needed required a rather precise combination of diplomacy and determination, with occasional outbursts of anger on my part. I now thank them warmly for their help and cooperation. Moreover, very precious help and logistic support has been offered throughout the years by the Italian Benevolent Society of

Alexandria of Egypt, and especially by its President, Mr Francesco Monaco.

In the course of my research I had the chance to discuss my work and receive comments and precious practical help from a number of people. The list is long and justice cannot be done to all here. Emad Hilal and Jennifer Derr shared their thorough knowledge of the Egyptian Archives; Liat Kozma, Mario M. Ruiz, Will Hanley and Joseph Viscomi discussed their common research interests with me, offering important insights; Liat Kozma, Hanan Hammad, Camila Pastor and Simon Jackson have become very important points of reference during these years, and I really enjoyed working with them on multiple projects branching out from parts of this work.

My gratitude also goes to all my friends and colleagues whose support has helped me in so many ways and at times when the end of this work seemed very distant: my dearest friends Amélie Barras, Jasmine Gani, Igor Cherstich, Massimilano Trentin, Marco Saggioro, Adil Radoini, Shahrazade el-Far and Martino Lovato. Thanks also to Gennaro Gervasio, Francesco Correale, Enrico De Angelis, Marco Lauri, Paola Rivetti, Marina Calculli, Lucia Sorbera, Gabriele Proglio, Sara Borrillo, Estella Carpi, Nicola Perugini, Amro 'Ali, Marina Romano, Joseph Viscomi, Serena Tolino and Ashraf Hassan, all talented scholars I was lucky enough to meet on my way. Thanks to my first mentor, Professor Marcella Emiliani, for her energy, passion and wit: it all started with one of her trance-inducing lectures.

I am very grateful also to my editor, Sophie Rudland of I.B.Tauris, for her constant assistance and help through all the stages of the work. Thanks to Andrea Hajek for her care in copyediting the manuscript.

Finally, my family has provided me with constant support and encouragement all the way through these years. Endless thanks go to my mother Danila Ottani, a powerful source of inspiration, my sister Carlotta and my step-father Giuliano.

My gratitude to Alberto, love of my life.

NOTE ON TRANSLITERATION

I adopted the *International Journal of Middle Eastern Studies* (IJMES) system, where only the Arabic letters *'ayn* (') and *hamza* (') are marked, and all other diacritics are not indicated. The Arabic letter *jim* has been transliterated as *j*, with the exception of those names that are normally pronounced according to the Egyptian parlance (for example Gamaliyyah, 'Abd el Gawwad).

The titles of all primary and secondary sources in Arabic have been translated in the bibliography; I have applied English capitalisation rules to transliterated titles, according to the IJMES system.

Please note that I translated all quotations from languages other than English. I am therefore solely responsible for any mistakes.

All financial amounts are given in Egyptian Pounds (LE), 1 Egyptian Pound corresponding to 100 piastres. Between 1885 and 1914, LE 1 equalled 7,4375 grams of pure gold. From 1914 to 1962, the Egyptian Pound was pegged to the British Pound and the exchange rate was LE 0.975 = £1 sterling ($4.86).

ABBREVIATIONS

AIF	Australian Imperial Forces
AMSH	Association for Moral and Social Hygiene
ANZAC	Australian and New Zealand Army Corps
EFU	Egyptian Feminist Union
IAW	International Alliance of Women
IBS	International Bureau for the Suppression of the Traffic in Women and Children
IWSA	International Women Suffrage Alliance
LNA	Ladies' National Association
NVA	National Vigilance Association

INTRODUCTION

THE MAKING OF MODERN PROSTITUTION IN EGYPT

From 1798 to 1801, during the French Expedition to Egypt, Baron Dominique Vivant Denon was in charge of Napoleon Bonaparte's archaeological mission: his duty was that of documenting Egyptian historical heritage. In 1802 he published a travelogue, *Voyage dans la basse et la haute Égypte pendante les campagnes de general Bonaparte*, where the detailed narration of his fieldtrips was accompanied by a series of beautifully engraved plates.[1] As the French troops took physical possession of Egypt, Vivant Denon appropriated the country's history by incorporating the scattered remains of a glorious, distant past into a historical trajectory that connected the most durable form of rule in human history with contemporary imperial France. A different type of colonisation took place, what we may call an epistemic one, whereby the material and intellectual resources of the West were deployed to secure its monopoly over the representation of the Orient.

In his travelogue, Vivant Denon did not only draw ruins and temples, palms and exotic landscapes; some plates represent images of Egyptian people and everyday life scenes. Among them, table XXXV (Figure I.1) caught my attention.[2] It shows an Egyptian woman, 'a female native, married to a Franc', Vivant Denon tells us in the caption. This picture is striking for many reasons: primarily, and paradoxically, for its being just so ordinary. Firmly placed within an orientalist figurative canon, Vivant Denon's lady is identical to many other Middle Eastern women sketched by Western painters like Ingres, Delacroix and their epigones. Aloof,

Figure I.1   Native lady married to a Franc, Vivant Denon (1803), Vol. 1, Table XXXV.

inattentive and stretched languidly on a carpet, with her staring gaze she is almost expressionless as she is 'captured' by the artist's charcoal. Something in her pose seems to betray a certain indolence, a sense of laxity that pervades so many nineteenth-century depictions of the Orient, with their ubiquitous scenes of languid eunuchs and women in *harims* and dimly lit hammams. Once and again, Vivant Denon is representing an idea, not a real woman; once and again this lady is a stereotype, her image the product of multiple gender, race and class-based power relations, which allow a white bourgeois man to represent – or just imagine – this woman.[3] Yet, in this case it appears that the portrait originated from an actual encounter, and my interest in the picture also stems from that little piece of information that the author purposely gave us in the caption. Fond of her master, yet unable to restrain her erotic drive, the Egyptian woman – married to Vivant Denon's neighbour – was, he tells us, not

> amiable enough to love him alone; his jealousy was the cause of continual noisy quarrels; on her submission, she constantly promised to renounce the object of his jealousy; but the next day there was new affliction; she would weep, and repent again; still, her husband had always some fresh cause for scolding.[4]

The epilogue of such a moral tale was intentionally tragic: when the plague broke out in Rosetta, the couple's hometown, the woman contracted the disease from one of her lovers and passed it on to her husband, who died an innocent victim of his wife's licentiousness. This Egyptian lady therefore seemed to fatally embody all the potential disasters awaiting those who fell prey to the lethal, erotic temptations of the 'Orient'.

Beyond the essentialist construction of the woman's thoroughly gendered and racialised body, I was struck by the utter lack of any explanation or presumption offered by Vivant Denon for her promiscuity, other than that of a 'typically Oriental', unrestrained sexual appetite. For example, no mention is made of the fact that, at the time of the French Expedition, a number of local women entered into multiple transactional sexual liaisons with French men who they took as their 'sugar daddies' in order to improve their economic circumstances.[5] The Egyptian historian al-Jabarti (1754–1825) wrote that when the French came to Egypt, 'loose women and prostitutes of low breeding became attached to the French and mixed with them because of their submission to women as well as their liberality with them'.[6] From a later account by Carlos Bey, *nom de plume* of a British army officer who witnessed the flight of the French from Egypt in 1802, we learn that a vast number of Egyptian women 'lived with the French soldiers and almost invariably destroyed by medicine before birth the creatures that would otherwise have seen the light, but would have been the children of Christians'.[7] Colonisers and colonised alike clearly talked of 'transgressive' female sexuality and interracial sexual relations as a way to express fears of subversion of the political and social order. Al-Jabarti, for instance, argued that

> because of the advantages offered by the French, these women renounced all sense of shame and self-respect, all deference to public opinion. And they enticed females of their like, particularly young girls, bewitching their minds and exploiting the penchant to sin characteristic of human nature.

When the black slave girls, he went on, 'learned about the interest of the French in loose women [. . .] they jumped over the walls and escaped to them through windows and informed them of the secrets of their masters and of their hidden treasures, concealed properties and so forth'.[8] Upon their return to France, French port officials at Rosetta sold their native women to British soldiers for one dollar each. Carlos Bey commented that 'in truth it was more of a transfer than a real sale, so that these women could find shelter from Turkish vengeance, since laws were passed calling for the execution of all native women that had intermingled with the foreigners'.[9] Some gruesome cases of execution are reported by al-Jabarti.[10] Fortunately, though, not all women were doomed to a tragic fate. Many went back to their previous husbands, or returned to their families and were eventually married off: in short, they reintegrated into their native society.

These stories, albeit anecdotal, were invaluable in providing me with a point of entry into the main themes of this book, that is, the social construction of transgressive sexualities in modern Egypt and, more pointedly, the making of a specifically gendered subjectivity, the *prostitute*'s, as a site of modern biopolitical governmentality.

In pre-modern Egypt, profiles of women carrying out morally 'dubious activities' such as public dancing and singing, the so-called *ghawazi*, communal dancers and singers of sometimes alleged Gypsy origin, can often be encountered in orientalist travelogues: here they were juxtaposed to other conventional images of the 'Oriental feminine', that of the heavily veiled women, impervious to the Western gaze.[11] Alongside other working-class women of casual or indefinite occupation, communal performers occupied a sort of grey zone, and increasingly fell under the scrutiny of the authorities as they were 'known' (*mashhurat*) for providing sexual services outside the wedlock on a more or less regular basis, as a way to survive. The occupational status of women selling sex in pre-colonial Cairo is a pretty elusive topic for historians.[12] The combination of ephemeral documentation and literary descriptions can sketch but the contours of this type of activity, and only to a certain extent. Whether these women were described as dangerous and sly, or passive and subservient, the transactional and contractual dimensions of their work are generally concealed behind highly eroticised descriptions. French writer Gustave Flaubert, for example, gives no background information about the presence of the 'Triestina', an Italian prostitute he encountered in a Cairene, 'dilapidated' brothel room during his authentic Middle Eastern sex tour in 1850.[13] In the same way, Kutchuk Hanem, the Syrian *'alimah* Flaubert met in Esna, may once have been one of the most renowned courtesans of her times, but we are not told anything about the circumstances that brought her to practise prostitution in a dull and languid provincial town: once again, voyeuristic descriptions of firm bronze breasts and sexual intercourse are all we are left with.[14] Towards the end of the nineteenth century, by contrast, sex work stood out as a manifest, exposed feature of a rapidly changing urban space. In the streets of red-light districts such as Cairo's Wass'ah or Wagh el-Birkah, professional prostitutes plied the trade under the public eye. In his masterpiece *The Cairo Trilogy*, Naguib Mahfuz, for example, describes a stroll in the area in terms of a spectacle:

> The men swivelled their heads from right to left at prostitutes who stood or sat on either side. From faces veiled by brilliant make-up, eyes glanced around with a seductive look of welcome. At every instant, a man would break ranks to approach one of the women. She would follow him inside, the alluring look in her eyes replaced by a serious, businesslike expression. Lamps mounted above the doors of the brothels and the coffee-houses gave off a brilliant light in which accumulated the clouds of smoke rising from the incense burners and the water pipes. Voices were blended and intermingled in a tumultuous swirl around which eddied laughter,

shouts, the squeaking of doors and windows, piano and accordion music, rollicking handclaps, a policeman's bark, braying, grunts, coughs of hashish addicts and screams of drunkards, anonymous calls for help, raps of a stick, and singing by individuals and groups [...] Every beautiful woman there was available and would generously reveal her beauty and secrets in exchange for only ten piasters.[15]

These accounts give evidence of a stark contrast between the elusiveness of transactional sex in pre-colonial Egypt – as suggested by the story of the Frenchman's Egyptian wife this book starts with – and its manifestations in colonial times, when sex work became an evident feature of the new modern city, and women selling sex tended to be seen by the general public as a specific 'type' of women, that is, defined by the peculiar kind of commercial and promiscuous sex they were engaged in. This begs for a discussion of the political rationality behind this momentuous change: how to make sense of this macroscopic transformation?

On one side, the change was quantitative and structural: sex work expansion, that is, the increase in the number of women selling sex, was triggered by the integration of Egypt's economy in the world market; by the rural crisis; by migration, both domestic and international; and by the instability of women's economic roles in a period of sweeping economic change. As occupational prospects for women outside the family economy were limited or poorly paid, a growing number of women turned to sex work as a coping strategy for themselves and, often, for their families. On the other side, the transformation was also qualitative, as sex work, now commodified and fetishised, was placed at the centre of competing discourses about social regulation. Gender and sex became critical areas for hegemonic intervention within the frame of an emerging modernist biopolitical governmentality in Egypt. The new paramount importance of biopolitics, a distinct marker of modern governmentality, in Cairo as elsewhere resulted in the introduction of a complex, albeit largely ineffective, system of sex work regulation starting in 1882. Women selling sex thus turned into 'prostitutes' as part of larger projects of societal control. Moreover, a whole host of discourses on prostitution, and its dangers for both the Empire and the Egyptian nation, started to proliferate.

By tracing the transformation of gendered economic roles and mobility in the rapidly changing urban environment of fin-de-siècle Cairo, this book tells the story of how subaltern women selling sex as a survival strategy were increasingly turned – by both colonial and local authorities – into objects of control, through a range of disciplinary practices which, I argue, made for a quite extensive, though ultimately flawed, biopolitical apparatus. In order to do this, I take into account the whole trajectory from the beginning of prostitution regulation in 1882 to its eventual abolition in 1949, so as to understand the dissemination of modern biopolitical governmentality in Egypt. The book thus engages in a critique of modernity and of the biopolitical as a distinctive feature of modern power, and the role prostitution plays in this process. More pointedly, I argue that prostitution regulation in Cairo constituted a peculiar biopolitical regime, whose meaning can be better understood at the junction between imperial concerns for public hygiene, military welfare, migration, public order and local nationalist politics. Women engaging in sex for money were increasingly subjected to forms of control, often based on their ethnicity, but they did not passively undergo this system of regulation. The book therefore also tells a story, necessarily fragmentary but nonetheless substantial, of how these women inhabited these disciplinary practices, submitting to them, escaping them and manipulating them, in order to achieve their material goals.

Scope of the Study and Theoretical Influences

This study aims to elucidate the inextricable link between facts, discourses and historical narratives about sex work in the Egyptian colonial period, in order to understand how colonial and nationalist anxieties – fears of social disorder, racial degeneration, imperial decadence, national crisis – were inscribed in the bodies of women considered sexually transgressive. A similar deconstruction of hegemonic representations of sex workers' dangerousness for the political and civic order is premised on some theoretical reflections. Non-economistic, culturalist Marxism and feminism initially sparked my interest in the examination of a type of gendered subalternity, whose story had long been excluded from the historical record. While subscribing to the view according to which there is much to know outside historical grand narratives, critical reconsiderations of the rather fixed notion of 'social margins' and 'dangerous classes' as postulated by orthodox 'history from below', prompted by the so-called 'culturalist turn', significantly impacted my understanding of social marginality.[16] I not only conceptualise it as a shifting, positional and productive construct; I see the construction, and normalisation, of marginal positions and subjectivities through disciplinary projects of various types as constitutive of hegemonic power structures. Marginality and hegemony are therefore interdependent and produced by the same generative process.[17] A similar process, and the resulting forms of governmentality, constituted a salient feature of Western modernity. The unprecedented stigmatisation of non-conformity to newly imposed norms of social behaviour was key to this process: idlers, vagrants, lunatics, homosexuals and prostitutes, all those deviating from bourgeois conventions were morphed into targets of power supervision and repression through the creation of specific institutions and normative discourses.[18] Modern disciplinary practices replaced medieval marginalisation rituals: if in earlier times lepers were excluded from the human consortium *tout court*, modern plague victims were carefully contained, monitored and subjected to a regime of power based on supervision.[19] Shifting away from the concept of power as a simple polarisation between coercion and consensus, repressive technologies of domination were paired with productive technologies of self-cultivation. Power was thus conceptualised as the capacity to control, regulate and expand the productive capacities of the individual and collective body: in short, a biopolitical type of power characterised by a new interventionist, transformative thrust upon reality. As Timothy Mitchell put it, modernity meant the 'spread of a new political order that inscribes in the social world a new conception of space, new forms of personhood, and a new meaning of manufacturing the experience of the real'.[20] Sex work represented then a particularly sensible biopolitical issue. Firstly, it implied the use of the body for sexual practices intentionally disconnected from their reproductive potential within the family, even if, as I will show, in many cases it was not external to the reproduction of household economies. Secondly, the danger of venereal contagion that was attributed to the prostitute's body, as amply illustrated by a rapidly expanding genre of scientific or pseudoscientific medical literature on public health and epidemiology, carried the risk of annihilating the entire social body. Sex therefore constituted an important medium for the articulation of normative ideas about social control, deeply classed, gendered and racialised at once.

Sex Work Regulation between Empire and Nation

A first aim of this research is to explore the relationship between the construction of social marginality and biopolitics by looking at a specific case study: the regulation, and subsequent abolition, of sex work in colonial and semi-colonial Cairo, and its unique positioning at the croassroads between imperial and nationalist forms of governmentality. In doing this I clearly engage in a conversation with a very rich corpus of revisionist, historical essays on sex work.[21] As Timothy Gilfoyle aptly remarked, one major shift in the historiography of prostitution was that of historicising sex work, which showed how modern prostitution can't be understood separately from disciplinary and subjectification processes. Far from being the 'world's oldest profession', prostitution has a precise historical genealogy which goes hand in hand with the transformation of forms of governmentality and political rationalities. Previous works have called into question the conventional incorporation of prostitution analysis into broader narratives of crime and deviancy, thus exposing the constructed nature of sex workers' scapegoating as an integral part of the production of the national order, and the imperial one as an extension of this order.[22] My research thus fits within a global history of modern prostitution, as it places the transformation of sex work in the midst of sweeping economic globalisation, modernisation of the urban space, and modern forms of political rule and social control.[23] The heightened vulnerability of female economic roles in the transition from 'traditional' to market-oriented and increasingly globalised economies turned sex into a type of labour which growing numbers of women worldwide could easily mobilise as a means of subsistence (like men, although the main focus of my research is female prostitution). Egyptian cities were no exception to this process. The expansion of sex work in Cairo was part and parcel of a global modernity characterised by the extension of capitalist relations of labour, production and consumption; the diffusion of new forms of political power and social order; novel conceptions of subjectivity and individual agency; unprecedented urban change; and increased mobility of people and commodities. Under Muhammad 'Ali's rule (1805–1848), Egyptian sex work was disciplined by on and off fiscal supervision and temporary confinement of sex workers to provincial areas; these measures were already dictated by nascent biopolitical concerns, and constituted vital parts of the *wali*'s project of defensive modernisation. Yet, no coherent disciplinary apparatus was in place before the British occupied Egypt in 1882. Just 15 days after the British Army invaded Egypt, a *manshur 'amm* (general decree) on prostitution was promulgated. This act constitutes both a point of departure and arrival in the historical narrative presented here. It is an arrival point because the system of regulation brought in by the British had historical local antecedents, as mentioned earlier; it is a point of departure because it marks the advent of a full-fledged biopolitical project whose imperialist connotations and nationalist implications were not lost on the local political elites. The *manshur 'amm* of 1882, in fact, can be understood as a product of coloniality; as a distinctively modern type of political rationale aimed at enhancing the productivity of the population through the regulation of their biological collective processes; and a product of colonialism, that is, a historically and geographically specific example of British colonial policy.[24]

The colonial modernity of sex work regulation in Cairo was also evident in its relation with the global market and urban space, thus presenting itself as the emerging setting of a world economy. The expansion of sex work in Cairo, in fact, brought together the local and the global, the rural and the urban; after 1882, and especially during the investment boom of 1897–1907, the city's colonial economy attracted thousands of subsistence migrants, both domestic and international, in addition to a class of foreign expats, businessmen, speculators and imperial administrators. Hence, mobility and migration represent an important part of the historical narrative presented here. New forms of female mobility, especially when they did not involve male supervision, haunted the new Cairene urban space according to the dominant, elite imagination. Migrants, in general, and women migrants in particular, aroused biopolitical anxieties, thus calling for specific forms of supervision and control often based on racial distinctions.

Between the end of the nineteenth century and the first half of the twentieth century, girls and women coming from economically depressed rural areas of Egypt and Europe alike (especially the south of France, Greece, Italy, Poland and Russia) moved to Cairo in search of an occupation. Sex work featured prominently among their professional options. In colonial Cairo, sex became a decidedly multiethnic trade, whereby local and foreign practitioners shared similar sociological profiles, motivations and aims, but were subjected to different working arrangements conspicuously defined by their racial profile. While Capitulary legislation shielded foreign prostitutes from unwanted state intervention, local ones were the target of the most intrusive aspect of regulation, which took the form of sanitary supervision. On the one hand, such a legal 'double standard' limited the effectiveness of regulationism, and seemed to threaten the imperial order by failing to contrast the spread of venereal disease among the occupational army, and to secure the public order; on the other hand, ongoing disciplinary efforts were instrumental in the consolidation of the racial fiction on which the entire imperial enterprise was based. Such imaginary hierarchies were simultaneously created and contested by the mutually constitutive relationship between disciplinary apparatuses and everday practices of evasion from below. In this sense, prostitution and its regulation were absolutely integral to the production of the colonial order in Cairo. Both local and foreign sex workers were represented by colonial and local authorities as a major metaphor of social unrest, a serious threat to imperial domination and political legitimacy on one side, and to the physical and moral welfare of the rising Egyptian nation on the other. Until World War I, regulationism was considered vital for the preservation of the military capacity and physical health of imperial troops that were dislocated in the Empire, and thus of the racial order. The shift from regulationism to abolitionism, which in Cairo started with the Purification Campaign of 1915–16, can be seen as the product of multiple negotiations between colonial authorities, imperial and international social reformers and local nationalist elites. The definition and regulation of normative and heteronormative, gendered roles and sexualities became, especially after Egypt's formal independence in 1922, nodal points in the making of the nationalist project for both secular and religious local elites.

The centrality of sex and gender in the articulation of an imagined homogeneous, national community and nationalist discourse, none-theless, was far from being purely derivative: on the contrary, I argue that it stands as an example of how exogenous cultural materials (namely a paternalistic discourse of humanitarian intervention and reformation with mature, biopolitical concerns) were manipulated and rearticulated into a locally inflected abolitionist idiom. Broadly speaking, my contribution to such a vast comparative approach entailed the in-depth exploration of a non-metropolitan context that has not yet been studied extensively, as a way to bridge the seemingly entrenched dichotomy between structural, systemic analysis and close areal readings. Colonial and semi-colonial Egypt after 1922 seemed to me a fascinating case study for pushing the boundaries of Foucaldian governmentality theory beyond its Eurocentric focus and homeostatic tendency.[25] The colony was a laboratory where imperial disciplinary strategies were tested and contested, interiorised, then manipulated and rearticualed by local hegemonic groups and ordinary people in the formulation of their own types of vernacular modernity.[26] With its subtle and complex interplay between a colonial power and a formally sovereign, yet *de facto* externally controlled, local form of rule, its emerging modernist, nationalist movement and the problems arising from the existence of large numbers of non-local subjects protected by Capitulary legislation, Egypt offered an interesting example of the provincialisation of sex work regulation as a facet of typically Western governmentality and its imagined order. The issue of the circulation of cultural materials between the metropolis and the colony, and indeed the question of the mutual constitution of the European self and the colonial Other, is thus central to my research.

Leaving Women Aside?

Post-culturalist historiographies of sex work have de-essentialised prostitution by deconstructing hegemonic discourses and symbolic formations, thus showing how the stigmatisation or pathologicisation of sex work in public discourse was historically and culturally constructed. Framing prostitution within different processes of state- and nation-building thus meant, on one side, the working through of multiple dominant discourses: on the other, it also meant – as other seminal works have done more emphatically – the taking into consideration of prostitutes' sociological profiles, daily lives and survival strategies. The analysis of prostitution in the context of coeval job markets and working-class culture implied a shift from the idea of prostitution as abnormal, dangerous or unmentionably seductive, to that of prostitution as something ordinary and banal.[27] However, according to Luise White, author of a radical materialist history of sex work in colonial Nairobi, the failure to formulate a forward critique of their sources' positionality led most of these works to reinforce, if unintentionally, the analytical categories through which prostitution had been made sense of and controlled: exploitation, sickness and poverty. By asking the fundamental question of how a corpus of literature on sex work can speak only of women's victimisation and passivity, instead of women's earnings, White explored the relationship between patterns of economic change, urbanisation and sex work in its various forms. With the aim of writing 'a history of prostitution without isolating women in the categories of deviancy and subculture',[28] she established a link between the dislocation of agricultural and pastoral economies and the expansion of sex work, a successful strategy available to women who sought to accumulate resources, either for the reconstitution of their families' shattered finances or in order to invest in urban estate properties.

For all the importance of trying to scrutinise agency beyond discourse, I subscribe to the view that materiality and discourses cannot be known and studied separately. Hence, I aim to complement the corpus of prostitution studies that focusses on the agency of sex workers, based on the premises that hegemony is never monolithic and that the exploration of subaltern lives does irremediably substantiate a space of complex and fragmented micro-resistances. At the same time, the way in which these forms of micro-resistance can be known and made sense of is open to scrutiny. In particular, the limit imposed by the type of sources available to the historian must be acknowledged and conceptually explored.[29]

My work has been heavily influenced by Gail Hershatter's methodological claims about history writing as a meta-discourse, and her critique of 'history as retrieval' methodology.[30] I agree on the fact that material and ideological changes cannot and should not be examined separately, as if social change was in essence pre-discursive. Neither can social change, Hershatter warns, 'be regarded as determinative in the last instance of the conditions of the prostitutes' lives in a mechanistic and predetermined way'.[31] I will therefore combine materialist bottom-up and discursive top-down approaches, while remaining aware of the inherent, unsolvable – but, I believe, productive – contradictions between the two approaches. As it has been noted in reference to some important developments in the epistemological trajectory of the Subaltern Studies collective, including its shift to post-structuralism,[32] although it assigns an important role to non-elite agency, discursive methodology – if pushed to the extreme – can cause any subaltern subjectivity, as fragmented and multiple as it may be, to drop out of focus. Yet, in colonial Cairo real flesh-and-blood women, under a multitude of arrangements and with different motivations, sold their sexual services; within the interstices of discourses about social decay and venereal peril, the dangers of Westernisation and moral crisis, women were trying to improve their working conditions and living circumstances.

Prostitutes, like other people of humble origins or illiterates, rarely recorded their life experiences or left firsthand accounts of their circumstances: they were mostly written about. Marilyn Booth, who has worked extensively on fictional first-person narratives by memoirists of 'fallenness', rightly speaks of this genre as an exercise in ventriloquism. Thus elite men 'spoke' for the subaltern and the feminine as part of a precise project of nationalist pedagogy. Some of these accounts did not resort to the rhetoric device of fictional female authorship: rather, from the point of view of a subaltern observer they presented to the

> voyeuristic reader, a journey into the underworld, the low-life sites of Cairo's urban fabric, from the gambling dens of Rawd el Farag to houseboat brothels on the Nile, and from the opulent facades harboring illicit sex on the boulevard Wishsh al-Birkah to the hashish dens behind al-Azhar mosque.[33]

Muhammad Ahmad Yusuf's *Yawmiyyat saqita* (Diaries of a fallen woman, 1927) and Muhammad Ra'fat Jamali's *Mudhakkirat Baghi* (Memoirs of a prostitute, 1922), instead, made explicit reference to their male authorship, a typical flâneur, enhancing the plausibility of his social commentary by inserting fictional entries from prostitutes' diaries. Female pseudo-memories written in the first person, lastly, claimed to convey the unmediated point of view of women in distress, who roamed the public space: they functioned as powerful cautionary tales of social unrest.

Given that registration lists containing quantitative data on sex workers' names, ages, previous occupations, family background, civil status and so on are not retrievable in the case of Cairo, biographical information must be sought in a different way, most notably through the combination of heterogeneous sources: these include governmental reports, judicial proceedings, police investigations, documents produced by benevolent societies and the press. Indeed, information about prostitutes' social profiles or firsthand testimonies by prostitutes must be extrapolated from documents of different types, which have been written by others and often in a heavily standardised, bureaucratic language. Yet, sources like court cases and police minutes can prove productive when trying to locate, within the interstices of a dominant normative discourse, instances of a prostitute's point of view and perception. I believe that an exploration of the lives of women who lived and sold sex in Cairo offers a reading of prostitution that complicates the language of victimisation and passivity, which has been uncritically adopted for a very long time, and in doing so illuminates possible sites of women's agency. It is nevertheless important to reflect on how such agency must be understood, and especially on the extent to which the subaltern women's agentive activities can be disentangled from the dominant discourses in which they are encapsulated. As Hershatter has argued, the search for subaltern agency is, in essence, somewhat quixotic:[34] the risk of plunging deep into the 'romance of resistance', to quote Lila Abu Lughod,[35] is ever-present. Prostitutes' actions, circumstances, possibly also their perceptions, were paradoxically shaped by, and shaping, hegemonic power. Historians cannot but work them out from sources written from highly patronising positions. When we are able to locate prostitutes' voices, as for example in court cases, these are of course also heavily mediated. Historians do not necessarily serve these subjects well when putting them on a sort of pedestal, comprised of a kind of political agency we actually cannot know in full.[36] Still, for all its limits I am convinced that the exploration of the scattered evidences telling us how disadvantaged women coped with legal, moral and social systems of patriarchal subordination can yield important information on the ways in which marginality and hegemony actually interacted in complex ways.

I located a number of consular court cases related to pimping and other crimes, where prostitutes figure as plaintiffs, defendants or witnesses. These cases concerned offenders of foreign nationalities, who were subjected to their national penal code because of extra-territorial rights granted by the Capitulations. Nonetheless, the proceedings also feature local subjects, and what we then encounter in these sources is a wide range of everyday interactions between subaltern local and foreign subjects who seem to share, to a very large extent, the same lifestyles and values, chiefly the exact same concern for subsistence. Foreign prostitutes who appeared in these cases described a working environment they shared with native ones. Although they undoubtedly articulated stories of exploitation and deprivation, they did not represent themselves simply as victims, but as working women strenuously trying to defend their role as breadwinners, whether for themselves or for their families. The availability and positionality of the sources that were at my disposition constrained my analysis. The most easily accessible sources, primarily reformist papers and consular court records, were concerned more with the activities of 'poor whites' than with indigenous women. I have retained these categories – which I derived from colonial sources – for descriptive purposes, especially with regard to the functioning of the system of regulation (which greatly discriminated between Egyptian and foreign sex workers), but this certainly requires some further explanation. The dichotomy between 'native' and 'European', which is so pervasive in hegemonic accounts, seemed misleading to me, not only because the circumstances of European and native prostitutes were determined by class and the social construction of gender, more than by race, but above all because the very same category of 'European' in Cairo's colonial context is questionable.[37] As recent scholarship on migrant communities in the late nineteenth and early twentieth century has posited,[38] Maltese, Italian, Greek, French and other 'subsistence migrants' (or 'white marginals') in the colony, who played a very important role in Cairo's political economy of prostitution, hardly fit the normative description of 'European' civilisational superiority, and were considered only marginally European. As for the use of the term 'sex worker', here it is used mainly as counterpoint to the legal category of 'prostitute' and the taxonomyc concerns of regulationism. It refers to a type of activity performed by women who sell sex as their main or prevalent way of supporting themselves and those dependent on them outside of the system of regulation. Although in today's postmodern usage the term is laden with an agentive potential, and deeply imbued with political claims to decriminalisation, social protection and labour rights, I believe the term can be used in historical contexts as a way of acknowledging the economic potential of sexual trade for disadvantaged women, whithout anachronistically projecting on to them a sort of class and political consciousness they did not possess.[39] I am not implying, though, that any type of labour equals agency: I argue that for most of the women whose stories appear in this book, commercial sex was a tactic, a form of labour they engaged with while hoping for better opportunities, either in the form of a salaried job, a husband or a profligate lover. Other expressions, such as 'women selling sex' or 'engaging in commercial sex', could and are, in fact, applied with the purpose of going beyond the labelling implicit in the uncritical use of the term 'prostitute'. As the process of constructing the prostitutional category is unravelled throughout the book, it becomes clear how multiple and diversified the social profiles and working arrangements of women grouped under this description were. Sex work was constituted by the different material conditions in which this labour took place as much as by the meanings and the imaginative repertoire mobilised by the term 'prostitution': ideas of social decay, disorder, threat and violence. In the interstices of historically constructed discourses about victimisation and passivity, empowerment and agency, ordinary women have been selling sex simply as a way to survive and make ends meet. To acknowledge that what they did was indeed a form of labour, without isolating them because of the lack of resistant or emancipatory movements, allows us to avoid obliterating their historical actions, even if these were motivated by the sheer need for subsistence.

Structure of the Book

Chapter 1 deals with the emergence of modern prostitution in late nineteenth-century Cairo as both a quantitative and a qualitative, new phenomenon against the backdrop of a rapidly changing urban space. Structural factors such as the integration of Egypt's economy in the global market on an unequal base, the restructuring of household economies and family relations, the heightened economic vulnerability of previously autonomous, extended families, and women in particular, can explain why growing numbers of women depended on sex work to earn a living. The expansion of prostitution was also encouraged by the unprecedented demographic growth and increasing social stratification of Cairo; the demands of expats and a rising local middle class with greater purchasing power and new consumption styles; massive imperial military presence; mass tourism; and international migration. These elements constituted the background against which prostitution was assigned new critical social meanings by the elites, both local and foreign. It led me to reflect on the role of international migration within Cairo's commercial sex industry and the extent to which prostitution could imply the weakening of patriarchal relations of power. Thus sex workers' heteronormativity was partly defined by their being mobile and transient, both in the public space and across national frontiers, in a way that was perceived as problematic by patriarchal forces. Female migrant domestic labour tended to be seen as morally suspect, despite a certain overlap with sex work. If prostitution, as any type of income-generating activity, could potentially have had an emancipatory effect on women, provided they were free to accumulate and reinvest their earnings, in reality this seldom happened. Sex work, mainly performed by internal or international migrants, tended to be mediated by patriarchal forces, that is, men whose fortunes were intertwined with 'their' women's in a very complex web of reciprocal exploitation (as many sex workers' narratives concerning their pimps seem to confirm). Chapter 2 zooms in on the geography of sex work in modern Cairo. It analyses the Azbakiyyah, known for its red-light districts, as a heterotopian space essential to the production and reproduction of the imperial and national order. Chapter 3 looks at the actual material and discursive strategies – spatial segregation, labelling, quantification and medicalisation – deployed by both colonial and local authorities in order to turn women who engage in commercial sex into disciplined and docile objects of control. By looking at race as a constructed category and the main regulatory force in a colonial context, I demonstrate how foundational racial hierarchies were threatened, though ultimately reinforced, by the regulationist logic. In Chapter 4, I go beyond the nominalism of sex work regulation by taking a look at the actual organisation of the trade. An alternative reading of primary sources, especially a number of individual micro-histories, seems to challenge received stereotypes of racial superiority and narratives of female victimisation and coercion. This chapter also addresses the question of sex workers' agency and shows how women in the trade, although caught in a system of subordination, did manage to resist and circumvent unwanted state intervention and pimps' exploitation.

The emergence of mature biopolitical concerns led to the shift from regulationism to abolitionism. The precedent of abolitionist practices can be recognised in the Purification Campaign waged by colonial authorities in Cairo during World War I, with the aim of safeguarding public order and curtailing the rampant spread of venereal disease among Dominions and British troops garrisoned in the Egyptian capital. The relationship between colonial warfare prostitution and venereal contagion is the subject of Chapter 5. This analysis will allow me to elaborate on the delicate link between sex, morality and power, by focussing on the struggle between abolitionists from civil society and the pragmatic military authorities. Chapter 6 deals with colonial reformists' attempts to reform and reintegrate prostitutes into society by converting them to disciplined and reliable servants. Paying specific attention to foreign prostitutes and 'fallen' women in Cairo, this chapter explores the colonial dimension of Victorian social purity by showing how these specific categories of gendered, subaltern actors discursively played a very integral role in the preservation of besieged notions of colonisers' racial and civilisational superiority. Chapter 7 focusses on the abolitionist turn, and does so in two ways. It traces the evolution of the abolitionist option within an increasingly vibrant printing press industry, which became – in particular after the nationalist revolution of 1919 – a fundamental outlet for the diffusion of multiple and competing ideas about the 'homogeneous' and 'authentic' national community. Prostitution was used by nationalist leaders of different orientations to formulate a trenchant critique of Western imperialism and Egypt's political subordination, while delineating the contours of their much sought-after autonomous, national community in the local press. Here a number of themes were woven together: the fear of social anarchy; the growing discomfort with increased female mobility and irruption in the public space; the spread of venereal contagion and its related biopolitical risks; and the degeneration of the national community due to rampant immorality and debauchery. In the context of Egyptian nation-building, debates about prostitution represented a medium through which local notions of citizenship and cultural authenticity, mainly defined by religion, found expression. Public discourses on commercial sex, sexuality, gendered roles, marriage, the family and public health in the formally, newly founded, independent nation of Egypt were inseparable from the attempts to define its modernity and political maturity, and to legitimise local nationalists' hegemonic role. To attain these goals, a typical discursive strategy created the figure of the 'national villain', as a dense metaphor for the spreading of social malaise: for this purpose the book concludes with a discussion of the cases of the 'King of the Underworld', Ibrahim al-Gharbi, and of traffickers in women and children. Ever since 1932, when a special governmental commission officially pronounced itself in favour of abolition, Egyptian political elites and middle-class commentators have considered prostitution as intolerable. Egyptian nationalists' abolitionism was part and parcel of a global hyper-regulationist disciplinary project, which adopted a paternalistic humanitarian approach to heteronormativity as a way to ensure social order and stability.

CHAPTER 1

SELLING SEX IN A CHANGING CITY

A Japanese passing through Cairo asked, I presume out of curiosity, if there was such thing as a 'yoshiwara' in the town. 'My dear sir', said the English officer to whom the question had been put, 'it would be quite unnecessary. We have here so many ladies quite *comme il en faut*.[1]

A.B. De Guerville, *New Egypt*, 1906

The shift from 'traditional' to 'modern' sex work encompassed both changes and continuities. An exact quantification of the increase in the actual number of practitioners is very difficult, not to say impossible, to establish due to the fragmentariness of the data at hand. Yet, the last quarter of the nineteenth century surely saw the emergence of a qualitatively different type of sex work. Prostitution was comprehensively commodified, and the – legal – selling of sex in brothels was placed in public thoroughfares in the centre of the newly planned, modern city. This process should not be understood as a linear trajectory, through. The transformation of sex work in the colonial period was an irregular phenomenon, whereby transactional sex was restructured through the articulation of different and complex degrees of interaction with the State and the market, from formal institutionalised brothel prostitution to informal and casual, clandestine sex work. While transactional sex continued to be a choice that women could make more or less deliberately, in order to alleviate their harsh economic constraints, the structure of sex work and its social meaning deeply changed due to its increased integration within the realm of market forces and state intervention.

In this chapter I introduce an analysis of the emergence of modern Cairene prostitution as a consequence of globalisation, colonialism, domestic and international migration, urban modernisation and social change. These structural factors, I argue, constituted the broad canvas against which prostitution came to be seen by an increasing number of local as well as foreign women in Cairo, as a viable strategy to cope with female economic vulnerability. At the same time, a novel social meaning was assigned to sex work by both the political elites and the general public.

Urban Transformation

Throughout Mamluk and Ottoman times, Cairo underwent a remarkably steady and continuous development. From the 1860s onwards, however, it rapidly grew into a global metropolis. According to a prevailing historiographic perspective, Khedive Isma'il was the promoter of a radical transformation of the city along European – and more specifically, Parisian – aesthetics, especially after his visit to Haussmann's 'new' Paris in occasion of the Universal Exposition of 1867.[2] Supported by the visionary and energetic Minister of Public Works 'Ali Mubarak (1823–1893),[3] Isma'il launched an unparalleled programme of urban renovation. His frenzy with Cairo's upgrade was made all the more pressing by an imminent occasion such as the opening of the Suez Canal in 1869. As historian Khaled Fahmy rightly observed, though, such emphasis on the catch-all term 'Europeification' risks obscuring not only the fact that the origins of Cairo's transformation predated Isma'il's accession to the throne, but also that this process was far more complex, hybrid and gradual than usually portrayed.[4] For all the influence that Parisian urbanism may have had on modern planning in Cairo, the renovation of the city was in fact largely defined by a mixture of conjunctural circumstances, such as budget constraints imposed by the *Casse de la Debte Publique* after Egypt's bankruptcy in 1875; the interests of private companies; and the peculiar structure of local governance, notably the complex relationship between the khedive, private investors and a number of administrative bodies with overlapping competencies. Modern urban planning in Cairo also implied the manipulation of the local legal system, especially in relation to *waqf* buildings, prioritising interpretation over strict literalism because of pragmatic considerations. In 1866, a *La'ihat al Tanzim* (Tanzim Ordinance) further specified the criteria for the organisation of public space in accordance with the dominant medical and political ideas of the day; the sanitation of space equalled the deployment of a correct functioning civic order. Straight, ample streets and spacious squares structured the urban space, allowing free circulation of people and fresh, healthy air. As Timothy Mitchell aptly remarked,

> Open, well-lit streets were a benefit not only to health but to commerce, for they embodied the principle of visibility and inspection [. . .] The dark 'interior' of the city, cleared of its human agglomerations, would become easier to police, and artificial lightning would enable the new shops and places of entertainment to do business into the night. Financially, the need for cleanliness in the streets reflected the newly envisaged relationship between the city as a site of consumption and the countryside as a place of production.[5]

Change was undoubtedly fast and selective. The demolition of unsanitary, narrow streets and old houses in order to make space for neat thoroughfares and new apartment blocks in European style meant relocating low-class Egyptians to the margins of the new modern city: in the words of American diplomat Thomas S. Harrison, Cairo offered 'the spectacle of two distinct cities in one, each filled with a different people, unlike in race, customs, and religion'.[6] All those trends that had already marked Cairo's development during Isma'il's reign – expansion of built-in areas, urban planning and increasing Western economic and cultural penetration – intensified on an unprecedented scale after British occupation. The British invaded the country in response to a broad proto-nationalist movement in 1882. They quickly enthroned a pliable ruler, the young and dull Khedive Tawfiq (r. 1879–1892), and set about developing a form of colonial enterprise that lasted formally until the country's unilateral independence in 1922, in fact ending only after the Free Officers Revolution. As Egypt was further integrated into the global market, as a supplier of raw materials to the British textile

manufacturing industry and as a purchaser of finished goods, a
plantation economy was fostered with the aim of maximising cotton
export to the global market. Small cultivators saw a rapid increase in the
pace of dispossession they had been subjected to since the middle of the
nineteenth century.[7] For many, the choice was between staying on as
sharecroppers or leaving the countryside in search of new employment
opportunities in cities. Rural exodus to Egyptian urban centres was a
major consequence, and one that greatly changed the face of cities such as
Cairo and Alexandria.

According to urban historian André Raymond, Cairo's population
increased from 374,000 in 1882 to 1,312,000 in 1937, that is,
250 per cent over a time span of 45 years.[8] Much of the demographic
influx was constituted by rural migrants seeking employment
opportunities and better living standards.[9] They usually settled in the
poorest neighbourhoods of the medieval Islamic city, such as Gamaliyyah,
Bab-al-Sha'riyyah, Darb al-Ahmar and the northern commercial district
of Bulaq, where they could rely on the social networks of urbanised
co-villagers, who could offer material and psychological support.
However, a significant number of newcomers also consisted of foreigners.
Due to favourable investment conditions under the Capitulation laws and
as a result of better occupational possibilities, European presence in the
city increased constantly: aggregate data given by Raymond show that the
number of foreign residents in Cairo rose from 18,289 in 1882 to 76,173
in 1927.[10] The British (11,221 individuals in 1927, tenfold their number
in 1882) and French communities (9,549 units in 1927), wielded most of
the political influence and economic power. Over time they also became
increasingly stratified, as wealthy businessmen and speculators were joined
by a growing number of working-class people in search of a better life in
the Empire.[11] The largest communities, namely the Greek (20,115
individuals in 1927),[12] and the Italian (18,575 individuals in the same
year),[13] had deep historical roots that could be traced back to the
early nineteenth century.[14] In the last quarter of the century, though, the
incipient crisis of agrarian economies in the South of Europe sustained a
steady emigration towards the booming North African countries. Other
than these four main European communities, many other national groups
were present in Cairo as well: the 1927 census of Egypt enlisted
23 nationalities,[15] not to mention the *shawwam* community that
originated from *the bilad al-sham*, which shared the Ottoman nationality

with native Egyptians. Moreover, in that same year 23,103 Jews lived in the Egyptian capital,[16] the majority being local subjects from the Egyptian diaspora community that had established itself in Cairo in ancient times: although it had preserved its cultural identity, it was fully integrated within the local society.

Steady population growth resulted in a dramatic expansion of Cairo's built-up area (i.e., from 1,000 hectares in 1882 to 16,330 hectares in 1937),[17] accompanied by blatant speculation in the real estate sector. During the speculative boom of 1897–1907, when the inflow of private, foreign and local investments was considerable, Cairo became known as a sort of El Dorado.[18] The combined effect of the increase in agricultural output and the confidence in the realisation of high profits from any kind of business related to rural lands or urban properties generated an investment upsurge in all types of sectors, from mortgage and banking to transport. Visiting Cairo in 1906, freelance journalist and commercial agent Amédée Baillot De Guerville thus described Cairo's speculative bubble:

> The whole population seems to have been bitten with a mania for building. The streets are crowded with builders' carts, full of material, and on all sides, surrounded by scaffolding, are houses under construction. Huge flats, immense palaces, super hotels, have arisen where, a year or two ago, nothing but gardens were to be seen. Egypt, at this moment, is passing through a period of great prosperity. Everyone is coining money and, as the value of land and property is increasing daily, all those who have capital, and they are many, hasten to build.[19]

Circulation within the city was made easier thanks to the paving of large tracts of the street system, to the effect that by 1917 public taxicab-driving constituted the single most common occupation in Cairo,[20] while municipal utilities like sewage and gaslights were introduced in the newly planned parts of the city.[21] Modernisation impacted the urban fabric rather selectively, though. The old city quickly overpopulated. Between 1882 and 1927, the population of Gamaliyyah increased by 44,788 residents, while the number of people living in Darb al-Ahmar increased by 52,544 units during the same period. In 1927 the more recent, highly popular commercial area of Bulaq accommodated 79,681 people more than in 1882.[22] Here services and infrastructures, not having been subjected to any significant modernisation, quickly collapsed under demographic pressure. Colonial elites, a foreign-comprador bourgeoisie and rich locals populated the newly built wealthy quarters, which seemed to combine European high society life with the exoticism of the Orient. The main commercial district around Shari 'Kamal and Midan al Opera, with its big Department Stores displaying *ifrangi* goods of every type, seemed to defy – in De Guerville's words – the stereotype of the dual city, with a rigid separation between colonials and natives:

> it would be impossible, even in dreams, to picture anything more animated than this living panorama, where East meets West, and meeting seems to mix one in the other. The eye is first struck by the thousands of little red spots on which hang tassels of black silk. It is the tarbouche, head-covering of so many different types that it seems as if all Africa had given rendezvous here. The majority are of the sterner sex, with nothing Oriental in their dress but the tarbouche; otherwise they are clothed as the ordinary European, whilst many of them attain to the last thing in elegance. In this extraordinary crowd are negroes, Arabs in their flowing robes, Jews with shifty eyes, eunuchs, Egyptian soldiers, well set up; and, making their way amongst all these Orientals, tourists of every country and speaking every tongue, young foreign girls with a knowing look about them, *mondaines and demi-mondaines*, the latter with a smile indifferently for black or white. Here and there a native woman, hidden beneath her veil, passes rapidly, silently, mysteriously.[23]

Nearby one could find the Azbakiyyah Gardens, and the international hotels catering for the throngs of tourists 'doing' Egypt in the season.[24] In 1914 Elizabeth Cooper, an American writer, described the exterior of the famous Shepherd's Hotel – a veritable institution of Cairene modern mass tourism – as a display of 'cosmopolitan cool':

> During the season, that is from November until March, there is always a well-dressed crowd sitting around the little tables on the big verandahs of the hotels. One sees the French woman with her

exaggerated styles, the American, looking as if she had just come from her Fifth Avenue milliner, the heavy but practical German frau with her heavier husband and uninteresting daughters, and finally the English woman with her *blasé* air and feather boa.[25]

Women and Labour

Life in the city exposed men and women to the vagaries of the market, and especially to harsh competition for waged labour, in the absence of a strong industrial sector. Unskilled and untrained as most of them were, women were extremely vulnerable on the job market, and occupational possibilities for them were particularly scarce. In 1907, for example, 103,856 women in Cairo were unemployed as opposed to 32,843 men, while the largest female occupational group was constituted of unpaid labourers (domestic workers in their own households numbered 126,919).[26] Women generally – and often casually – found occupation in the informal economy as providers of services, such as domestic workers, peddlers, hairdressers, seamstresses and so on.[27] Poor wages and lack of alternatives might have led a growing number of women to turn to sex work, whose demand was sustained by the unprecedented growth of Cairo and Egypt's socio-economic change. Hence, the expansion of prostitution had much to do with the encroachment of global economy and state power on the lives of poor Egyptians and Europeans, men and women, during the long nineteenth century. In such a context, not only women who were deprived of the support of a husband (e.g., divorcées and widows) might have had recourse to the selling of sexual services for economic reasons, but also women whose husbands, pauperised and in menial unstable jobs for most of the time, were simply not able to fulfil their duties as household heads. In this sense, the idea that there is a direct causal link between the spread of prostitution and a crisis of patriarchal values and forms of control on women, a favourite argument of middle-class reformers and social workers, misses the point. Indeed, prostitution was not only the labour of women coming from 'morally degenerated' working-class families, as maintained by bourgeois observers; more accurately, it was the labour of women coming from economically weak, patriarchal families. Luise White has forcefully driven the point home, arguing that in times of social and economic upheavals, prostitution was

often the response to the precarious position of unskilled women
[...] not the failure of families as institution. The women who
became prostitutes in order to support their families through hard
times, or the abandoned wives who prostituted themselves to
support themselves and their children, even the women who
were thrown out of their homes because they were 'ruined away'
were not victims of week family; they were the victims of strong
ones [...], living testimonies to a belief in families that they
should continue and prosper at any cost.[28]

In other words, having recourse to sex work because of personal
predicaments or systemic transformations constituted an adaptive
strategy, more than a break with a consolidated patriarchal sex/gender
system. A brief analysis of the impact of slavery abolition on the
expansion of Egyptian prostitution enables us to further elaborate on this
point, as well as to illuminate the relationship between labour and
gender, especially to what pertains the conflation of domestic service
with sex work.[29] In 1877, a first Anglo-Egyptian convention on the
suppression of slave trade was signed, and British officers had been given
free rein to target slave merchants. Manumission bureaus opened in four
Egyptians cities, with the task of examining applications from slaves
who wanted to be freed. As Diane Robinson Dunne suggested, British
officials had a very ambiguous approach towards the manumission of
female slaves, their objective being the eradication of human trafficking
managed by powerful networks of slave dealers in trans-Saharan areas,
not women's emancipation.[30] Using a moral argument, British officials
cautioned that 'a precipitous manumission campaign would contribute
to the increase of immorality in society'.[31] Along the same line, the
British Consul Barker stated that his rejection of nine out of ten requests
for manumission was grounded on the fact that, on inspection, the
applicants' living conditions had been ascertained to be 'fair', and that
'so few opportunity existed for outside work that most likely (they)
would become prostitutes if freed'.[32] These fears seemed unfounded: to
quote Tucker, 'the vision of large numbers of slave women thrown
headlong into prostitution by lack of skills, knowledge, and ambition
simply failed to materialize'.[33] This can be gleaned from the records of
the Home for Freed Female Slaves that the British established in 1884,
in order to assist manumitted slaves in their search for employment and

to prevent them from drifting into prostitution. During the 1890s, no more than 30 to 40 women per year sought assistance, which made up one-fifth of all manumission cases processed by the Cairo bureau. This suggests that former slaves, once freed, were able to support themselves without the Home's assistance, either by finding a job or getting a husband. Finding an exact explanation for this is not an easy task, and requires a closer analysis of the nature and meaning of slavery practices in Islamic societies, and of Islamic jurisprudence.[34] The relationship between a slave and her master was not primarily defined by economic factors. Slave concubines and/or domestic servants were marginal to economic production but central to the reproduction of labour through their care work. In fact, although lacking the legal rights of free women, female slaves were considered members of the household. Moreover, female slaves' rights to family and reproduction after manumission were acknowledged, and a slave background was not stigmatising. Slaves' material circumstances during bondage and after manumission, finally, were dramatically defined by their masters' social status and the kind of social network made available to them. Thus a Circassian slave from an elite family had very high chances to marry into the upper class after manumission, without undergoing changes to the lifestyle she was used to. For black slaves, by contrast, things must have been much harder. Racial discrimination, scarce occupational prospects, lack of social networks or guild protection – all these factors combined to restrict the number of available alternatives: without means of support or community networks, many freed slaves had to fend for themselves. Some chose to remain with their former masters as servants, fearing the economic insecurity of freedom. Domestic service was the kind of work they were expected to find anyway, outside of the context of slavery. Some women settled into marital life, others resorted to prostitution; this, I would add, also meant the commodification of an integral aspect of a lawful matrimonial contract, that is, the provision of sexual services.[35] In the brothel, a locale I will discuss extensively further ahead, despite the existence of highly hierarchical power relations between the keeper and her women, new bonds of solidarity could be formed between inmates, almost like a surrogate family where the *madame* acted in the paradoxical role of a *pater familias*.

Female slaves thus tended to respond to structural changes in a conservative way, namely by relying on pre-existing support networks whenever possible. This does not mean that life in bondage was pleasurable: unless they were born into a household as second-generation slaves, experience of slavery entailed a traumatic eradication from one's own original environment, adaptation to and socialisation with a new one. Slaves could and often did endure various forms of violence; yet, complete freedom also meant a further transformative experience and a new beginning.

Migration

In the course of this transition towards freedom, women rethought their vulnerable status, redefined their subjectivities, exerted rational choices and manoeuvred within newly formed spaces of agency, at the intersection of micro- and macro-historical changes. The same can be said of those foreign women who, because of these momentous transformations, left their places of origin in search of a life overseas.

It is estimated that 60,000 Europeans left labour-rich but resource-scarce Europe between 1870 and 1913, and settled in labour-scarce and resource-abundant, non-metropolitan areas.[36] Many of these were working-class women, and some of them were active in commercial sex or got into it because of the most desparate circumstances. If, for many poor Europeans, Egypt made an interesting destination because of its bustling economy, a whole class of sex work entrepreneurs and labourers gravitated around the booming Egyptian cities, shielded by the special legal status the Capitulations had granted them.[37] Governmental authorities, abolitionists and purity campaigners referred to these women as victims of the so-called 'White Slave Trade', the massive smuggling of women from Europe to other parts of the world, which became a prominent concern of bourgeois reformers from the end of the nineteenth century onwards. Popularised by a number of pamphlets and publications portraying the commerce in the lewdest and flashiest of tones, a powerful propaganda was orchestrated by purity and abolitionist activists who portrayed unattached women roaming the globe as wretched women and deceived girls: in other words, living examples of 'weak' female and working-class morality and indecency, at best, dangerous symbols of political and social decay, at worst. European prostitutes travelled to Egypt from a number of countries, most notably from the most economically depressed areas of Southern Europe

(Italy, Greece, the French *Midi*) and Eastern Europe, through international networks of pimps working in collaboration with local procurers, who liaised with brothel owners. The main traffic routes departed from Germany, Austria, Spain, France, Greece, Italy, Poland, Romania and Turkey, and headed either to South and Central America – Argentina, Brazil, Mexico, Panama and Uruguay – or North Africa and Egypt. Through the Suez Canal, women could then travel all the way to the Orient, India and the Far East, mainly Shanghai.[38] In fact, as a report issued by the Central Office for the Repression of the Traffic in Women and Children of the Italian Home Office clarified in 1927,

> the majority of women involved in the traffic are professional prostitutes, although minors. A significant number of trafficked women is made up by *demimondaines*, living at the fringes of professional prostitution [. . .] while a third category of women is represented by music-halls artistes. A fourth group is made up by tricked girls, who marry adventurers who force them to practice the infamous trade abroad.[39]

Traffickers resorted to a number of strategies in order to evade the control of authorities and deceive their victims: fake marriages; religious marriages with no legal effect in the case of Jewish girls;[40] false promises of employment opportunities, especially as maids or artistes; tampering of passports and birth certificates. Smugglers would know special spots to embark and disembark their 'merchandise' without being impeded by major controls. For example, Italian prostitutes would normally travel to Marseilles to board the steamers leaving for Egypt and South America, so as to circumvent tougher checks at Italian ports.

Despite local authorities' attempts to conceal the dimension of this illegal traffic,[41] Egypt had been known since the end of the nineteenth century as 'a country of large demand for women and girls of all nationalities for prostitution'.[42] In 1905, a report on the 'White Slave Trade' was presented by a Greek subject resident in Alexandria, Madame Tsykalas, at the International Conference of the Union Internationale des Amis de Jeunes Filles.[43] According to Madame Tsykalas's report, in the preceding 20 years Alexandria had come to be the major international centre of the trafficking of European women, thanks to Egyptian economic and population growth and, more importantly, to the existence of the

Capitulation system as well as the structural weakness of the indigenous penal code in dealing with offences by foreigner traffickers. Thus the Capitulations granted foreign communities a privileged fiscal and legal status, allowing their members to evade persecution from native courts. As for cases involving offenders of multiple nationalities, it was occasionally possible for the Egyptian Parquet, the Native Court of Appeal, to conduct the enquiry on its own, after being granted a permit by the relevant consulates. The norm was that the case be divided into as many trials as the nationalities of the involved offenders, and that they be tried by their consular authorities separately, in a way that was often 'derisory', according to Cairo City Police Chief Russell Pasha.[44] Ultimately native Egyptian investigations were hindered by a number of cavils, due to the existence of a dual judicial system: 'no entry into a foreign domicile could be made without the presence of a consular representative, and in the case of Greeks no permission could be obtained for perquisition by night as this under the Greek constitution was illegal in Greece itself.'[45] Moreover, the efficiency of the security apparatus, in particular its capacity to bring criminals to justice, was jeopardised by the lack of collaboration between the police and the judiciary. According to the Napoleonic Code that was adopted in Egypt, the police – under the aegis of the Ministry of Interior – could only proceed to open a crime scene investigation with the authorisation of the Parquet, which was dependent on the Ministry of Justice. Consequently, in many instances the police failed to bring offenders to justice because the Parquet authorities did not collaborate. Thus criminals of every kind, from women's procurers to drug dealers and smugglers, especially if non-Egyptian, were free to ply their trades in a sort of legal vacuum.[46] Foreign brothel owners, profiting from the virtual immunity bestowed upon them by the Capitulations, relied on a vast network of international traffickers to provide them with new attractive girls, especially during the tourist season when they were most in demand. It seems that French procurers took the lion's share of the business, particularly in Cairo and Alexandria, given that they controlled the main port of departure, Marseilles, and could count on the collaboration of stokers and chauffeurs working on board of the steamers to Egypt. Women travelled as stowaways on the Messageries Maritimes vessels and disembarked mainly at Alexandria, where ships were moored along the quay; this made it easy for women to go ashore, disguised as seamen or wearing army uniforms.[47] Next, they were sorted by local procurers, often through fake employment agencies, and directed to their destined workplaces. Other women got off at Port Said on their way to Eastern destinations further afield. Older prostitutes that had been in the trade in Europe before being taken to Egypt, usually via Marseille or Naples, tended to be employed in local brothels and end their careers there. More marketable younger women would spend some time in Egypt, before being transferred to India and the Far East. Some girls were inveigled by international traffickers and eventually forced into prostitution. Many Greek girls, for instance, were said to be lured with the promise of a job or a marriage match; upon their arrival they were welcomed by local intermediaries disguised as the groom's relatives.[48] After some days, the women would be told to get ready for travelling in order to meet their future husband, and eventually they were taken to their destined brothel. Many were, nevertheless, fully cognisant of their circumstances. In a 1927 Report of the League of Nations Special Committee of Experts on the Traffic of Women and Children, the following statement made by a Greek prostitute was reported: 'Greece is quite different from all other countries. It is actually overpopulated and they are glad to see us go. If a girl has a good reason of going (*sic.*), that it is all is necessary.' Another prostitute (named 91-G in the report), while commenting on two prostitute friends who had left for Egypt on forged passports because they were minors, put it quite clearly: 'It is there one must go to make money. I should be going myself but it is too late in the season.'[49] Reliable quantitative data about the dimension of the 'White Slave Trade' are not offered in the report, but Madame Tsykalas estimated at 500 the number of foreign girls – mainly of Romanian, Austrian, Russian, French, Italian and Greek nationalities – sold to brothel owners in Egypt every year. Women's trafficking was a highly seasonal market, with the largest number of women being imported into the country during the tourist season, from December to the end of February. During that period, the demand for new girls to be employed in brothels, dancing halls, cabarets and the like increased dramatically, and the procurers' profits skyrocketed. In Naples, a traffic ring was active that smuggled women from Italy to Athens, Salonica, Alexandria and Cairo.[50] Led by Maria Pica, a former artiste known as 'Marie d'Argent', the network was exposed when a tampered passport was found in the name of Annina Morghen, a *demimondaine* from Naples whom Pica had sent to Athens to work in a dancing hall. Pica seized Morghen's real passport to prevent her from leaving Greece. Originally hired on the agreed monthly salary of 50 liras, she would instead receive 90 drachmas, the equivalent of 12 liras, plus a percentage on every bottle of champagne sold to customers in the club. Investigations into Pica's activities revealed how she held contacts with local impresarios in Egypt and Greece, countries for which passports were issued relatively easily by Italian authorities.

Increasing globalisation of the Egyptian economy due to colonial policies after 1882, powerful waves of rural and international migration, real-estate speculation and the intensification of state and private initiatives in urban planning; all these factors significantly changed Cairo, the Egyptian capital, since Isma'il's khediviate. Peasant families migrated to the city due to a protracted trend of rural dislocation. Macro-historical changes in Egypt thus deeply impacted the lives of millions of rural Egyptians who adapted to new lifestyles in booming cities. Men and women tried to enter new job markets, but the opportunities for generating female income were very limited. This is why sex work figured as an extreme but viable income-generating strategy for women in distress, either as a form of contribution to their families' shattered economies, or for themselves. Since the last quarter of the nineteenth century, female migration to Cairo expanded. Usually unattached, foreign women migrated to Egypt especially from Southern and Eastern Europe, attracted by Egypt's economic growth. Some of them were trafficked into the country by enterprising international networks of pimps, who thus supplied local brothels, both clandestine and legal. The presence of women openly marketing their sexual services in the public space, that is, outside the enclosed space of the brothel, considerably troubled political elites, both colonial and local. Cairo's urban rejuvenation was premised on the idea of controlling the rapidly expanding fluxes of people and products into the cities by rationalising, mapping, ordering and sanitising the urban space. At the same time, administrative elites were also concerned with disciplinary actions and supervision of contacts between respectable citizens and social types considered antithetic to progress and modernity: the urban poor, migrants, vagrants and sex workers thus became symbols of the sense of disorientation produced by such rapid and aggressive social change. The next chapter will zoom in on the geography of prostitution in modern Cairo, and on the role sex work played in the construction of the new urban space.

CHAPTER 2

THE GEOGRAPHY OF SEX WORK

On a bright morning of 1870, Thomas S. Harrison, the American diplomat whose diary makes for a colourful account of urban change in late nineteenth-century Cairo, while looking out of his hotel window could not help but notice how

> the *coup d'oeil* is entirely changed from what it was a few years ago. Where the hotel now stands and far beyond, it had been an uncultivated garden. In the place of the ragged sycamores which stood some distance in front and which surrounded a public ground, a receptacle for filth and a haunt for dogs, with here and there a little drinking booth for the low foreigner and dirty Arab, now stands one of the most enchanting gardens in the East, with a broad avenue between it and the hotel. This garden is laid out with beautiful pebble walks, adorned with fountains, and decked with rare exotics, flowers and trees [. . .] a silvery lake in its centre with graceful swans [. . .] boats for the amusing of the passing stranger [. . .] which render it a diminutive *Bois de Boulogne* to the Egyptian capital.[1]

The Azbakiyyah Garden, which Harrison is describing here, was located on the original site of the Birkat-al-Azbakiyyah, the Azbakiyyah Pond: during the annual floods of the Nile, in Mamluk times this lowland filled with water, while during the rest of the year it provided a green area and rallying point for festivals. This area remained abandoned until 1837, when Muhammad 'Ali decided to have it drained and transformed into a garden. The nearby cemetery was closed in order to render the area more agreeable to those foreign travellers, mostly businessmen and diplomats, who already resided and operated there. The first hotels, an enduring feature of the Azbakiyyah, were established around that time, notably the Orient Hotel and the famous Shepheard's. From the 1840s onwards, a growing number of constructions imitating Western architecture replaced the traditional buildings. Cafés, taverns and dancing halls mushroomed, where a mix of Italian, Turkish, Greek, Arab and French songs were played and heavily made-up European women welcomed customers. A heterogeneous crowd of travellers and locals, street vendors of various types, mountebanks, snake charmers, storytellers and so on populated the esplanade until Khedive Tawfiq decided to transform it into an ordered, well-designed park, a focal point of the new city he had in mind. Foreign capital was essential in bringing about the rejuvenation that turned the Azbakiyyah into an integral part of Cairo's overall urban planning scheme. The new Azbakiyyah garden was created together with the new gaslit boulevards, the districts of Isma'iliyyah and Tawfiqiyyah and the monumental Opera. The octagonal park was surrounded by large streets and four ample squares: Opera, 'Atabah al Khadra', Khazindar and Qantarat al-Dekkah were placed to the south, south-east, north-east and north-west respectively. All the trappings of fin-de-siècle cosmopolitan life concentrated in the new Azbakiyyah: the hotels frequented during the winter months by hordes of international tourists; the large, foreign-owned department stores like Cicurel, Chemla, Rivoli and Tiring; the Opera; the local branches of major European companies and societies; and the stock exchange. The Azbakiyyah was inaugurated in 1872; a green oasis of exotic species such as baobabs, Bengal figs and other rare varieties, it contained a lake, a grotto and a pagoda. The park was fenced and late-night admissions were charged at one piastre per person. Open-air cafés and restaurants catered to different tastes, both European and Oriental. Discipline and order was imposed on space and social practices, thanks to technological progress: the new Azbakiyyah, a site for refined and civilised middle-class leisure and amiable sociability, was made safe through the dissemination of gaslights. Street lamps in the shape of giant tulips holding translucent porcelain bulbs, for example, were scattered all through the park. The outside of the park was equally flamboyant, with 'its pavements and its park railings as exhibitions of native life rank next to the bazaars':[2] the donkey boy, the pavement restauranteur, the peripatetic dealers of beads and scarabs, the postcard sellers, the rug picker, the chestnut roaster, the whip maker, the tarbush maker, the fortune teller – all populated the exteriors of the Azbakiyyah Garden, trying to make good deals with the foreign tourists on their strolls outside the hotel.

In modern cities, flows of people, capitals and desires intermingled and structured a new spatial order. Cairo was clearly part of a global history of urban transformation, marked by the changes that an unprecedented acceleration in the circulation of goods, people and ideas worldwide had brought about in urban life and public space.[3] Sex workers, together with other marginalised groups, embodied the ambivalence of the modern city, a disorder which came into being with the increased social stratification and inequalities in wealth distribution that were typical of modern capitalism, in the midst of a panoptic regime. The urban landscape, in fact, was conceived and structured as a space to be seen and scrutinised by the masculine middle-class gaze of the *flâneur*, the bourgeois prototype that typically strolled around a clean, orderly and mappable city. Straight streets, ventilated boulevards, agreeable parks and pleasant coffee houses formed the backdrop to a bourgeois sociability that was deeply gendered. On one side, men's agency in the public arena contrasted with women's protected domesticity; on the other, interactions between the sexes in public were coded and performed through carefully staged social choreographies. With their openly displayed heteronormative sexuality, sex workers thus defied gendered norms and called into question men's authority over public space, their ambiguous position in the cityscape urging authorities to contain their potentially subversive practices spatially. Zoning, or the spatial marginalisation of sex workers in red-light districts, was in fact a measure taken by a number of municipal administrations in nineteenth-century global cities, 'an important symbolic and rhetoric means of isolating urban problems' in modern cities.[4] As discussed in an imposing corpus of literature on sex work, space and colonial governmentality,[5] prostitutes were often displaced from their central, although enclosed, location in the city centre to the outskirts of the city, a move that human geographer Stephen Legg – in his work on sex work regulation in India – has called 'civil abandonment'.[6] This, however, never happened in Cairo. Some forms of sex work were certainly practised in very peripheral areas, like the Acqueduct ('*Ubur al-Mayyah*), but not because of some distinctive form of institutional intervention; sex work was placed at the centre of the urban space and of the production of a normative understanding of citizenship, materially and discursively.[7] This reflected the specificity of Egypt's coloniality, that is, the presence of conspicuous numbers of non-local Capitulary subjects active in the trade, who could not simply be deported outside the city walls, and of a formally sovereign local government.[8] Cairo's main red-light district was in fact situated at a stone's throw from the Azbakiyyah and its big hotels, taverns, restaurants and dancing halls, which catered to native customers, foreign residents, tourists and, especially after 1915, an increasing number of imperial soldiers. In this chapter I look at the Azbakiyyah area, the heart of cosmopolitan Cairo since the last quarter of the nineteenth century, as a 'heterotopian' space,[9] whereby the production of two dominant orders – the national and the colonial – occurred through a subtle and constant interplay between normativity and heteronormativity, a marginal non-hegemonic space whose role in the production of the dominant order was nonetheless essential.

Zoning

Descriptions of the Azbakiyyah and its 'red-blind' district are easy to locate in old travel books and personal narratives of contemporary observers, as the area was considered a 'spectacle' of the city, one of the spots tourists had to visit during their tours of Cairo. According to Miss Cicely McCall from the British National Vigilance Association (NVA), who run a refuge for street women in Cairo in the early 1930s, Egypt – and Cairo in particular – was

> notorious for its houses of ill fame and the practice of perversions. Even nowadays, tourists are sometimes taken round the segregated quarter by their obliging dragomans to see the sights. Yet few people realize the full horror of the segregated quarter and in particular the native quarter. In Cairo, the quarter is close to a main thoroughfare in the centre of the town. Most of the streets are for pedestrians only, some are not more than two yards wide, and nowhere is there any water laid on in any of the houses. At night,

the streets are so densely crowded that a client coming out of one of the hovels onto the street can hardly push his way among the passersby.[10]

Steeped in voyeurism and a certain aversion-cum-fascination with regard to the beastly and hyper-sexualised East, the image of which they obsessively tried to evoke, orientalist travelogues and reformist documents nonetheless constitute interesting sources for the reconstruction of the appearance of the regulated area at the beginning of the twentieth century, and in the interwar period.[11] Moreover, a number of Egyptian literary sources can be fruitfully used to explore the sexual geography of the Azbakiyyah as depicted by native, as opposed to colonial, eyes, in particular the writings of modernist writers such as al-Muwaylihi and Naguib Mahfouz, who most forcefully rendered the *flâneur*'s gaze and the aestheticisation of the urban space he navigates in literary terms.[12] Cairo's brothel area was divided into two zones: the Wagh-al-Birkah, or Wish el Birkah in local parlance (meaning the 'front of the lake'); and Clot Bey Street (see Figures 2.1 and 2.2) and the Wass'ah, the area for regulated native prostitution. The Wagh-al-Birkah concentrated most of the foreign prostitutes endowed with a licence. The street was flanked with

Figure 2.1 Cairo, Clot Bey Street. Max H. Rudmann, no. 148. (Courtesy of Heather D. Ward.)

Figure 2.2   Caire, Rue Klout-Bey, dated 1914. (Courtesy of Heather D. Ward.)

three-storey buildings in Mediterranean style, with balconies stretching out onto the streets. Women would lean on the balconies wearing light dressing gowns, trying to catch the attention of those promenading the street. Just off Wagh-al-Birkah, Shari' Bab-al-Bahri was a blaze of electric lights. The street was full of music halls and cafés chantants. Female entertainers, the vast majority of them European, sang and danced while native dancers performed a sexy variant of Oriental dance for the intoxicated and uproarious crowds. To the north of the Wagh-al-Birkah and not far from Shari' Clot Bey, by contrast, the indigenous quarter of prostitution was located in the area usually known as the Wass'ah, with an extension into the Harat-al-Ruhi and the Fishmarket (see Figure 2.3). Women in the Wass'ah either solicited in front of their 'shops', that is, one-room shacks (*akhwakh*), or assembled in front of the bigger establishments. William Nicholas William, a former Australian politician who had left Australia on charges of corruption and had started a publishing company in London, where he specialised in racy publications, noticed that

> the front or street flat generally has an open window near the doorway. In this great opening, without any glass or covering at

Figure 2.3   Cairo, Fishmarket. Lichtenstern and Harari, no. 71. (Courtesy of Heather D. Ward.)

all, in fact quite open, like the big fish-shop windows in London, several women sit bedecked with the most gaudy garments that even the showy splendour of the East can produce. At the back of one great window, I noticed seven women 'on show'. In centre sat a very tall negress, whose face was as black as the devil's hoofs are reputed to be. She was splendidly proportioned, with regular and evenly cut features, and large expressive eyes. She was, as I say, jet black, with an oily shine or polish on her face. She came from the Upper Sudan, stood six feet seven inches high, and was altogether a fine picture of Nature's handiwork, even for the borders of Sudan and Abyssinia. She was a licensed woman, and had under her protection six girls, two of them came from Syria, two from the land of Goshen, and 2 from Greece, all licensed and registered.[13]

Zoning provisions stipulated that brothels could be opened only in such reserved areas of the city.[14] Brothels could not have more than one door opening onto the street, and should be completely detached from other buildings, shops or public places, in order to avoid grievances from respectable people. They also had to be far from churches and schools, so that religious sensibilities and the young generations' morals would not be harmed. Women had to avoid standing in the doorways or in the windows. Ideally, they had to be invisible. There was, however, a striking contrast between the strict segregation prescribed in legal texts and the reality described by the sources at hand. Russell Pasha recalled that the Wass'ah

> reminded one of a zoo, with its painted harlots sitting like beasts of prey behind the iron grilles of their ground-floor brothels, while a noisy crowd of low-class natives, interspersed with soldiers in uniform and sight-seeing tourists, made their way along the narrow lanes.[15]

Women would solicit openly in the streets and invite their prospective customers into the buildings lining the alleys. In the *quartier réservé*, vices were meant to be confined to the brothels, with the anticipated effect of removing all provocation from the public thoroughfares and ensuring the safety of 'decent citizens'. In reality, sex work was far from removed from the eyes of passers-by. According to a contemporary description,

> so familiar is the sight of brazen women, lost of all womanly feelings, lost to all shame and often perverted by a sexual lunacy into sexual monomaniacs; so common and so familiar is their presence, hanging from their windows almost in the nude, smoking, cursing, screeching like fiends or laughing like mocking devils; so accustomed have the inhabitants, young and old, become to all the signs of their business that they now pass, as a matter of fact, as something necessary for the use of man.[16]

In relation to slippages in the segregation system, the view of Arthur Upson (a missionary from the Nile Mission Press) is also revealing:

> When I began my purity efforts two years ago, there was not only public solicitation in the public streets, but the 'manual signs' of coitus were publicly demonstrated from both balconies and doorways, while the statistics per VD cases were not only alarming, but disgraceful.[17]

From the Wass'ah, multiple alleys departed towards inner areas whereby the coexistence of 'respectable people' and those active in 'not so respectable' activities, amid bursts of complaints on the part of reform-minded individuals, was the norm rather than the exception. Florence Wakefield, a social worker from the British Association for Moral and Social Hygiene, wrote in a report on the British Army and prostitution regulation in Egypt that:

> children live in and frequent the segregated areas. I saw three little boys sitting down for the night against the wall of one of the narrow, crowded streets. Throngs of men, many of them at student age and appearance, saunter through the streets, when the women sit at their doors in scanty garments calling to each other and the passers-by. Some of them disappeared as we approached, some stood up respectfully and greeted the police officer as a trusted friend – as indeed he was [. . .] The area impressed me as a sort of moral swamp, spreading contamination over the whole town.[18]

The physical proximity of vices to 'decent honourable families' and young generations would later be discussed in newspaper columns by ardent pro-abolitionists. For example, an article published on 8 December 1923 in the main Egyptian daily *al-Ahram*, entitled 'Chastity screams!' ('al-'Afaf intahib'), acknowledged the problem of the physical vicinity between respectable people (*al-ahrar*) and 'traders of vice'.[19] A particularly problematic spot was Shari' Clot-Bey and its adjoining alleys. Here houses of ill fame, taverns and hashish dens were placed in close proximity to the Coptic Patriarchate and the Franciscan convent, along with its school.

State officials, although rather reluctantly, eventually addressed the problem and took action: the Minister of Communication stated that public health, wealth and young generations had to be effectively protected by the government, being the foundations of the State's power, whereas the Minister of Public Works declared that the insalubrious houses near the Coptic Patriarchate would soon be demolished,

> to make space for a wide thoroughfare where decent people and families can live, instead of those wretched creatures [*hasharat*,

literally 'insects', referring to prostitutes and pimps}. At the same time, al- Khalig street will be widened by forty metres, in order to purify it from the filth it is notorious for, and to restore it to its original dignity.

The article mentions a petition started by the residents and addressed to the Azbakiyyah police station (*qism*). They had decided to

stand up as a sole man and call upon the Azbakiyyah police and the hakimdar of Cairo City Police. We complained about this most serious situation to His Excellency Vice Minister of the Interior in the month of September last, and we made an official complaint to His Excellency the Minister of the Interior.

While this source attests the direct link between citizens and institutions, the photograph of the original petition published by the newspaper allows us to understand which social groups self-identified as *ahrar*, that is, free and respectable members of civil society: 'owners, merchants, residents, religious and school authorities' acting on behalf of 'decent people and students, God's angels on Earth.' Not only is it clear that property constituted an unequivocal marker of social respectability. The concern for a clear zoning of sex workers, in terms of a spatial confinement intended to distinguish between areas for refined sociability and areas marked by vice, is tightly linked with those exclusionary policies and practices which lie at the core of the modern State, its rhetoric of civic natural rights and the making of a disciplined 'public space'. In time, various proposals were made to extend this type of regulation to other areas of the city, in an attempt to circumscribe and bring under State surveillance larger portions of clandestine sex work: in 1926, licensed brothels also existed in 'Abbasiyyah and Sayyidah Zaynab, while in 1927 brothels were opened in Bulaq, al Wa'ili and al Khalifah areas too. These measures did not prove successful, as by 1928 regulation was restricted to the original zoning areas (al-Azbakiyyah and Bab-al-Sha'riyyah). If the spatial organisation of sex work in Cairo followed a typical, disciplinary model, it was overall inefficient. The geography of commercial sex in colonial Cairo was far from being insular and restricted to the Azbakiyyah. Quite the contrary: it was dual, circumscribed and highly visible on one side; decentred, multiple, pervasive and absolutely undefined, on the other. In truth, the vast majority of the sex trade took place outside the segregated areas, hidden under a cover of decorum in anonymous flats of 'respectable' neighbourhoods, or disguised as entertainment in clubs and cabarets. From 1926 to 1936, Cairo City Police detected and raided 2,654 clandestine brothels, which were probably only a tiny fraction of the many illicit establishments in the city. On 13 December 1923, a letter was published in *al-Ahram*, concerning the diffusion of clandestine brothels (*buyut sirriyyah*, secret houses) in the city. A reader had drawn a map showing the locations of these brothels, which he had discovered while walking around Cairo. He had been able to identify 159 houses, scattered across the whole urban fabric. Apparently very few areas of the city, if any, were devoid of these houses or 'places', as the reader called them, 'for the resident and the traveller, where sinners, men and women, lie together illicitly'. However, according to the reader, most of these – albeit clandestine – houses were in fact known to the neighbourhoods' residents, and to the police itself. Hence, as long as the public order was not disrupted, and no complaints were raised by the people living nearby, public security officials were happy to turn a blind eye on clandestine sex work. Public morality was clearly in a very bad condition, the reader argued, given that a robbery case could be solved in just 16 hours, while the police did not bother to take any action to protect the 'country's virtues'.[20] Transient, disguised sex work was the real subversive vice, as it was more resistant to incorporation into the microphysics of power than anything else. The perceived threat posed by the mobility of women selling sex clandestinely, and their capacity to infiltrate the spaces of respectable people, ended up reinforcing the notion of the essential dualism between civilised bourgeois classes and unruly, dangerous and low social classes.

Conclusion

Unlike those colonial cities where sex work was pushed to the margins of the urban fabric, thus placing the articulation of the civic dialectic at the border of the urban space, Cairo's liminal – or heterotopian – places marked the existence of a much subtler dynamic, as we have seen in the case of the Azbakiyyah and its red-light district: central and within easy reach, it is fully integrated in the urban fabric. Despite the existence of specific regulations aimed at enhancing the enclosure system, prostitutes were perfectly visible and navigated the public space. Brothels may have complied with laws prescribing one access door only and fenced windows, but prostitutes would shout for customers from the balconies or thresholds, and even solicit in the streets. It is evident that Cairene sex work regulation totally missed its self-proclaimed aims of circumscribing and supervising the practice of commercial sex. Yet, regulation and zoning were organic to the realisation of a gigantic heterotopic order, as they constantly conjured up the idea of subversion, or quiet encroachment, which legitimated the imposition of that very same order. Moreover, sex work was far from being insular: in its most pervasive form, namely as disguised and clandestine sex work, it was diffused all over the city. Prostitutes and gaudy women became dense metaphors of civic disorder, paradoxically destabilising and at the same time reinforcing gendered, racial and class hierarchies and conventions.

CHAPTER 3

REGULATING PROSTITUTION IN COLONIAL CAIRO

Anxieties about the influx of rural migrants, manumitted slaves and foreign, unattached women engaging more or less overtly in the selling of sexual services haunted modern urban life in cosmopolitan Cairo. Mass free movement, the intermingling of socially disparate human types and unsupervised physical contact among the sexes raised serious suspicions in the authorities: popular crowds and individual bodies were conceived, by the dominant elites, as dangerous sites of moral degeneration and physical pollution, to be actively patrolled. Nonetheless, the Egyptian authorities and, after 1882, the British colonial administrators who came to exercise real power over the country tried to implement a whole array of disciplinary techniques in order to ensure public order and health.

This chapter introduces the theme of the regulation of prostitution in Egypt as a specific type of colonial and biopolitical project. The term 'colonial', therefore, carries two interrelated but distinct meanings. Firstly, and primarily, it is used to indicate the expansion of the purview of the State, its capacity of controlling and disciplining broader areas of social practices, and its turning the modular logic of individual confinement or disciplinarisation into an expansive regulatory apparatus. Secondly, the adjective 'colonial' qualifies a historically specific and situated case of imperial rule, which Great Britain established as a 'veiled protectorate' over Egypt after 1882.

Prostitution regulation in Egypt had some pre-colonial antecedents, which implies that biopolitical concerns were already part of

Muhammad Ali's modernisation project. Yet, the extension of sex work regulation as a self-conscious disciplinary project was an imperial policy, aimed both at preserving colonial troops from venereal contagion and preserving order. According to regulationist thinkers, prostitution was a 'necessary evil', which could not be eliminated from society, only contained and supervised, sanitised and spatially circumscribed to minimise its consequences on public order, morality and health. Thus a number of techniques, which will be described and analysed in this chapter, were deployed to realise such a scopic regime in addition to spatial zoning, described in the previous chapter: labelling, quantification, medicalisation, confinement and racialisation. The emergence of a distinct subjectivity for sex workers, namely that of professional prostitutes, was both the result of and the necessary pre-requisite for regulationism. The simultaneous deployment of a number of disciplinary practices produced its object of control, whose normalisation required the unceasing reproduction of the disciplinary mechanism itself. If panopticism is taken as a quintessentially modern way of exercising power through the continuous circulation of it, prostitutes not only became 'metaphors of modernity', to use Timothy Gylfoyle's expression.[1] They were also representative of a typical paradox of modernity: discursively constructed, as much as thoroughly embodied and sexualised, by a wide host of material, corporeal and invasive practices they were subjected to (sanitary inspections, incarceration, medical treatments etc.), regulation was based on the epistemological distinction between the 'real' world and an abstract concept of order to be forced upon this world. The relevance of sex and race politics for the stability of the colonial enterprise will be extensively discussed in the last part of the chapter. Sex and race, in fact, served as referent for the articulation and reproduction of civilizational hierarchies which, far away from the metropolis, did not seem as stable as usually maintained by the official colonial rhetoric. Interracial relationships, generally accepted in early imperial times, came to horrify the colonisers with the looming threat of miscegenation in the late age of Empire.[2]

Labelling

As shown by Khaled Fahmy,[3] the emergence of state interest in sex workers' activities can be traced back to Muhammad Ali's defensive modernisation reforms: in 1834 a ban targeted sex work, expelling Cairo's prostitutes and performers – albeit temporarily – to Upper Egypt.[4] This was a decisive break from the previous Mamluk and Ottoman practices of *de facto* toleration, when sex workers were grouped as a profession and, despite being excluded from the guild system, taxed. Taxation was carried out by tax farmers, communitarian leaders who had free reign in adding or erasing women's names from the registers, often depending on the payment of a good bribe.

The advent of regulationism resulted in a dramatic, qualitative change in the way sex work was managed in modern Cairo, and it signaled a momentous transformation in the relationship between the State and the people. By starting to regulate sex work directly, the State expanded its reach over society in an unprecedented way. The institutionalisation of prostitution through the establishment of state-licensed brothels in reserved urban areas, where registered sex workers offered their services, lawfully entailed the creation of a system of oversight: this was constituted by the brothel, where prostitutes worked under the supervision of brothel owners and were subjected to weekly medical inspections, and by the so-called lock hospital, used for the enclosed treatment of venereal sex workers. This system was framed by a broad medical discourse on social hygiene, reflecting the emerging political priority of creating a normative knowledge corpus about the biological and the social.

Systematic regulationist policies were introduced in Egypt by the British, as a local variant of the French-style, state-licensed brothel system, immediately after the British occupation of Egypt in September 1882.[5] At that time, the modular logic of individual confinement and regulation of abnormal social practices was turned into an expansive regulatory apparatus for reasons of sheer imperial governmentality. Based on the acceptance of the existence of a double standard for male and female sexualities, and on the Augustinian conception of prostitution as a 'necessary evil', the modern system of regulated prostitution conceived prostitutes as a clear-cut, separate category of marginal social actors. Removed from the working class they originally belonged to, they were increasingly stigmatised as agents of moral corruption and physical contamination. The Malthusian logic of social productivity came to bear on this subaltern group in such a way that regulation was seen as the key method to transform these 'indolent', disorderly elements into disciplined workers, thus making their activity both socially and morally acceptable. Unlike France, Great Britain was not a regulationist country: the closest the British had gotten to sex work regulation was in the form of the Contagious Diseases Act(s) in 1864, only to be repealed in 1883 thanks to the vocal opposition of a variegated abolitionist front. Yet, regulationism was invariably put into place in the colonies, where racist notions about the cultural inferiority and sexual primitivism of native people were coupled with the paramount importance of colonial security. Utilitarian concerns about public order and the spread of VDs among imperial troops made regulation mandatory, all the while 'offering a counterargument to the notion that British liberalism was largely responsible for the limited engagement with regulationist pratices'.[6]

The first law disciplining sex work was drafted in Egypt on 31 October 1882, that is, only a month-and-a-half after the British victory against the nationalist uprising led by Colonel Ahmad 'Urabi at Tell al-Kabir, and the occupation of Egypt by 13,000 colonial troops. According to the Egyptian social historian 'Imad Hilal,[7] British authorities forced the Egyptian government to adopt an overtly racist discrimination against sex workers. Since the 'Orient' was commonly associated with images of sensuality, lust and unrestrained vice, the colonial imagination constructed local women as subhumans. As one Lieutenant Olliver, on duty on the HMS *Calypso* of the Mediterranean Fleet during World War I, had it:

> perhaps people in England do not realize the effect that the immense inferiority of foreign women – compared to our own – has on men; more or less according to the meridian of longitude of the place so is the woman either a beast of burden, a chattel of her man, or more or less his equal. Tho' one may respect ones' equal, one has not the same feeling for the chattel of a man who is decidedly inferior to oneself and who does not respect herself. And the whisky or vodka inside one tends to take away the objection to her *dago* nationality or her yellow skins.[8]

Given the enthusiasm with which rank-and-file soldiers on leave tended to patronise brothels and taverns throughout the Empire, authorities felt the need to take measures that could help prevent the physical degeneration of the occupational armies, before steering toward abolitionism in later times.

Security reasons were combined with public order and health considerations. According to N.W. Willis, an Australian author of pamphlets on moral reform in the interwar years, Cairo was reeking with violence and disease before the arrival of the British:

> The Wazza [the Wass'ah, the Cairene area for licensed native prostitution, *mine*] bazaar was to be found a fearful death-trap of iniquity [...] and the Egyptian police was afraid to enter [it] in response to the cries of the unfortunate who were being done to death. It was then – in the dark days of Egypt – quite a common thing to discover the mangled body of one of the poor unhappy women in the roadway at Wazza bazaar as the beneficent sun cast its morning rays on this plague-spot. Then, no man or woman was safe in such dens. Many went into the dark, dirty lanes and came out no more [...] this state of things has been abolished, until today the place is safe for a European to walk through as Piccadilly Circus or Leicester Square.[9]

In other words, according to Willis the introduction of regulationism in Cairo was tantamount to a philanthropic act, which not only benefited the city's ordinary residents but, most crucially, sex workers themselves, as they could now ply their trade in a safe environment. Apart from the gross falsification of the actual state of public order and security in the reserved areas, as later revealed and discussed by Willis himself,[10] and in spite of the beneficial impact of regulation on women's conditions (it is no coincidence that most of them decidedly resisted state intervention by keeping or going underground), this testimony highlights the extent to which themes of crime prevention and public order played a distinct role in discourses about the desirability of regulationism in the colony. According to such a narrative, sex work regulation in Egypt was part and parcel of the British civilising mission.

The *manshur 'amm*, or 'general decree', of 1882 profoundly changed the practice of sex work in Egypt.[11] Thus it formally established sex work as a 'profession', by creating a juridical difference between women who were legally authorised to exchange sex for money in state-licensed brothels, and unauthorised clandestine prostitutes and streetwalkers. Regulationism introduced a system of supervision which was constituted by the brothel, where prostitutes worked under the control of a *badrona*, a brothel owner, and the inspection room, *maktab al-taftish* (two were opened in Cairo and Alexandria, managed by the central Health Administration). Women's names had to be listed in special registers, together with the results of their medical check-ups. If found affected by disease, women would be hospitalised for treatment. They could resume work only after being dismissed from the lock hospital and issued a medical certificate. Prostitutes had to obtain licences as a proof of their professional status; more importantly, third parties were granted the right to legally run brothels by applying for a regular licence. According to Article 3 of the decree, every prostitute (*imra'ah 'ahirah*) working in a locale known for prostitution was obliged to register her name with the local police, in the bureau of medical inspection. She was given a card with a progressive number, which clearly showed her name, age, address, personal characteristics and the name of the brothel owner she was working for. The woman had to undergo weekly sanitary inspections, whose results were reported on her unique card. Inspections took place on a daily basis, from 8 a.m. to 1 p.m. in the summer and from 10 a.m. to 2 p.m. in the winter. Doctors were prohibited from carrying out sanitary check-ups at the woman's domicile. Those prostitutes who were unable to attend the weekly sanitary inspection due to illness would send a certificate from their doctor, on the day designated for the scheduled check-up, proving that their conditions prevented them from being present at the medical inspection. The same kind of provisions also applied to female brothel owners, with the exception of women over 50 years of age. The concern for a clear definition of the marginal status of prostitutes is evident in Article 13: every prostitute who wished to leave the trade, as a result of marriage or repentance (*tawbah*),[12] had to produce two witnesses and apply to the Public Health Administration in order to have her name removed from the registration list. Pecuniary fines were applied to enforce the law: all women who failed to attend medical examinations, or did not produce their certificates, were subjected to a 50-piastre fine in the first instance, 100 piastres in the second, or imprisonment from two to eight days.[13] The regulation concerning the issuance of brothel licences was also laid down by the 1882 law. Article 16 stated that whoever desired to establish a house for prostitution (*karakhanah*), whether they were local or foreign subjects, would have to submit a specific application to the local administration in order to get a licence. After a grace period of three months, any non-licensed brothel would be closed down by police authorities. The owners of brothels were required to notify the police and the Medical Inspection Bureau about the number of women employed (their names, age and provenence), as well as to supply information about all the women coming, going or temporarily residing in their establishments within 24 hours from the issuance of the licence. Brothel owners also had to keep a ledger, to be made available to authorities upon request.[14] The 1882 decree was followed by a number of legal texts elaborating upon its main provisions. In July 1885, for example, an ordinance on the medical inspections of prostitutes was promulgated by the Minister of Interior, 'Abd al-Qadir Hilmi Pasha.[15] It stipulated that the inspection bureaus of Cairo and Alexandria were to be staffed by one or two doctors, one nurse, a secretary with knowledge of Arabic and French, a police officer and a suitable number of guards. On 15 July 1896, finally, a comprehensive Law on Brothels (*La'ihah Buyut-al-'ahirat*) was issued.[16] This law marked the real beginning of licensed prostitution in Egypt (*bigha' rasmi*, literally 'official prostitution'), and it constituted the basis for the 1905 Arête which, being the ultimate legal text on state-regulated sex work, disciplined the activities of licensed prostitutes resident in brothels until the abolition of prostitution in 1949. Article 1 of the 1896 law defined a brothel as 'the place where two or more women are living permanently or assembling temporarily for the purpose of prostitution'. According to Article 5, in order to open a brothel a written request had to be submitted to the Governorate, or the Provincial Administration, at least 15 days prior to the proposed opening date. The name, birth place and nationality of each applicant, as well as information about the location and number of rooms of the establishment, and details about the legal owners of the premises, were also to be included in the request. The actual licence consisted of a certificate of registration in a specific brothels' register. Both foreigners and locals could apply for a permit, provided they were not minors or interdicted. Indeed, those who had been convicted of a crime in the five years prior to application, as well as commercial sex entrepreneurs whose establishments had been closed down by police authorities for not complying with existing laws, were forbidden from applying for a licence. The brothel owner also had to supply a detailed list with the names of registered prostitutes and other people living and working in the house, such as servants, to authorities. Prostitutes had to be at least 18 years old. Every prostitute received a photo card from the police, which was to be renewed annually. Finally, according to Article 15 women had to submit to the weekly medical examination (*kashf tibbi*) described earlier on. In sum, the whole text was characterised by an emerging preoccupation with labelling prostitutes as such, and stamping them out as a specific sociological type.

Counting

Before moving to the description of the spaces and procedures associated with the regulation of sex work in Cairo, I would like to explore a different type of disciplinary technique, whose cumulative effects impacted the ways in which public opinion made sense of prostitution to no lesser extent than law enforcement. Over time statistical thinking has proven to be a powerful governmentality tool, and it has been used to construct normative corpuses of knowledge in any field of the social sciences. The importance of counting for the creation of a biopolitical system is conspicuous. Demographic statistics and censuses, the science of counting the population, are key measures for the enhancement of the productivity and wellbeing of a people, by virtue of their capacity to study, understand and regulate patterns of reproduction, labour, residence etc. The practice of counting has been inclusive as much as it has been exclusionary: it was used both to demarcate belonging and to circumscribe difference. Such statistical knowledge, a real tool of power, was constructed through the accumulation of data and information, which materialised into voluminous digests.

Being a regulationist country from 1882 to 1949, Egypt produced a distinct type of documents concerning prostitution and its place within society. Authorities tried to monitor and discipline sex work by turning it into a quantifiable phenomenon as much as possible. Police and sanitary officials were instructed to collect detailed information about sex workers' social profiles, while brothel owners were requested to keep registers with their employees' names, provenance and age. Unfortunately, none of these materials seem to be available to researchers today. What historians can make use of, in an attempt to reconstruct the dimension of the phenomenon, are the aggregate data that can be detected in the censuses (available for the years 1917 and 1927) and, more significantly, Public Security and Public Health yearly reports from the Egyptian Ministry of Interior (available for the years ranging from 1921 to 1946 inclusive). These sources have in fact been used and compiled in a number of publications on prostitution and venereal diseases, by abolitionist societies and public health experts respectively.[17]

According to the 1917 census, prostitutes in Cairo were 1,395 (with a greater concentration in Bab-al-Sha'riyyah, Azbakiyyah and Sayyidah Zaynab), that is, a number much smaller compared to other coeval estimates: writing in 1915, Guy Thornton, Chaplain of the Australian and New Zealand Army Corps garrisoned in Cairo during World War I, talked of at least 2,300 native plus 800 European women being registered as prostitutes, 'without considering clandestine prostitutes numbering in the thousands'.[18] Two years earlier, Major Frank Young, Honorary Secretary for the YMCA National Committee, told the *Egyptian Gazette* that 'with the increasing prices in all directions in Egypt, thanks to the popularity of the country as a tourist and a winter resort, one thing remains cheap: vice'.[19] It may be that a major Purification Campaign carried out under martial law in 1916, during World War I, had significantly reduced the numbers in the trade. However, without detailed information on this specific episode, beyond some media coverage, it might be safer to say that, despite the enforcement of state-licensed prostitution in Cairo, the numbers of actual women practising the trade can only be estimated. Moreover, it is commonly accepted that a decrease in licensed prostitution may not reflect but a significant increase in clandestine sex work: in other words, not a decrease in the actual number of sex workers, but simply their 'going underground' as opposed to practising as registered prostitutes. In the 1927 census, which was the first to enlist prostitution as a separate professional category, that is, separately from 'unproductive' activities such as begging and vagrancy, the registered prostitutes consisted of 749 women: 680 locals and 69 foreigners. Once again numbers must be treated with great caution. In 1926, two years after a crackdown on clandestine prostitutes and procurers in the native quarter, Cairo City Police reported the existence of 1,184 licensed women: 859 Egyptians and 325 Europeans. According to the report, 102 clandestine houses had been raided in 1926. In this case I was not able to verify the coeval trend in clandestine sex work, which would give us a more exhaustive picture of the phenomenon. Contemporary observers described prostitution in

Cairo as an unabated and flourishing phenomenon, thanks to the relative post-bellum prosperity.[20] Moreover, according to Russell Pasha, *hikimdar* of Cairo City Police, in 1931 the enforcement of state regulation on prostitution did not have any positive impact on public security, as the bulk of commercial sex trade was underground and out of reach of public authorities. Russell Pasha stated that brothels catered for working-class customers and the 'baser kind of tourists', while '99 per cent of respectable middle-class Egyptian men consorted with clandestine prostitutes'.[21] In fact, he maintained that the general standard of morality in the city was so low that 'there was no need for any but working-class men to cohort with licensed prostitutes because there was an ample supply of other complaisant girls'.[22] If we bear in mind that in the 1927 census, almost 400,000 people in Cairo figured as unpaid workers, the vast majority of them women, it is utterly difficult to estimate how many of those women engaged in some form of transactional sex work in the clandestine sector. The available data document only the expansion or contraction of the licensed sector, the relative presence of local as opposed to foreign women employed as prostitutes and the number of clandestine houses raided every year. They reflect the contours of the extent to which Public Security officials were able to scrutinise the trade, not what was really going on. Public Health bureaus for the sanitary inspection of licensed prostitutes recorded the numbers of Egyptian licensed and unlicensed sex workers they interacted with in the years 1921–1927, while yearly reports of Cairo's City Police reconstruct trends in the trade between 1928 and 1946. These data are collated and shown in the following table.[23]

Since 1925, the number of unlicensed sex workers raided in clandestine houses or caught in the streets while soliciting has always exceeded the number of registered women. Hence, looking at licensed prostitution data only, one could inadvertently think there was a decline in sex work at first. However, available data on clandestine prostitution have revealed an entirely different picture, namely an upsurge in sex work in the 1930s and again during World War II, concentrated in the casual and informal sector. More and more often, women seemed to avoid licensed sex work as they did not want to comply with the sanitary medical inspections they would be subjected to, which severely affected their ability to work and make an earning, if affected with desease. This was especially true at times when sex work was sustained by increased

Table 3.1   Number of licensed and unlicensed prostitutes in Cairo, 1921–46.

Year	Number of unlicensed prostitutes known to police	Number of licensed prostitutes
1921	906	1,210
1922	651	1,243
1923	840	1,070
1924	735	843
1925	884	718
1926	–	745
1927	723	641
1928	–	620
1929	–	628
1930	–	653
1931	–	338
1932	2,497 (Azbakiyyah area only)	726
1933	–	745
1934	2,278	848
1935	2,009	804
1936	2,899	821
1937	2,893	823
1938	–	699
1939	–	582
1940	2,124	606
1941	–	742
1942	2,624	758
1943	4,319	631
1944	2,909	571
1945	3,772	555
1946	1,219	462

demand and, therefore, became a particularly interesting occupation: during World War II, for example, when thousands of soldiers were stationed in Cairo, the census detected 4,319 unlicensed prostitutes against 631 licensed ones: two years later the number of unlicensed prostitutes was recorded at 3,772 as opposed to 551 licensed ones. This is undoubtedly useful information for the description of general trends, but it is far from indicative of the phenomenon. While there was a general agreement among experts on the fact that clandestine prostitution was several times the size of licensed sex work, very different estimates were made. N.W. Willis argued that

> to every licensed woman in Cairo or Alexandria there are at least ten, perhaps, twenty unlicensed, uncontrolled, women of every colour or nationality *except British and Americans* [my emphasis] [...] most of the women are French; next in numbers come Italians, and there are also Germans, Swiss, Greeks and Spanish.[24]

Similarly, a prominent specialist on venereal diseases, Dr Fikhri Mikha'il Farag, gave the most disquieting estimates, arguing that the number of unlicensed prostitutes could be 35 to 40 times that of registered women: this means that, if in 1921 licensed prostitutes were 906, the number of unregistered sex workers would be around 35,000 to 40,000.[25] Finally, Louise Dorothy Potter, an abolitionist social worker active in Egypt in the 1930s, wrote in a leaflet *Egypt is awakening. Is it true?* that 'Cairo has, it is officially stated, about five times as many "secret" as "registered" women. This is true in different degrees of every regulated city. In practice, therefore, vice is not confined by the system of licensed prostitution'.[26] Once it is established that data on licensed prostitution far from reflect a balanced picture of the diffusion of sex work in the city, it must be noted that key information, as for example the actual diffusion of clandestine sex work and its proportion to licensed prostitution, is not retrievable and bound to remain unknown. Moreover, such a proliferation of haphazard and fragmentary data is interesting in itself, as it points to dominant anxieties with and concerns about quantification and control.

Medicalising

Egyptian and colonial authorities claimed that one of the main reasons for the adoption of a regulationist legislation in the country was to protect public health from the spread of sexually transmitted diseases; according to this logic, only the containment of the brothels' inmates and the strict supervision of their medical conditions could prevent the diffusion of syphilis, and its degenerative effects on the entire social body.

The discourse about the sanitary supervision of sex workers can be framed, of course, within a much larger debate on public health, an integral facet of Egypt's defensive modernisation project since the beginning of the nineteenth century. The link between a scientific medical discourse and modern state-building, in fact, has been extensively studied in order to show how modern clinical medicine was introduced and developed in Egypt under Muhammad Ali's rule, as a tool of self-strengthening state reform.[27] By the 1820s, French consultants were hired to set up a modern medical school in Egypt, Qas al 'Aini, under the direction of the French doctor Clot-Bey. Students were taught the medical profession through a four-year medical curriculum modelled on the French one. Clot-Bey's reforms were not meant to Frenchify Egyptian medicine, but simply to introduce modern medical knowledge and practices in the country. In other words, French doctors were to instruct a native class of professionals whose competences were based on Western standards. The process of institutionalisation of the medical profession went on under a different guise after the British occupation of 1882. In 1893, Qasr al-'Ayni hospital was taken over by the British on the pretense of its poor management by the Egyptian government, to be returned to Egyptian authorities only in 1929. The Anglicisation of medicine in Egypt resulted in a dramatic reduction of the number of Egyptian doctors, with access to the Medical School of Qas al 'Aini being limited to a small elite of upper-class, English-speaking locals because of the introduction of yearly fees and the requirement of English as the language of instruction. Clearly, the British wanted to encourage the practice of medicine as a trade, not as a service to the benefit of the Egyptian population. Legal regulations, for example, privileged foreign practitioners who could work in Egypt freely, as medical diplomas obtained from any medical school in the world were the sole requisite for obtaining a licence in Egypt. More importantly, the School curriculum was not designed in a way that students could obtain a specialisation, but for the training of general practitioners employed in state health care facilities: those who graduated from the School were considered simply as 'graduates', and not doctors.[28] At the same time, the top echelons of the profession became the precincts of specialist graduates from institutions other than the Medical School of Qas al 'Aini. As el-Azhary Sonbol reports, the number of Europeans working in Egypt rose from 109,725 in 1897 to 147,063 in 1907, an increase of 35 per cent in 10 years. The number of Greeks increased by 65 per cent; Germans, 35 per cent; Italians, 43 per cent; Swiss, 35 per cent; and Belgians, 33 per cent. In addition, a great number of Syrians and Armenians, all of whom were Ottoman subjects, settled in the country.[29]

Foreign doctors formed a powerful professional class catering for the needs of wealthy urban elites, while the sanitary needs of the vast majority of poor, and rural, Egyptian people were deserted almost completely. Thus knowledge of Western medicine was not only a toll of social control, but also constituted a form of power capital, jealously guarded by colonial elites and their associates. Here, we can see an interesting parallelism between sex work regulation and the institutionalisation of modern medicine, and the medical profession, under colonial domination: although disciplinary techniques imported from the West were already deployed in Egypt before the colonial period, their consolidation into self-conscious, biopolitical regulative apparatuses driven by the increasing scientification of local culture, and based on racial hierarchies, was definitely a colonial endeavour.

With the increasing stratification of Egyptian society and the emergence of a nationalist elite, namely a specific group of self-identified agents of modernisation, Egyptian medical doctors – often educated or trained abroad – started to act as mediators between local sensitivities and imperatives of Westernisation, and cultural imitationism. In the 1920s, that is, one century after the first encounter between European and local medicine, Egyptian doctors established themselves as recognised specialists; this professional elite of upper-middle-class men began questioning the predominance of European doctors and institutions, asserting themselves as pioneers of a truly local, nationalist medical science at the service of the well-off members of the Egyptian population. Liat Kozma excellently explained how 'reformers and medical doctors who started writing about sex in Arabic, presented themselves as liberating their readers from the hold of customs and organized religion and thus situated themselves as the vanguard of a modern and enlightened East'.[30]

Experts in reproductive health and sexology (*'ilm al-tanassuliyyat*, 'science of reproduction') clearly intervened in the debate on the rational management of sex work as an issue of national interest. In 1924, Berlin-educated dermatologist and self-proclaimed sexologist Fakhri Mikha'il Farag wrote that Egyptians needed to be taught about sexual health and reproductive matters, exactly as they had been acquainted with technological innovations such as the wireless telegraph one generation before. In his tract on the diffusion of venereal diseases (*amrad tanassuliyyah* or *zahriyyah*), he provided vital information on the medicalisation of prostitution in early twentieth-century Cairo. Faraj described the three sanitary bureaus for prostitutes in Cairo: one in the Darb-al-Nubi, for sex workers plying the trade in Bab-al-Sha'riyyah and the Azbakiyyah areas; one in 'Abbasiyyah; and one in Sayyidah Zaynab. He compared them to their counterparts in Berlin, in an attempt to reveal the serious limitations of sanitary policies in the Egyptian capital. In 1921, for example, 1,381 prostitutes were listed in the registers of the Darb-al-Nubi bureau. During that year, 390 women were stricken off the list for various reasons: as a result, the actual number of prostitutes that were regularly inspected in the bureau was 991. As the clinic was open four days a week, and the total number of inspections that year was 29,208, it is possible to derive a daily inspection rate of 143 women.[31] Moreover, it is important to consider that bureaus were open only from 10 a.m. to 1 or 2 p.m., depending on the season, and that during opening hours medical staff also had bureaucratic responsibilities, in addition to the carrying out of medical inspections on women. Thus, we may conclude that every medical check-up would last for a few minutes, instead of the 60 minutes that were necessary for a thorough internal and external examination and, accordingly, a correct diagnosis of venereal diseases. Doctors in the sanitary bureaus themselves lamented that they were virtually unable to detect any infection. Under these difficult circumstances, regulations concerning the frequency of medical check-ups (once a week) were also evaded. Local women were checked 20 times a year (i.e., every 18 days), while foreign women were subjected to medical examinations 30 times a year (i.e., every 12 days). Burtuqalis Bey, a gynaecologist specialising in the treatment of venereal disease in Cairo during the first decade of the 1900s, claimed that a medical inspection would take him at least 30 minutes, while in state-run bureaus a doctor would check tens of women in the same timespan.[32] Foreign women were exempted from medical inspection if they were able to provide a certificate signed by a private practitioner: this resulted in frequent forgeries. If found affected by disease, the doctors would notify the woman's consul, who would then prohibit her from practising the trade until recovery. Given that free clinics were not available, and treatment in venereal wards for European women was not enforced by law, foreign prostitutes were largely allowed to keep working provided they went underground, and were not caught prostituting themselves in the *quartier réservé* or soliciting in the streets.

In addition, prostitutes resorted to a number of strategies in order to escape supervision and work undisturbed. Thus some women disinfected themselves prior to the check-up or used special ointments to conceal the external manifestations of syphilis, in the hope that they could deceive their doctors. Traditional barbers and midwives played an important role in these elusive practices, as they had some knowledge of traditional medicine. In 1934, for example, a barber was arrested in Alexandria; he was known for being a specialist in the camouflage of syphilis marks on the bodies of prostitutes. Over a period of time, a new practice was introduced: rich customers would ask private doctors to test prostitutes before consorting with them, so as to be certain that the women were not infected. For a considerable sum of money, specialists would inspect the women and sign a certificate valid for 24 hours, stating that the prostitute was free from infection. Obviously such medical inspections had no diagnostic significance. Women, Burtuqalis Bey wrote, were treated like fresh fish, to be consumed within one day after being bought.[33]

In 1904, a hospital for the treatment of native syphilitic prostitutes was opened in Sayyidah Zaynab. The hospital, called al-Hod al-Marsud ('haunted basin'), occupied the site where the current Skin and Venereal Disease Hospital is situated today, at 22 Shari' Qadri, and contained 200 beds. The hospital was staffed by three doctors only, and women were hosted in crowded common rooms with barred windows, to prevent the possible escape of inmates. Any sex worker found infected with a venereal disease, whether during a routine medical inspection or while she was prostituting herself (in the streets or in a clandestine brothel), was confined to the lock hospital for treatment. The hospital was equipped for the diagnosis and treatment of venereal disease throughout its different stages and in accordance with medical practices.

For instance, large quantities of mercury and potassium permanganate were used to suppress the infections. Reports from Public Health authorities point out the constant increase in the number of patients; from 1925 to 1931 the number of women treated in the al-Hod al-Marsud lock hospital rose from 2,830 to 5,783.[34] As stated by Muhammad Shahin, author of a work on the system of venereal clinics established across the country from the mid-1920s, the rise in the number of treated people may have reflected a greater awareness of the necessity to cure infections promptly and in accordance with the correct sanitary practices. However, the high number of inmates who stopped treatment upon the disappearance of external symptoms, that is, without full recovery, does not corroborate Shahin's hypothesis.[35] In other words, the number of syphilitic patients was constantly on the rise, which means that regulationist policies did not curb the spread of sexually transmitted diseases, as medical techniques of infection control were avoided and evaded by patients whenever possible. In addition, we learn from Shahin's report that in al-Hod al-Marsud, between 1925 and 1932 the average percentage of diseased women who interrupted the treatment beforehand was 44 per cent.[36] The reasons for this were manifold: not only was hospitalisation perceived, by the women, as an unwanted form of confinement which restrained their freedom of movement, but it also severely affected their economic circumstances. Moreover, treatment was not free: in 1918 inmates paid 47 millims per day, 50 millims in 1919 and 78 millims in 1920.[37] Brothel owners often advanced money to pay for the prostitutes' hospital fees, charging very high rates of interest in return. We must also take into consideration the fact that a significant number of foreign practitioners were not subjected to sanitary control, and were thus left virtually free to prostitute themselves despite being diseased. Moreover, the vast majority of sex workers in Cairo engaged in clandestine prostitution in an attempt to avoid control by state authorities. Sanitary officials believed that the treatment they provided in the clinic was a medical failure; they were perfectly aware that no full recovery was possible for the majority of women, without costly therapies that usually lasted several years. Secondary and tertiary syphilis, for instance, was to be treated with mercury and potassium permanganate tablets for the duration of three years, in addition to the patient being kept under observation for two years, with blood tests taken at regular intervals. In reality, though, women would often be discharged from hospital after only a few days, or upon disappearance of the most evident, exterior symptoms of syphilis.

Confinement

In theory, the Egyptian regulationist system was informed by principles of enclosure and hierarchical supervision. However, none of these requirements were respected in Cairo. As we have seen, the *quartier réservé* in fact only hosted a limited number of establishments, since prostitution in Cairo was largely scattered across the urban fabric. The majority of licensed brothels were opened in the touristic and nightlife areas of Cairo, Azbakiyyah and the surrounding neighbourhoods, thus underlining how the expansion of prostitution was intertwined with rising upper-middle-class purchasing power and global commerce. Nevertheless, sex work was practised illegally all over the city. Despite the existence of specific regulations aimed at enhancing the enclosure system, sex work was not segregated. Due to a specific clause in existing regulations, doctors were forbidden from making house calls: as a result, medical check-ups did not take place in brothels. The effects of this were that Cairene prostitutes enjoyed liberty of movement to a degree unknown to sex workers subjected to the same regulationist system in other countries. There was certainly a hierarchy within the brothel, but nothing comparable to the French system; the Madame was often a prostitute herself, and the presence of men – whether husbands, pimps or paramours – was not exceptional. In the case of clandestine establishments, in particular, brothels were often akin to family businesses, with the owner's family and servants occupying one storey of the building, while sex workers and customers used the rest of the house. Hence, rather than there being a careful separation between prostitution and the domestic economy, this implies an overlap between sex work and family work. In the French system, the brothel owner was considered to be an agent of the central government, indeed, the very antithesis of elusive procurers and pimps, who evaded supervision and tried to prevent police control over the prostitutional milieu.[38] In Cairo, by contrast, the alliance between brothel owners, local pimps and bullies was considered essential for the evasion of state control. Indeed, in some cases, police officers were known for creating secret dealings with brothel owners and prostitutes.[39]

Prostitutes who were caught while soliciting in the streets, or those who failed to turn up at medical check-ups, were taken to the local police section, *qism*, to be sentenced and eventually transferred to the relevant *niyabah*, the prison of the Public Prosecutor's Office. Unlike French prisons, Egyptian penitentiaries did not have a separate section for prostitutes. Segregation was not enforced due to infrastructural constraints: in the *niyabah* of Bulaq, the isolation cell was designed to contain no more than 15 people, but in reality it accommodated 40; in the penitentiary of Old Cairo, isolation cells contained no lavatories; in the 'Abdin *niyabah* there were no windows; in al-Khalifah's the isolation cell had a shattered roof.[40] The efficiency of the regulationist system in Egypt was jeopardised, above all, by the very existence of unequal colonial power relations, as those at work in the Capitulary legal system. The Dual system,[41] and the privileges granted to foreign communities by the Capitulations, severely curtailed the capacity of both local and British police to enforce the law effectively. Since its inception, sex work regulation in Egypt applied to local women and foreign nationals very differently. Such a difference was based on the colonial logic behind the Cairene regulation of prostitution, and the limits imposed on it by the specific forms of local government.

Racialisation and the Colonial Order

Prostitution in Cairo was extensively described in contemporary sources as a two-tier trade, where the hierarchical distinction between European sex workers (*afrangi*) and their native counterparts was spatial, juridical and cultural. Discourses on the prostitutional milieu by Western puritan reformers and imperial authorities maintained that European prostitution in Cairo was mostly squalid and deplorable, but still civilised if compared to native, 'Oriental' abjection and filthiness. They subscribed to a fiction of imperial and racial superiority, while pointing to the necessity of converting and correcting working-class female sexuality and moral weakness, in the context of metropolitan campaigns for moral purity and social regeneration. Many accounts routinely stressed this point: the aforementioned Russell Pasha wrote in his service memories that the Wagh-al-Birkah, the area of European prostitution in the Azbakiyyah, was populated with European women of all breeds and races *other than British* [my emphasis], who were not allowed by their consular authority to practice this licensed trade in Egypt. Most of the women were of the third class category for whom Marseilles had no further use, and who would eventually be passed on to Bombay or the Far-East markets, but *they were still Europeans* [my emphasis] and not yet fallen so low as to live in the one-room shacks of the Wass'ah which had always been the quarter for purely native prostitution of the lower class.[42]

In the Wagh-al-Birkah, European prostitutes did not offer a more edifying sight, at least not according to Douglas Sladen who, in any case, doesn't seem to have been entirely immune to the fascination of the scene:

every floor has its balcony and every balcony has its fantastically robed Juliet leaning over. As the street, in spite of its glare, is not well lighted, you cannot see how displeasing they are; you get a mere impression of light draperies trailing from lofty balconies under lustrous night blue of Egypt, while from the rooms behind lamps with rose-coloured shades diffuse invitations.[43]

Like the Wass'ah, the nearby Harat-al-Ruhi contained many low-class brothels, which featured a more diverse ethnic make-up. Here, Jewish women could be found next to Italians and Levantines. Prostitutes soliciting in the streets were described by travellers as rapacious, dangerous beings: 'wild-eyed, lithe creatures, human leopards' or 'night birds seeking whom they may devour.'[44] Local women were not considered as morally degenerated, but devoid of any sense of morality. More than as 'fallen women', a category which was later introduced by the activists of foreign benevolent societies and local feminist associations, Egyptian prostitutes epitomised widespread beliefs about the typical lasciviousness of uncivilised, backward Oriental peoples.

European observers were certainly more concerned with the presence of European women, mostly French, Italian, Greek and Austrian women, selling themselves unabashedly to black, brown or white men, than with the plight of Egyptian sex workers who were ordinarily described as beastly creatures or freaks. Both foreign and native sex workers were essentialised by the colonial gaze, although in distinct ways. European women were portrayed as victims of the 'White Slave Trade': mindless or retarded girls whose typically low-class lack of morality or sound moral judgment ultimately accounted for their present situation. Local women, instead, were often described as voluntary sex workers. In social commentaries penned by local modernist publicists such as al-Muwaylihi, sex workers were in fact described in terms of the typical, ambiguous mixture of grotesque, beastly repulsion and seduction:

> When a brazen tart took the stage, a whole hubbub ensued. She was emaciated and ugly, flat-nosed, and big mouthed, bleary-eyed and nearsighted. With pencilled eyebrows, she presented a riot of colour – red cheeks, white forehead, and dyed fingers. Using greasepaint, she had decorated her face with a veil of makeup and plastered on it a false, multicoloured covering in a variety of hues – from gleaning white to pitch black and deep red. In fact, she displayed as many different colours as the chameleon in the midday heat of the desert. The exposed part of her body and naked flesh were covered with necklaces, bangles, bracelets, supports, armlets, bells, belts, and anklets. She started skipping and dancing to the beat of the music, twisting and turning like a snake [...] Between her to-ings and fro-ings, she kept making lewd and disgusting comments to the audience, treating them to all manner of filth and lechery, and mouthing taunts and nonsense. Their mouths simply gaped, and their hearts were enthralled. Everyone was stunned and full of admiration.[45]

Ethnicity and race were constructed as determinants of sex work practice by the very same institutions of colonial control. Yet, the efficiency of the regulationist system in Egypt was jeopardised above all by the colonial underpinnings of the legislation: its inherently racist logic. On the one hand, the existence of a dual legal system – with separate courts for local subjects and foreign nationals, legal privileges enjoyed by non-Egyptians and the notorious 'leniency' justice that was administered within consular courts – hindered the capacity of both local and colonial police to combat illicit sex work effectively. Colonial power relations allowed Capitulary subjects in Egypt to profit from any sort of illicit activity in the country, boosting the consolidation of transnational networks of traffickers in whatever merchandise, women included. As we have seen, foreign women could receive medical examinations from private practitioners, instead of going to the local *maktab al-taftish*. If found diseased, Egyptian subjects were confined to the al-Hod al-Marsud lock hospital, while foreign women were expected to notify their consular authorities and undergo medical treatment on their own. Of course, this rarely happened. Foreign sex workers normally went underground or obtained false health certificates from complacent doctors. On the other hand, the differences in treatment between local and foreign sex workers in relation to health checks made medicalisation untenable. The closest to a medicalisation of European prostitutes ever reached in Cairo was the opening of a 'European Bureau de Moeurs' and a dedicated lock hospital in the predominantly Coptic area of Shubra, as part of a major Purification Campaign carried out under martial law, in 1915: military authorities advocated a 'pragmatic approach' to regulation in order to curb the diffusion of venereal diseases among the troops. Consuls grudgingly agreed to these measures, provided they were temporary, as they feared that sex work regulations could call into question the whole system of privileges that Capitulary subjects enjoyed in Egypt. This bespeaks the racial hierarchy constitutive of the imperial enterprise. The British introduced sex work regulation out of concerns for colonial governmentality: while the racial hierarchy that was at the core of the colonial order made sex work regulation absolutely inefficient, the ordinary practices of evasion made possible by this racial hierarchy turned regulation into an apparently necessary method of social control.

Conclusion

As Cairo became a cosmopolitan, global capital city caught between the contradictions of an emerging nationalist political culture and the reality of colonial domination, the introduction of regulated sex work in 1882 marked an effort to stamp prostitutes – labelled as a new and specific, sociological type – out and contain them through a specific disciplinary system. Egyptian regulationist policies reflected the expansion of biopolitical concerns from the metropolis to the colony, and the ways in which these policies were inflected in a new context defined by local relations between power and cultural norms, and by the imperatives of colonial governmentality. British authorities enforced sex work regulation, as they did in other imperial domains, for both pragmatic and ideological reasons. Pragmatic considerations concerned the preservation of Cairo's public order and the well-being of British occupation troops, which were fundamental, but so was the racist orientalist ideology and the belief in a Western civilising mission that also motivated sex work regulation.

Egyptian regulationism was a colonial disciplinary project linking sex, gender, public health and order, based on principles of quantification, spatial segregation and medical supervision, which proved to be quite fuzzy and unsuccessful. Contemporary sources well expressed the anxiety of ruling elites about labelling and quantifying sex workers. While these testimonies are certainly interesting, they far from allow us to get a clear picture of the quantitative dimension of the phenomenon, given that the bulk of sex work in Cairo always managed to stay outside the radar of disciplinary authorities. In other words, the question seems to be the poor inclusiveness of the regulationist system. Egyptian prostitutes avoided regulation in official brothels, and preferably practised sex work informally in clandestine houses, hence camouflaged in the urban fabric and often for limited periods of time. Foreign prostitutes, on their part, were shielded by Capitulary legislation and consular protection: consequently, they were almost free to keep plying the trade undisturbed and outside the system of licensed brothels. In practice, both local and foreign women strenuously resisted pigeonholing by state authorities. In fact, the question of the inclusiveness of the regulationist system seems to be very complex and almost paradoxical. The more regulation is inclusive, the more it is able to exclude, marginalise and alienate necessarily complex, fragmented, at times maybe even contradictory, forms of human agencies.

In the previous chapters, I have offered some discussion of the historical background to the emergence of modern prostitution in colonial Cairo, and the role of this not so 'marginal' activity in the making of the rapidly changing, Cairene social order. It is now time to turn our attention to the issue of how women decided to ply the trade, in which different ways and to what ends; in short, to the question of women's agency and autonomy.

CHAPTER 4

SEX WORK BEYOND PROSTITUTION

Elles passent, gaies, bavardes, agaçantes, avec une cigarette à la bouche, pas de voile, une profusion de colliers et de bracelets faux, les genoux en l'air et la bouche ouvert dans un large rire.

M. Fredolin, *John Bull Sur Le Nil*[1]

In Foucault's work, resistance is primarily a tool for the diagnosis of power; it is the subject's agency and a byproduct of relations of power which continuously remake themselves by ordering and normalising individuals, categorising them, attaching them to a certain identity, imposing a regime of truth that they 'must recognize and others have to recognize' in them.[2] At their most basic level, all struggles against disciplinary regimes are anarchic: they do not target a certain institution of power, but a form of exercising authority through a regime of knowledge. In fact, people inhabit, act and manoeuvre within the fissures of power apparatuses, sometimes in a self-conscious and anti-hegemonic way, sometimes not. In other words, emphasis on disciplinary techniques and biopolitical regimes often leads to neglect the complex phenomenology of ordinary, non-political acts of resistance individuals resorted to while negotiating their positions within these power structures, more or less quietly challenging the authorities' monopoly on 'government individualization' and 'mystifying representations'.[3] In this chapter, I will shift my focus from the state perspective to the lived realities of commercial sex in colonial Cairo.

I will look at the multifarious forms of sex work practised in the city, with the aim of moving beyond homogenising representations of prostitution and the nominalist practices connected with state regulation. In Cairo, in fact, diverse types of sex work were practised by women coming from a variety of backgrounds, with different aims and degrees of autonomy, in areas loosely defined by their practitioners' ethnicity. Three main types of commercial sex, namely enclosed regulated prostitution in brothels, 'disguised' transactional sex in public entertainment venues and casual clandestine prostitution, will be described here. Of course, these categories reflect the extent to which they were subjected, at least in theory, to the gaze of the authorities, which was more dominant in the case of enclosed brothel prostitution than with clandestine sex work in private houses. Yet, it is important to clarify that they should not be taken as monolithic and self-contained. Boundaries between the different types of sex work were in fact porous, with women practising different kinds of prostitution at different times of their lives, and with different aims. Emphasis on the diversity of working arrangements, then, helps to deconstruct the essentialist stereotype of the 'prostitute' and stress the notion of agency. In fact, it noy only highlights the fact that no unified category of 'prostitutes' actually existed: it also shows how women who were active in sex work more or less successfully manoeuvred within the limits imposed by a fundamentally exploitative system in order to fulfil their goals, namely economic independence for themselves and their families. The attempt to offer a fairly detailed account of the diverse circumstances of Cairene sex workers is essential to the endeavour of this book, in that it allows us to gain at least a glimpse of the agency this group of subaltern social actors has been systematically deprived of by pseudo-sociological, regulationist accounts, on the one hand, moralising abolitionist pamphlets on 'fallenness', on the other.

'Let down the curtain around us': The Kharakhanah[4]

Brothels situated in the Wagh-al-Birkah and the Wass'ah areas were run in accordance with Egyptian laws. Licensed prostitution in Egypt at the beginning of the twentieth century was regulated by the *arête* of 16 November 1905 on the *maisons de tolérance* (*buyut al-'ahirat*).[5] According to the decree, a maison de tolérance, or brothel, was a house where two or more women would cohabit or assemble for the purpose of prostitution.[6] As a simplified version of the continental regulation system, the decree stipulated that brothels could only be opened in specific areas (the aforementioned *quartier réservé*),[7] although segregation was never strictly enforced in Cairo and prostitutes generally failed to comply with legal provisions, which confined them to the brothel area and prohibited any form of visibility.[8] Brothel owners were to obtain licences from the *mudiriyyah* (province), and had to provide the local police section with a list of the employed women's names, ages and nationalities. The same legal provisions applied to brothel owners of foreign origin, with the major exception that, instead of getting a licence, they only had to notify their consuls of their decision to open a *maison de tolérance*. Women working in licensed brothels were registered prostitutes (*mumisat rasmiyyat*) and had to be at least 18 years of age and keep annual photo cards. As we have seen, they were also required to report for weekly medical inspections at the police infirmary (in 1937 a dedicated *Bureau de Mœurs* with medical equipment was introduced in Cairo, within the context of a major reform of public security measures).[9] The women paid for their registration fees and were charged for all medical check-ups. Infected women would be barred from prostituting themselves, and confined in the aforementioned al-Hod al-Marsud lock hospital in Sayyidah Zaynab, until three negative tests were taken. Foreign-registered women, instead, would notify their consuls, who would then prohibit them from practising their trade until recovery. As we have seen, since free clinics were unavailable, and treatment in venereal wards was not enforced by law for European women, foreign prostitutes were largely allowed to continue working provided they either went underground or avoided being caught prostituting themselves in the *quartier réservé* or soliciting in the streets.[10] Brothels (called *karakhanah*) would usually lodge five or six *maqturat* (resident prostitutes). Given the high density of the Cairene red-light district,[11] brothels would normally occupy small premises with a ground floor vestibule and a staircase leading to the first floor, where bedrooms were located. A fairly detailed description of a brothel is available in a British consular record concerning a murder in a house of ill fame.[12] This particular brothel was owned by a European prostitute, Santa Coppola, and was located in Shari' 'Abd al-Khaliq, in the Wagh al-Birkah. Five girls – plus the mistress – worked there, four of whom were Italians and one was Greek. The brothel had three steps leading down to the street, where some of the girls waited for customers while others sat in the hall. A five-metre-long corridor led to a bedroom. Taking the staircase to the first floor, one would find a large sitting room overlooking the hall and two adjoining rooms. In the sitting room customers waited for the girls to receive them, spent time in conversation with their mistresses, drank spirits and gambled. The rooms were quite simple: 'a bedstead, a table with marble top and some other things.' This description of the brothel closely resembles the setting of the sexual initiation of Kamal in Naguib Mahfouz's novel *Palace of Desire*:

> He went inside trailed by her. She was singing: *Let down the curtain around us.* Finding the narrow staircase, he started climbing with a pounding heart. At the top was a hallway leading to a parlour. Her voice caught up with him, saying now, 'Go right', then 'go left', and finally 'the door that's partway open'. It was a small room decorated with wallpaper, containing a bed, a dressing table, a clothes rack, a wooden chair, a basin and a pitcher.[13]

The song Mahfouz refers to in this well-known passage was a popular *taqtuqah*,[14] 'Irkhi al-Sitarah' (Let Down the Curtains), composed by Zakariyyah Ahmad and written by Shaykh Muhammad Yunus al Qadi, recorded by Abd el-Latif al-Bannà (1884–1969) for Baidafone around 1925.[15] In the song, a girl speaks to her lover, inviting him to close the curtains in order to protect themselves from the neighbours' gaze. Sexual innuendo and explicit references to the consumption of alcohol qualified these lyrics as indecent, almost pornographic. The song belonged to a specific corpus of commercial, light music, the genre of the *khala'ah wa dala'ah* (debauchery and flirtatiousness). Representative of the emergence, in the early 1920s, of a new commercial entertainment sector and a thriving music industry, these songs also articulated new ideas about gender, sexuality and desire. As noted by Frédéric Lagrange, these songs show the emergence of a new 'phantasmatic' femininity, synonym of social and moral chaos: '*une catégorie assurément marginale dans l'Egypte des années 20, qui prennent les devants face à des hommes-objects, boivent de l'alcool avec leurs amants et se donnent sans regret dans une felouque sur le Nil.*'[16] In sum, this type of femininity was the antithesis of the *masunah* (well-protected), the decent woman whose honour was safeguarded by segregation within the walled spaced of the *harim*. This song was often associated with the prostitution milieu because of its references to the privacy of the love nest; it parodied bourgeois values of decorum and domesticity in the same way that first- and second-class brothels, as well as *maisons de rendez-vous*, did with their appearance of dignified respectability.[17]

Brothels in the poorer area of the Wass'ah were certainly shabbier and more destitute. Prostitutes received clients in rooms directly overlooking the street. At the turn of the twentieth century, the British Police Chief in Cairo – Russell Pasha – described the Wass'ah as a place where sex workers were so miserable that they lived 'in one-room shacks [. . .] Here in the Wass'ah, Egyptian, Nubian and Sudanese women plied their one shilling trade in conditions of abject squalor, though under medical control'.[18] The indigenous brothel district consisted of

> hovels opening to the street like shops, with a dirty pink cotton curtain across the opening and a bed of the same enticing colour behind. While waiting for custom, the women sit in their doorways, and if a policeman passes 'they are just taking a breath of air'. In the doorways of some larger establishments sit other painted women, also just getting a breath of air. A prostitute knows nothing of the eight-hour day. She works every day of the month and all day even though perhaps suffering from continual haemorrhage.[19]

Until 1916, the Wass'ah district was overseen by Ibrahim al-Gharbi, a Nubian transvestite who controlled women's trafficking both in Cairo and in the provinces. Known as the 'King of the Underworld', he was imprisoned by the British during a crackdown on freelance prostitution in 1916. He was confined in the Hilmiyyah internment camp for one year, before being sent to his village in the South. In 1923, he was arrested once more, during a major Cairo police operation which exposed a local sex traffic ring. One hundred and twenty Egyptian men and women were indicted for participation in an organisation recruiting local girls, aged between 12 and 14, from the Helwan area, and turning them into prostitutes. Sixty girls were rescued, but it was thought that hundreds of girls and boys were involved, exploited as sex workers or sent to the provinces as virtual slaves to local landowners.[20] The news aroused a great deal of interest in the national as well as international press, with the British newspaper *Morning Post* reporting the 'revolting allegations' of the abduction of 60 Egyptian girls, kidnapped, sold or pawned by their parents.[21] Local judicial authorities, however, hastened to reassess the nature of the case. G.W. Hughes, the Chief Inspector of the Parquet (the Native Court of Appeal), in a letter to Miss Baker, Secretary and Director of the British National Vigilance Association (a reformist society active against vice in Egypt),[22] claimed that – unlike the information circulated by the British press – the girls involved in the case had not been kidnapped or sold to brothel keepers by their parents. Instead, he noted that they were 'volunteers', as 'practically the whole native prostitute world in Egypt is supplied by volunteers'. He went on to suggest that the vast majority of the girls had freely chosen prostitution in order to support their families, 'after having in most cases practised as unlicensed prostitutes for years'. In a number of cases, officers had supposedly been deceived by the girls with regard to their age, and had granted them a permit.[23] This is a significant example of the mild approach that local authorities adopted towards native commercial sex. Sister Margaret Clare, a British religious activist running the IBS Refuge in Cairo at the time, remarked that sex trade was 'encouraged and supported by the Egyptians in the highest positions'. According to her, al-Gharbi – the most important women's trafficker in the country – was 'looked upon as a little God by the Egyptians', and could rely on the support of political elites.[24] At the end of May 1924, the charges against al-Gharbi were dropped, and he was released on bail. Sources tell us that a bribe of 5,000 Egyptian pounds was paid to Maqrushi Bey, the Egyptian Head of the Parquet, to secure the liberty of al-Gharbi, who 'returned home, had a tremendous feast and was welcomed as a conquering hero'.[25] Years later al-Gharbi served a five-year prison term, during which he died. Russell Pasha wrote in his memoirs that

> his removal was not altogether a blessing for the brothel organization of the country. He had the reputation of being good to his women and fair, though severe, in his justice. Deprived of their king, the women had to find other protectors, without whom, however brutal they may be, a prostitute, all the world over, is lost and helpless.[26]

Disguised Prostitution, Nightlife and Legal Loopholes

With the increasing expansion of international tourism and business in the Azbakiyyah district, new forms of sex work developed. Moreover, the emergence of new patterns of middle-class nocturnal sociability, made possible by technological change including the introduction of gaslights and electrification of public transport, impacted the ways in which people made use of the urban space. Rising levels of consumption sustained the spread of venues where people of all walks of life found some form of amusement that was accessible to their pockets. Imperial troops constituted a permanent source of demand, especially during World War I and World War II, when the presence of soldiers on Egyptian soil dramatically increased. Indeed, soldiers regularly patronised brothels, and this resulted in a heated debate about the standards of morality among troops, leading to the imposition of a vigorous, albeit short-lived, campaign of 'social purification' in Cairo during World War I.

From this moment onwards, big brothels gradually declined. On the other hand, unregulated prostitution, whether disguised or clandestine, thrived. In the nightlife district of the Azbakiyyah, packed with *cafés-chantants*, music halls, cabarets and brasseries, disguised prostitution was practised by women employed as barmaids, waitresses and performers, the rank-and-file of 'a new form of procuring that [...] formed networks whose sheer size helps to explain the currency of the theme of the "White Slave Trade" during the early years of the twentieth century', according to the historian Corbin.[27] British journalist Alfred Cunningham, for his part, was scandalised by the situation, and made the following observation:

> If ever a city deserved the name of 'modern Babylon', it is Cairo. [...] There is none to compare with Cairo in the degradation, vice and depravity which are permitted to exist and flourish, even in the very midst of the city, under the nose of the authority, who make no attempt in the name of morality and decency to check these evils.[28]

In the Fishmarket, not far from the Azbakiyyah, low-class Europeans and locals mixed in grogshops, cheap cafés, music halls and brothels. In the words of Cunningham, here the nights were 'hideous with the orgies of these unfortunate creatures, who, under practically no police restraint, and with the open protection of their foreign soutenirs [sic.], can do exactly what they want'.[29] Cunningham clearly referred to the legal vacuum created by the Capitulations, the main obstacle the British administration had to deal with when trying to safeguard public order in town. Other than clandestine sex work, Capitulary subjects could engage in various illicit activities, such as the sale of adulterated liquors or drugs, often in collaboration with local subjects.[30]

Archival sources widely document the criminal activities pursued by the foreign types gravitating around the Azbakiyyha underworld because of their privileged legal status. Production and sale of adulterated alcoholics was rampant: Greek wine sellers, for example, cut cheap Greek wines from Cyprus and Athens with 25 per cent water and saccharine, selling them as pricey Italian wines.[31] Drugs were ubiquitous in the Azbakiyyah, and white drug dealers were often Capitulary subjects. The Bar Hamidiyyah, owned by Greek Theodoro Papparis and located in 67 Shari'ah Clot Bey, was known for being frequented by drug dealers and addicts. Jean Mamberti, a French national and a notorious pusher in the Akbakiyyah, was said to be a frequent customer. According to a Cairo police memorandum enclosed in a dossier of the Italian Consulate of Cairo, on 6 May 1932 Mamberti was drinking coffee with a local subject and Ettore Barone, a 22-year-old Cairo-born Italian subject at the Bar Hamidiyyah, when the police stormed and searched the place. Ten small sachets containing morphine salts were found under a painting hanging on the wall. Barone was accused of drug dealing and held in custody at the Italian Hospital due to his medical condition – he was affected by secondary syphilis. As the police were not able to prove there was a link between the presence of Mamberti and Barone and the drugs they had detected, they were both released.[32] According to a contemporary source, in Cairo several shops known as *dadakin al manzul* freely sold candies stuffed with morphine, opium, strychnine, cantharides and other substances to people who used them to 'entice homeless girls and minors for immoral purposes'.[33] Some others also used them for 'their young innocent wives, to put them under their influence, leaving them to sleep for days and in many instances forever in order to satisfy their beastly instincts', possibily an even more disturbing reality in the public opinion as it hinted to the fact that vice and immorality threatened women also in the domestic space, hence not only outside.[34] Nikita Cumbaro, a 27-year-old Italian subject from Leros and owner of a bar in Haret Habib, Clot Bey, was known for selling drugs with the help of a group of prostitutes and young boys. When the usual coterie of officers from Egyptian police and the Italian Consulate searched his bar on the morning of 6 June 1932, they found 52 grams of heroine inside a candy box in the shopwindow. Cumbaro sustained that the drug had been placed there by Hosnia, a prostitute frequenting his bar, out of revenge, as she was convinced he had played a role in the robbery of some gold pieces that she owned.[35]

In nightclubs and bars, transactional sex was based on a fictional game of seduction.[36] Unlike licensed prostitution, which mimicked domesticity while paradoxically entailing the extreme commodification of sex and female objectification, disguised prostitution was all about ambiguity. Disguised and clandestine prostitutes, in other words, those women who were not disciplined by the regulationist frame, in many ways embodied a new femininity haunting urban life with its transient, unruly nature.

Signposted with large billboards advertising the sale of different types of alcohol, Azbakiyyah casinos and bars opened their doors at 11 p.m. to the throng of locals, tourists and soldiers who packed the establishments until the break of dawn. Scantly dressed and heavily made-up women quietly sat around casting eloquent glances at potential customers. After being approached by a customer, a girl would then join him for a drink at his table. In addition, she often made him buy an indefinite number of drinks and packets of cigarettes, both for himself and for her. At the end of the *fath*, as the approach was called, the girl would have sex with the customer if requested to do so, either in one of the rooms of the venue or in a nearby brothel; many barkeepers had special agreements with brothel owners. Bargirls were, in fact, unlicensed prostitutes who freely plied their trade in agreement with the owner of the venue.[37] To be able to solicit on the premises, a girl had to pay the owner a fee, receiving a percentage of the customer purchases in return, plus the cash she earned for her sexual services. In cabarets and *cafés-chantants* women sold themselves under the cover of music and dance. Artist-prostitutes would first sing and dance on stage, thus displaying themselves before being invited to sit at a patron's table for a drink.[38] They next encouraged the patron to consume as much as possible: indeed, the opening of bottles, which could be champagne, whisky or beer depending on the venue and the customer's rank, actually constituted most of the womens' earnings. Due to the fact that they had low wages, they were forced to supplement their income by inducing their patrons to drink excessively with them. According to the press, in 1938 a café chantant performer earned 16–20 Egyptian pounds a month through singing and dancing, and 24–48 pounds from the percentage on customer drinks.[39] A drink in a bar cost 15 piastres, of which two were for the alcohol; five went to the girl; and eight to the venue's owner. Tabloid columns anecdotally commented on the process of *fath*. Occasionally girls were unable, towards the end of the night, to perform on stage due to the enormous quantities of alcohol they had consumed, while others preferred to sit and drink rather than to get back on stage. *Fatihat* also elaborated strategies to augment their own profits dramatically; for instance, if two girls sat contemporaneously with a customer, and one of them left at some point only to return a few moments later, it was customary that the gentleman should then order another drink for her.[40] The behaviour of an artist-prostitute was closely supervised by the managers of the venue, and carefully detailed in the contract. Normally women worked until 2 to 5 a.m., payed for their own dresses and, in some cases, they were requested to gamble with customers. The occupational status of artist-prostitutes was furthermore extremely vulnerable, since they could be fired by the manager without notice.

From the 1890s, when the entertainment industry in Cairo dramatically expanded, the city's nightlife and its excesses became a topic for social commentary in fictional form. In 1898 the journalist Muhammad al-Muwaylihi (1858–1930) started publishing, in the daily *Misbah al-Sharq*, a series of articles under the title *Fatrah min al-Zaman* ('A Period of Time'), which in 1907 were collected in a book called *Hadith 'Isa Ibn Hisham* ('A Narration by 'Isa Ibn Hisham'). Infusing the classical *maqamah* genre and its precious rhymed *sag'* prose with modern topics and debates, the work did not only constitute a modern proto-novel of sorts, but also provided an unparalleled, poignant description of social change in late nineteenth-century Egypt. Through the narrative device of the resurrection of a Pasha from Muhammad 'Ali's times, whom 'Isa Ibn Hisham – the narrator – takes on a stroll through the streets of fin-de-siècle Cairo, the novel depicts the capital's urban space as ridden by tensions and a growing sense of danger. Once again, such uneasiness is expressed by gendered figures and their subversion of traditional norms of decency. One night 'Isa Ibn Hisham and Ahmad Pasha al Manikali, the resurrected Minister of War, sit in a drinking den in the Azbakiyyah, watching a dance performance:

> She started skipping and dancing to the beat of the music, twisting and turning like a snake. Alongside her stood an assistant so repulsive that we have no doubt that he was the accursed Devil himself [. . .] Bottles in multiple pairs and rounds one after the other would appear, and he would uncork them and arrange them in rows at her feet. Her assistant kept pouring glasses for her, and she would quaff them and ask for more [. . .] Her leaps and pirouettes became more violent and her jumps and turns intensified [. . .] Sweat poured off her shoulders and sides, and foam thickened on her neck and mouth [. . .] As a result, the falseness of her appearance was exposed and the deception became clear; things that had been hidden were brought out into the open. She was transformed into the guise of a harpy, appearing in a desert mirage, a ghoul grimacing and leaping around, or a bear quivering and crawling. We turned away in utter horror and disgust, so powerful was our sense of revulsion.[41]

The sheer repulsion felt by 'Isa Ibn Hisham and his venerable companion was matched by their amazement at the power the dancer was able to exert over her admirers. A living symbol of social disarray, she 'managed to bring ruins to flourishing houses, to sully pure lineages, and to open the gates of litigation'.[42] A tragic and grotesque figure, she embodies the forces that were consuming the Egyptian nation, leading it, in the narrator's view, to a point of near-collapse. In the following scene, we find her surrounded by a coterie of exalted and intoxicated admirers, taking rounds from the customers, mouthing obscenities and slander and reaching out to grab and steal. She often slapped and punched people on with her outstretched hand, inflaming people's minds with deceitful wiles and using her hand to grab and swallow glassfuls. Her every move was aimed at profit and gain.

While her wretched assistant pops bottles of vintage wine, she cajoles and teases her suitors, until a quarrel breaks out and 'from a distant corner of the place a gruff-looking thug of a man sprang to his feet and came rushing over, brandishing a club'. It's the woman's husband, we are told, 'a Maghribi riff raff attached to a foreign government, a status that makes him immune to the authority of Egyptian laws'.[43] Dancer-prostitutes, the author explains, normally resorted to this working arrangement: they married Capitulary subjects so that they acquired their protected legal status as legitimate spouses. In return, men would receive a fixed amount of the woman's earnings in order to support themselves. It is easy to see how women's capacity to accumulate money was severely curtailed by the existence of a hierarchy of parasitic and exploitative figures, from barkeepers via assistants to legal husbands or boyfriends, men they would give up everything for:

> Just then, as everyone was getting ready to leave, an ugly, ill-tempered man came scowling his way in. With a thick neck, bulging eyes, flared nostrils and flabby lips, he was certainly not a pretty sight. Looking to right and left and scanning everyone present, he went over to the woman, started cursing and swearing at her, then gave her a slap.[44]

The man, we are told, was the woman's lover, sick of waiting for her in a tavern while it was well past her working hours. Yet,

> this woman prefers this raging beast over all those other domestic animals. He hurts her, he beats her, makes good use of all the money that she collects by various means [. . .] Then at nights' end he comes here and beats her right in front of all these worshippers who have been falling over each other to please her. She then submits to him and is led away.[45]

There is a striking contrast between sex workers' firsthand testimonies, which I will introduce next, and moralistic fictional accounts like that of al-Muwaylihi, of the way women managed to shrewdly manoeuvre within such a male-controlled exploitative system. In al-Muwaylihi's narrative, the only trait these 'monstrous' creatures seem to share with 'honourable', 'decent' women is an unfulfilled desire for romantic love. At the same time, regardless of the fact that they are represented as monstrous or pathetic creatures, sex workers are always de-humanised, reduced to irrational characters and lacking sound judgement. This assumption about the capacity of acting responsibly, the very same negation of autonomous agency, legitimates the need for some institution, usually the State or – as in al-Muwaylihi's Islamo-reformist view – the religious establishment, to educate sex workers to the precepts of Islamic religion and save them from their debauched life and eventual death:

> her entire life involves spending the night till early morning, as you have seen, drinking foul wine and contorting her muscles and limbs in a series of exhausting routines [...] Once she reaches home, she is utterly exhausted; her nerves are shattered and her body aches. She has no desire to eat and doesn't even look for food. Instead she throws herself on the bed, totally drunk [...] Next day she gets up at noon or later, with a terrible hangover. Once she has pulled herself together, she works on improving her appearance. Then she receives their daytime visitors. When evening comes, she starts the round all over again and so on [...].[46]

The existence of a social problem concerning cabaret girls, in fact, was extensively commented upon in the press. In *Black and White*, two Englishmen in a nightclub described the plight of another *fatihah*:

> One black-eyed Arab, of ugly but amiable countenance, sat down beside the Doctor and myself after her performance, and we conversed to the extent of our powers [...] The Doctor said: 'Well, my dear, how is your poor tummy now?' [...] And she said: 'Anglais-pint-bitter-bottled'. Thus, you see how truly expressive is our language even in the mouth of a Cairo dancing girl. She drank a pint of beer, then another half-pint; and no doubt her tremendous exertions required exceptional quantities of liquid support. Then she sent the empty bottles on to the stage, and they were set on a little table besides her place there so that all men might see she had been entertained and put money into the pocket of the proprietor. She smoked cigarettes for some time, failed to

make much conversation or understand ours, and bade farewell. My brother said that generally these girls die young, as their business is calculated to put a tremendous and unnatural strain upon their system.[47]

Over time the issue was addressed by a number of British moral purity associations, increasingly active in Egypt since the beginning of the twentieth century. In 1937, for example, the IBS discussed a proposal for the establishment of a pension for cabaret girls to grant them some form of assistance. Highlighting the firm, exploitative grip that managers had on girls, IBS abolitionist activists concluded that for any action to be effective, 'as the contracts of the girls often specified where they were to live, etc. it was absolutely essential to get the collaborations of the entrepreneurs'.[48] The IBS, as an emanation of metropolitan abolitionist campaigners within the League of Nations, was particularly concerned with the circumstances of foreign artistes in Egypt. Performers were brought in by procurers and theatrical agents during the tourist season. A well-known French procuress of the 1920s was Madame Marcelle Langlois, owner of the Casino de Paris and of a pension for female artistes. She was credited with having amassed such a considerable fortune that she was able to buy a castle in her native France. Every summer she brought five or six artistes, dancers and singers over from France for the seasonal opening of her casino, to which all prominent Cairene personalities were invited. She was known for being the mistress of an important Bey in Zaytun, and for introducing her complacent girls to other members of Cairo's elite. When some girls, upon becoming mistresses of wealthy beys and pashas, relinquished their contracts with Madame Langlois, she charged their patrons high sums of money.

In 1925, the Passport and Permits Office attempted to restrain procurement by introducing stricter rules on the import of artistes from abroad. A tax of 100 Egyptian pounds was levied on every performer, and their repatriation was made mandatory on the expiration of their contract. It seems however that the new regulations were far from being effective. It was also alleged that nothing could be done to clamp down on foreigner procurement as long as theatres and other entertainments managed by locals had to pay the exorbitant sum of 180 Egyptian pounds a year for a licence. With the exception of a few internationally renowned companies, such as the French and Italian operas, it was argued that earning an 'honest living' was impossible for a singer or a dancer in Egypt due to their meagre incomes. Performing meant disguised prostitution, and 'everyone knows this'.[49]

Karin van Nieuwkerk, author of an ethnography on present-day female entertainers in Egypt, argues that 'prostitution was not necessarily part of the performers' job, although several probably engaged in it in order not to lose wealthy customers'.[50] She reports some interesting stories from contemporary press, about romanticised anecdotes of virtuous singers who stubbornly resisted the advances of wealthy patrons, preferring instead their poor lovers.[51] Certainly not all female performers engaged in prostitution: a small group of artistes managed to become powerful *salat* entrepreneurs, carving an autonomous space within a very sexist field.[52] Tawhidah, for instance, started performing in the Azbakiyyah around the turn of the century. She married a Greek man who opened for her the famous 'Alf Laylah wa Laylah', where she was the headliner for many years. After her husband's death, she managed the hall until she died in 1932. Similarly, Na'imah al-Masriyyah – who came from a lower-middle-class family – started performing to support herself after she got divorced. She became one of the most acclaimed singers of the Shari'ah 'Imad al-Din theatre district, and eventually opened her own establishment, the 'Alhambra'. Another example is Badi'ah Masabni, a Syrian migrant who danced and sang in the Levant before moving to Cairo. There she became the star of Nagib al-Rihani's theatrical troupe, marrying him in 1923, before she divorced in 1926. Using the money she earned during her career, and thanks to the financial help from wealthy patrons, she opened her own salah in 1930, 'Salat-Badi'ah', which became a landmark of Cairo's nightlife. After a wrong investment in the film industry, she entrusted the management of the establishment to Bibah, one of her leading performers, and moved back to Lebanon in order to escape Egyptian tax inspectors. Ratibah Ahmad, finally, was a niece of Bamba Kashshar, one of the most famous *'awalim* at the end of the nineteenth century. She managed to open her own dancing hall and was known for her usual rowdiness and drunkenness. Women such as Tawhidah, Na'imah al-Masriyyah, Badi'ah Masabni, Ratibah Ahmad and Bibah, as well as several other famous public performers, constitute interesting examples of how gifted and charismatic individuals could actually manage to work an exploitative system to their own advantage.[53] While in many cases their early biographies remain obscure, and it is alleged that in some instances they were supported by powerful and wealthy patrons,[54] they were able to carve out their own space in show business, amassing considerable wealth and becoming powerful social *personae*. Nevertheless, these women constituted an (important) exception to the ordinary dynamics of the public entertainment business which, while using women as sexualised objects of desire, exposed them to public stigmatisation and disapproval. Very low wages, in fact, meant that for the majority of café chantant artistes in Cairo, engagement in sexual services was necessary in order to sustain themselves.

Even during the 1930s depression, nightlife in Cairo flourished despite the growing dissent of Egyptian nationalists (both liberal and conservative), colonial authorities and social purity reformers. Local concerns over the spreading of vices and immorality were increasingly framed within an anti-colonial discourse. Subordination to Western cultural influence and political subjugation was often considered central to the Egyptian political crisis. Throughout the 1930s and the 1940s, Islamism as represented by the Muslim Brethren, founded in 1928, played an evermore increasing role in Egyptian politics: the need for a moral regeneration of the country based on sound Islamic values was at the top of their social agenda. It is within this context that a wave of purity laws, targeting nightclubs and the entertainment industry, emerged. In 1933, for example, *fath* was prohibited to Egyptian performers, even if foreign dancers and singers continued plying their trade undisturbed, while clubs and nightclubs came to be patrolled and monitored by local police. Since police officers were relatively easy targets for bribes, enforcement of restrictive regulations was quite uneven, and periodic crackdowns alternated with periods in which the *fath* was publicly practised despite prohibitionist regulations.[55]

During World War II, Cairene nightlife boomed and the sex market further expanded because of the massive military presence in the city. Artemis Cooper, author of a brilliant account of Cairo's military and social history from 1939 to 1945, states that at the beginning of World War II there were 80,000–100,000 British soldiers on Egyptian soil. In 1941, the number of men that were stationed in Cairo had risen to 140,000. Allied troops were garrisoned in different camps around the city: South Africans stayed in Helwan, Indian soldiers camped in Mena and New Zealanders in Ma'adi. The British were stationed in

Heliopolis, Hilmiyyah and Al-Mazah. Their dwellings consisted of small squared tents with one window, ten men per tent. Venturing into the city, the soldiers would take a tram and head to the nightlife district in order to spend the money they had amassed during their time spent in action in the desert: 'bars and brothels cost money, but since there was nothing to buy in the desert and except the occasional egg from a nomad child, the men usually arrived in Cairo with a considerable amount of back-pay in their pockets.'[56] Popular venues like the Opera Casino, run by Badi'a Masabni, the Kit Kat or the Bosphore Club of Bab-al-Hadid, were conveniently located next to the main tram station and the brothels district. In bars and dancing halls, often adulterated spirits were sold to soldiers. Their drunkenness frequently caused brawls, to the extent that many troop cabarets along Shari' 'Imad al-Din erected barricades of protection in order to prevent drunk customers from climbing on stage.[57]

Clandestine Sex Work

As we have seen, licensed prostitution, although numerically significant, constituted but a small part of the Cairene sex trade. Reliable quantitative data about the diffusion of clandestine prostitution are extremely difficult, if not impossible, to obtain. However, police-generated figures concerning mandatory regulations and the number of raided illicit brothels suggest that clandestine prostitutes greatly outnumbered licensed sex workers. In fact, the vast majority of Cairo sex workers did not belong to the brothel system and plied the trade on a more flexible basis, in clandestine *maisons de rendez-vous*.

A Cairo City Police memorandum on prostitution of 1926 highlighted the existence of many such houses, particularly in periods when no public scandal or complaints were made.[58] The memorandum confirms that transactional sex, rather than being marginalised, was integrated into the everyday lives of popular neighbourhoods, as long as it did not disturb the public peace. The topography of Cairene clandestine prostitution was therefore hazy and elusive, as unlicensed brothels were camouflaged in Cairo's urban fabric. First-class brothels, under the cover of bourgeois respectability, could be found in districts such as Rod-el-Farag or 'Abdin, and often benefited from the patronage of influential members of the political and economic elite. The *'awamahs*, houseboats on the Nile, were known as places of debauchery where 'gay' young girls would entertain upper-middle-class and upper-class men.[59]

As we have seen, women engaging in prostitution in early twentieth-century Cairo did so out of necessity, in order to cope with situations of serious economic and social vulnerability. In doing this, some of them subjected themselves to state regulation and got licences to ply their trade as professional prostitutes in privately operated brothels, but approved by the State. The vast majority of women, by contrast, marketed their sexual services in the informal sector; in other words, they were clandestine sex workers in clandestine brothels. They successfully evaded state control by taking advantage of the porousness of the boundaries of social respectability. As Historian Liat Kozma points out, 'women and places of ill repute could be easily mistaken for respectable ones, and vice versa'.[60] As early as 1880, a Police Act had warned security officers and neighbourhood *shaykhs* that sex workers might try to rent a place under the pretense of being a respectable woman. In other cases, girls found in brothels often claimed that they had ignored the real nature of the place they had entered, thinking it was an ordinary house.[61]

Clandestine sex workers came from a variety of working-class backgrounds: most of the time they were women living on the margins of the peddler economy, working as seamstresses, washerwomen, dressmakers, servants or shop assistants. Despite the strain of economic hardship and impoverishment, these women retained their family ties; many of them were married and practised prostitution in order to supplement their meagre family income. According to Egyptian governmental sources, though, clandestine houses were frequented by married women (either with or without their husband's consent) whose incomes were insufficient for their luxurious tastes; by girls who were being exploited by unprincipled parents; and by young women who had fallen victim to procurers, and had continued in this mode of life. Women connected with procurers were also seen in these houses, as were women who had been previously registered but who, for some reason, had succeeded in eluding the supervision of the Bureau of Public Morals.[62] A similar description, apart from the classist disdain for 'dubious working-class moral standards', typically stresses the victimisation of women, while downplaying the importance of prostitution as a pragmatic survival strategy. Moreover, it fails to elaborate on an additional, important aspect of sex workers' motivations, one which certainly accounted for the expansion of clandestine prostitution as opposed to the regulated one. Women, in fact, turned to sex work to earn money for themselves and/or for their families in a context characterised by female economic vulnerability, but also by spreading consumerism. In other words, the concept of subsistence came to include the capacity to satisfy non-basic necessities as well, and sex was again the most available asset women could trade off for higher purchasing power or material comfort. These new desires are expressed by the literary figure of Hamidah, one of the most famous antiheroines conceived by the pen of laureate novelist Naguib Mahfouz, in a memorable scene from *Midaq Alley*: when she makes her daily promenade along the Musky, she admires 'the luxurious clothes' that she sees in the shopwindows lining the street, stirring 'in her greedy and ambitious mind-bewitching dreams of power and influence'.[63] Her path is then crossed by the factory girls from the Darrasah quarter, who,

> taking advantage of war-time employment opportunities, ignored customs and tradition and now worked in public places like the Jewish women [...] They imitated the Jewish girls by paying attention to their appearance and keeping slim. Some even used unaccustomed language and did not hesitate to walk arm-in-arm and stroll about the streets of illicit love. They exuded an air of boldness and secret knowledge.[64]

Such an unquenchable desire for material possessions will lead Hamidah to leave her alley and start a carrier as a first-class prostitute.

Rampant prostitution must also be placed in the context of larger patterns of socio-economic crisis, which afflicted Egyptian society since the end of the 1910s: this endangered the fundamental institution on which social reproduction reposed, namely marriage. As bachelors encountered growing difficulties in amassing the necessary wealth for the *mahr*, prostitution constituted a viable alternative to release their sexual drive when the financial burden of marriage could not be sustained. Rather unsurprisingly, prostitutes resisting state regulation enjoyed the greatest autonomy: both first-class elite prostitutes, or kept women, and clandestine prostitutes eluded registration. Thus they were not restricted in their freedom of movement, nor were they subjected to medical examinations. This was in stark contrast with licensed prostitution in legal brothels, where sex workers catered mainly for working-class locals and troops. Clandestine sex workers plied the trade as a part-time activity within the precinct of the clandestine brothel, adjusting their work schedule to other occupations, usually domestic chores and childcare. From the minutes of a court case concerning a raid in a clandestine brothel in Kafr el-Kafarow in 'Abdin, we can derive some interesting information. The house was managed by Giuseppe Mifsud, a Maltese shoemaker married to a French woman, possibly a former prostitute. The couple ran the brothel – with the help of two menservants – as a family business, in their three-storey house. The couple lived on the third floor, with their two children, while the first and the second storeys constituted the brothel. When the house was raided due to a complaint by the neighbours, six women were in occupancy. They were all Egyptian and came from nearby areas, such as Shari' Muhammad 'Ali and the Darb al-Ahmar in the Dawudiyyah. One of the women told the police that she had been working there for a month, and that she went there only at night, for the purpose of prostitution, while busy at home during the day; she would retain half of the money paid to her by the customer. Among the other women also present in the raided house there were a mother and her daughter, both unemployed and living on the income of half a house they owned elsewhere. They claimed to have been lured by Mifsud with an excuse and subsequently kept against their will.[65]

Pimps

As we have seen, while the majority of sex workers practised underground, regulated prostitution took place in state-licensed brothels. The role played by procurers was fundamental in both sectors: they maintained a regular supply of foreign women to licensed as well as clandestine brothels. Thus an international procurer commented on a local pimp, who was acting as intermediary between him and the brothels, saying that the pimp had him bring over from France at least eight young girls per year:

> He sells them to the tenants [. . .] Sometimes he obtains as much as 50 Egyptian pounds. The *souteneurs* also purchase them. In Egypt,

you can do whatever you like: this is why you find *souteneurs* from all parts of the world. They can change the ages of the women when they work in the houses for it is forbidden to register women under 21 years of age.[66]

In 1923, there were 312 registered prostitutes of European nationalities in Cairo: 98 Greek, 75 Italian, 47 French and 12 women of other nationalities. In 1924, of the 357 women registered in police records, French women figured as the largest group (127), followed by Greek (107), Italian (56) and five women from other nationalities.[67] In 1925, a list of pimps operating in a Cairene red-light district reported the existence of 16 men, of whom 14 were French, one was Greek and one British, while it was stated that more than 100 French pimps were in fact active between Alexandria and Cairo. Miss Saunders, warden of the IBS Refuge in Cairo at that time, compiled a report for the Cairo City Police about French pimps operating in Cairo, sketching out some vivid profiles:

Here are, under, a few names, or rather nick-names, some of the best-known pimps. These pimps frequent the Café Carillon and are to be found at midnight. They also frequent the Café Riche, and a small bar of Haret el Arbakhana, Ezbekiyeh. 1. Marious: exploits Marie Hoen, dite Mignon, his legal wife, and runs Pension Mignon, Rue Wagh el-Birka; George: fat, short, cleanshave; speaks French with an rrrrr accent. Exploits Georgette Lallier, dite Suzanne, who is running Pension Montmartre; Paul le Petit: exploits the woman named Raymond, Pension Montmartre; Joseph: short, thin, small black moustaches, black eyes, red face. Exploits the woman Juliette of 8, Rue el-Berka; Dominique Le Brun: exploits Mme Marcelle, of Pension Modéle in Rue Wagh el-Berka (travelling between Cairo and Alexandria); Louis l'Australien: exploits woman Gaby of Luxembourg; Louis l'Algerien ou Bouton: exploits his legal wife, Henriette Bouton Suzanne Germaine. She has lately run away from him with a native; Joseph: reforme de l'armée a cause de maladie mentale, exploits Odette, Rue Zaki, no. 7; Dominique Le Jacquot: who was expelled in 1924. His woman is Mado, who ran away lately with a native; Philippe: exploits the woman named Marie, who runs the pension 'Chat Noir' of Rue Wagh el Birka.[68]

All these pensions were located in the segregated area, meaning that the women practising there were all registered. Miss Saunders also noticed the 'boldness' and 'effrontery' of the French pimps who loitered around Azbakiyyah with their dogs, while the Egyptian police could do nothing against them.[69] She also explained that the large number of French nationals active in sex traffic was due to the quite favourable attitude their consular authorities held towards them, in particular the Consul General, Monsieur Labè. According to Miss Saunders, Labè had in various instances deliberately vetoed or delayed the deportation order of notorious traffickers. In the case of Madame Dora Norvalle, a famous procuress in Cairo, the Consul was reportedly in close confidential terms with the accused, as he regularly visited her clandestine house:

> One of the experienced workers called to see him in the winter 1924–25 about the repatriation and more adequate treatment for venereal disease of a young French prostitute whose family in France had been enquiring for her and that was under the age of 20. At her request, the girl and the padrona of the brothel were summoned but when this Dora Norvalle (now deported) came in, the Consul shook hands warmly with both women [...] shortly after this, the French Lady on the Committee of the Refuge of the League, who had drawn the attention of the Consul to the condition of the sick girl, was very indignant at the behaviour of the Consul to herself. Monsieur Labè, who was not sober, met her at the Opéra and came up to speak to her in front of her own daughter of 19 about 'his young friend, Rosalie V.', the prostitute referred to.[70]

Later that year, Monsieur Labè was notified by the native Parquet that a notorious French pimp was to be arrested along with other European traffickers, and that it was of necessity that the Parquet sent its kavasses in. Upon hearing the news, Monsieur Labè asked who the French subject was that was to be arrested. His name was Antoine Desanti, a Corsican living at 6 Shari' Galal with three women he exploited, among whom his first cousin. It is unknown whether the Consul General informed Desanti personally, but, according to Miss Saunder's informant, Labè was the only one at the consulate to know that Desanti's name was on the list. The Corsican pimp swiftly left the country the night before the raid was carried through.[71] The IBS had previously sent a letter, dated July 1925, giving details concerning a traffic case related to Desanti and asking the French Consul to arrest him. They requested a trial through the consular court, instead of simply having him deported, since deported pimps often remained at large for a while before returning to Cairo undisturbed.

Life in the brothel was often marked by the existence of vexatious ties between the *padrona* and her employees. In these cases, the prostitutes had to rely on a pimp for protection from greedy brothel owners and their relentless physical and economic exploitation, as well as from violent and rowdy customers. Getting a lover pimp meant even more protection, but it usually only added to the women's subordinate position, being yet another element of exploitation.

The ongoing difficulties encountered by Egyptian authorities in the enforcement of regulation and segregation, however, resulted in the ever-increasing diversification of the forms of sex work. A registered prostitute could also work as a self-employed professional, for example, provided she refrained from public soliciting, as this was forbidden by law. Although this gave her a greater measure of physical mobility and autonomy, it could also expose her to more dangerous situations, especially mistreatment and abuse by violent customers. While the brothel restricted prostitutes' independence, it also offered an institutionalised system of protection. Indeed, a brothel owner often resorted to local bullies in order to enforce a security service, where men would intervene in cases of fights over payments or brawls between drunkards. Self-employed prostitutes, by contrast, were forced to recur to a lover pimp, whose behaviour tended however to be exploitative and abusive.

The social profiles of Cairo's pimps were as diverse as those of the prostitutes. The vast majority of them were young, local and foreign men from working-class backgrounds, unskilled casual labourers living on the fringe of informal economy. Pimping provided them with the opportunity of securing a living without suffering the pressures of the local labour market. Most of the men had been gravitating around the Azbakiyyah district for some time, temporarily working in bars and taverns where they had made acquaintance with the prostitutes plying their trade in this area, drug dealers and pliable police officers. Among the cases I have come across, I found at least four instances of pimps who had previously served in the British Army, two of whom had been members of the Cairo City Police under the command of Russell Pasha.[72] For instance, Gordon Anslie Ness, a former lieutenant in the Lancashire Fusiliers, was appointed as a Constable in the Cairo City Police, before being removed for bad conduct. In November 1921, he was charged with living from the proceeds of Sophie Maltezaki's prostitution, assaulting her and disturbing the public peace on 14 June 1921.[73] It appears that he was resident at 6 Shari' Galal Pasha, the same address where Antoine Desanti, the notorious Corsican pimp, lived. Sophie Maltezaki was a Greek artist-prostitute at Guindi's café-concert in Shari' 'Imad al-Din. She had known Ness for a year, and lived with him for seven months. Giving evidence, she pointed out that she was not a prostitute, and that prostituting herself wasn't in any way part of her job: she only danced and sang. She denied having given Ness any money, and stated that she had returned to her aunt's house upon hearing that he was a married man. In June, Ness and Sophie met at a police station, where he asked her to get back together. Outside the station, he grabbed her with force and dragged her towards a taxi, while drawing his revolver. A police officer, Giuliano Santo, subsequently stopped him. Sophie's occupation and her relationship with Ness were described in very different terms by witnesses. Sophie was in fact a *fatihah*, a dancing hall girl who was paid for sitting with customers, drinking with them and occasionally going home with them.[74] As she did not wish to become a licensed prostitute, she desperately wanted to conceal that she engaged in paid sex, despite the danger Ness constituted for her. According to Arthur Marks Broome, Head Constable of Cairo City Police, during the quarrel at the police station Sophie lamented that there was no question of her moving back with Ness, since she was unable to support him any longer. Her job as 'waitress' at Guindi earned her ten Egyptian pounds a month plus 20 per cent of drink orders, and she furthermore had to maintain her son on that small amount. Eventually, Ness was found not guilty when he was tried before the Supreme Court in January 1922. He was subsequently repatriated under martial law.

John Charles Shalders, instead, was a sergeant in the Military Police; after his discharge from service he became the pimp of Rosa Lieben, a Jewish-Russian registered prostitute and owner of a licensed brothel on Shari' Wagh-al-Birkah. According to the sworn testimonies of Ragheb

Saad and Nico Gregorio, two members of the secret service who had been instructed to follow the accused, Shalders worked until 12.30 p.m. in a bar in Shariʿ Mahdi called the Union, a meeting place for British soldiers. After his shift ended, he would go to a brothel located at a distance of 150 yards, on a parallel street, to supervise the business there. According to witnesses, Rosa would give Shalders 20 piastres per night. Tried by the Supreme Court in January 1922, Shalders was found not guilty but soon repatriated under martial law.[75]

Subalternity, Sex Work and Agency

During the years I spent doing research for this book, I never expected to find prostitutes' personal testimonies, either in the form of private papers, diaries or letters. Yet, scattered voices and perceptions of sex workers, regarding their social profiles and their lives, can be extrapolated from documents written by others, usually representatives of disciplinary apparatuses such as police officers, judicial officials or social reformers. These sources were shaped by the biopolitical concerns of the authorities, both local and colonial. The accumulation of data was instrumental for an understanding of who a prostitute was, where she lived, whether she was healthy or not: in other words, to carry out those nominalist, segregation and medical practices I have analysed in detail in the previous chapters of this book. Yet, as Stephanie Sippial pointedly observed, sex workers 'were indeed targets of state agendas, but they were also moving targets'. A strategic reading of hegemonic archival sources, despite their partiality and disciplinary obsession, can yield at least a glimpse of the ways in which sex workers inhabited those power structures. Court cases, police minutes and abolitionist papers, if read against the grain and beyond their heavily standardised, bureaucratic and patronising language, can be used to locate instances of sex workers' agency. In some cases, repeated encounters between specific individuals – sex workers or pimps, and the legal system – allowed me to retrace at least segments of their life trajectories. From the State's point of view these were no more than criminal records, but to me it was particularly interesting to explore the repertoire of everyday strategies that people who struggled for survival would resort to in order to avoid unwanted attention from the authorities. Prostitutes, for example, used different methods to evade the authorities' gaze while remaining visible to potential customers: spatial mobility, clandestinity, the establishment of fictive kinship relations, the use of nicknames and the like. Such information, although fragmentary, may help us go beyond plain nominalism and gain a more complete understanding of the politics of the trade.

Despite the didactic tone and the moralistic vein in which abolitionist accounts of the 'White Slave Trade' were written, some cases are reported that shed light not only on the structure and dynamics of women's trafficking, but also on the way women adapted to their circumstances.

Augusta Pellissier, for instance, was a 17-year-old French girl, brought over from Marseilles under the pretense of finding her a partnership in a café. The man who smuggled her over from Marseilles was called Adé, alias Amédée Desanti, brother of Antoine Desanti. She had met him in Marseille in July 1928, in a restaurant she used to lunch at. Her story is so vivid and detailed that it is worthy being reported in full. Augusta Pellissier told the authorities the following:

> My acquaintance with Adé grew closer and closer and he started making some proposals, like leaving to Egypt with him to open a ball-room there. Three weeks later, once I had decided to accept his offer, he asked me to go and live with him, at Rue de la Cathédrale 1, where we planned our journey. I went and live with him for fifteen days all in all, during which it did not occur to me there was anything seedy with him. This is how we travelled to Egypt [. . .] Adé embarked our luggage the day before the departure. On that day, at 7 a.m. he got on board on his own. One hour later, I went to the ship with a certain M. Michel, who lived with Adé and whose wife did some housework for him. I was given a small packet I was instructed to deliver to Jules Arency, a chauffeur on board, pretending I was his wife. When I got on the ship, I was taken to Arency's cabin: he was there with Adé and another boy. Adé made the gesture of keeping my mouth shut. Arency went out of the cabin and took a look around. One hour later they took us down to the storeroom. They put us in a chest and put weights on top of it. Some hours later, when we reached the open sea, the storekeeper came and picked us up and we moved to his cabin. We spent all the crossing in there, except for some walks at night and a couple of

times when we had to be hidden because the cargo was being inspected. The first time, we were hidden in a cabin, on the side of the anchorage, almost buried alive by canvas bags. The second time, they put us at the bottom of the bridge, among planks and one ton iron rims [. . .] We reached Alexandria on 28 September on the Lotus [. . .] At 7 a.m. Adé set foot on land dressed as a chauffeur and came back with a friend of his to pay the storekeeper. He gave him 3.000 francs, then they drank champagne together to celebrate the arrival at Alexandria. And then a chauffeur called Joseph gave me an identity card. My picture was on it but the stamped papers accompanying it were in the name of a certain Virginia (I don't remember the surname), Italian, housemaid. I disembarked around 7 or 8 at night. Three chauffeurs were waiting for me on the quay, a tattooed big man, Arency and Joseph. They told me to go through the custom on my own and that we would have rejoined after that, which I did. At the custom, I was not checked nor searched at all.[76]

In Alexandria, Augusta was handed over to a woman who suggested she could make money as her 'partner', since Adé did not yet have sufficient capital to buy a ballroom. The girl objected and when persuasion failed, she was beaten. She was then made to go on the streets from 8 a.m. to 1 p.m., from 4 to 7 p.m., and again from 8 p.m. to 1 a.m. or later, and always with someone watching her. After a month in Alexandria, Augusta was visited by a woman, Jeanne Maury, alias Josephine Emilie Maury. She paid Amédée Desanti seven Egyptian pounds on the spot, and took the girl to her clandestine brothel at 2 Sekkat-al-Manakh in Cairo. Augusta started prostituting herself there, travelling once a week to Alexandria to give Amédée the money she earned. Her testimony is extremely vivid and reveals a considerable amount about her life in the brothel and the tricks of the profession. This included the *vol à l'entôlage*, or pilfering, which constituted a common way to augment the income of the business in low-class brothels:

Mme Maury instructed me to pick up only native types in *galabiyeh* or elder married-looking men because they don't make difficulties about the price and they are fine with paying 20 or 30 piastres. Once in my room, I must be paid in advance for the service and a tip. Making himself comfortable, the punter puts his clothes on a sofa, specially placed before a door opening into another room. While the man is busy with me, Emile Maury is pilfering, lifting the wallet from behind a tent, that looks as if it sticks to the wall, but it is in fact loose. She takes some bills but she leaves some in place, so that the man doesn't realize he has been robbed if he opens his wallet. She puts the money she stole under the sofa, so that, if the man finds out the theft, I pretend I am finding the money. If the man doesn't find out, Mme Maury gets the money, and every time I go to Alexandria I bring Adè his share. We use a code between us: for instance, if she doesn't find anything in the wallet, she makes me understand saying: 'Renè needs you'.[77]

There is certainly a considerable difference between Augusta's firsthand account of prostitution and the way in which female stories were popularised in literary accounts of 'fallenness': women who had failed to conform to Victorian sexual and social norms and who were enthusiastically patronised by abolitionist associations. Despite their moralistic emphasis, abolitionist pamphlets did not altogether fail to recognise the role of material causes in orienting women towards prostitution, especially the lack of occupational opportunities and the meagre wages women received for their work. On the contrary, the earnings of prostitutes were quite favourable if compared to ordinary wages. With prices varying per area, prostitutes generally charged ten piastres a head in the Wass'ah, double this amount in the European Wagh-al-Birkah. Depending on the number of customers, a woman could even earn between 80 piastres and approximately one-and-a-half Egyptian pounds per day.[78] These are striking amounts if we consider that, before World War I, a (native) mason would earn 6–12 piastres per day, a painter 14–15 piastres, while a railway worker's family of six people living in three rooms maintained itself with about six piastres per day.[79] While prostitution constituted a quite lucrative activity in terms of wages, many of the women normally had their earnings swindled by their *padronas* or *souteneurs*. Thus brothel inmates managed to keep half of their earnings to themselves, the other half went to the owner for board plus various extras, usually charged at very high prices. In some cases, women would retain their earnings, but would then have to pay a monthly rent for the room they used. Average rent was calculated at 30 piastres a day for lodging, although it was possible to rent a room in the Azbakiyyah for only 10 piastres a day.[80] Prostitutes also had to buy clothes, undergarments, shoes and cosmetics in order to attract more clients and increase their earnings. Often, however, brothel owners provided the women with these articles, acting as an intermediary between women and dealers. Other expenses sustained by prostitutes included medical fees and annual registration fees. In many instances, they had children and relatives depending on them, or they had to give up part of their earnings to pimps and bullies. Consequently, many women soon became indebted to their *padronas*, or struggled to accumulate private money in order to reinvest it, for example in trade or in an exit strategy. Only a small number of particularly successful prostitutes could hope to earn enough to be able to accumulate money and emancipate themselves, starting other income-generating activities. In some cases, former sex workers turned to sex service management, that is, they became brothel owners. Here money and connections in the criminal underworld became essential for crossing over. When a woman could count on the right type of protection, nonetheless, she could earn really well, depending on the type of clientele that frequented her establishment.

Prostitutes were thus in a weak and subordinate position, but this does not mean they did not try to resist or renegotiate the terms of their exploitation. Strategies of resistance were multiple and related to the different brokers who controlled their work, whether these were *padronas*, state officials (i.e., policemen or public health officers) or pimps. Women who chose to resist unwarranted state intervention remained in the informal sector, instead of obtaining government-issued licences. When sex workers attempted to subvert the power relation with their pimps, they did not hesitate to make use of the law system, for example through plaintiffs in courts. Among the consular minutes that I have consulted, there are cases that provide interesting insights into the relationship between prostitutes and their pimps. In these cases, women were self-conscious enough to sue their pimps and haul them before a court in the case of mistreatment. Take, for example, the aforementioned case of Antione Desanti, the notorious Corsican pimp and women's trafficker who succeeded in making a daring escape out of Egypt, thanks to his well-placed political connections. The allegations against him were based on the testimony of Nelly Plummier, a 23-year-old dressmaker and former prostitute in a *maison de rendez-vous* in Marseilles, who had made Desanti's acquaintance in a dance hall there. They began a relationship and Desanti suggested that they moved to Egypt, where he would open a milliner's shop for her. She travelled as a stowaway on the Messageries Maritimes steamer *Lotus*, protected by some members of the crew. Upon her arrival in Alexandria, Desanti, who had travelled on the same boat, gave her a visitor permit and had her disembarked. Once ashore, he put her in a clandestine brothel run by an Italian; she protested and was brutally battered. Upon the return of the *Lotus* steamer from Beirut, on its way back to Marseilles, Nelly got aboard in a desperate attempt to talk to the captain and ask for his assistance. Immediately recognised by one of the shipboys who had helped smuggle her into the country, it did not take long before Desanti seized and took her to another clandestine pension in Rue Cleopatre. She was then transferred to Cairo, where she started working in a French clandestine brothel in Shari' Mahdi. She lived with three other women: Desanti's cousin, a woman called Eliana and Desanti's mistress, Pepé. The women were evidently exploited, as all their earnings went to Desanti. Nelly eventually met a young man and decided to move with him to a pension, but when Desanti found her, the young paramour disappeared and she was forced to return. Desanti claimed that he was ready to take her back, but only if she paid 100 Egyptian pounds to him as a refund for the expenses he had sustained for her. Alone and without money, she eventually decided to denounce him as her pimp.[81]

Obviously, licensed prostitutes – given their recognised professional status – were particularly prone to make use of the consular courts system in their struggle against exploitation by pimps: in 1914, for example, an Italian registered prostitute called Francesca Collavita sued the 21-year-old Maltese Giuseppe Vassallo, accused of living from the earnings she gained from prostitution, while he also repeatedly threatened her with a razor. The woman worked in the Fishmarket, under the name of Angiolina, while she rented a 'shop' to receive her customers. She lived with Giuseppe in a small room nearby, in Darb-al-Nur, where she paid for rent, food, washing and her pimp's expenses. After she asked for assistance from the police and denounced him, Vassallo fled to Alexandria, where he was caught. Leaving Cairo he had robbed her of a dress, a sheet and a pair of cushions. Vassallo was found guilty and sentenced to 12 months of imprisonment, with prison labour, in Malta.[82] Similarly, in 1917 Alexandra Calloubi, a French national working as a prostitute in several houses in the Azbakiyyah, filed a complaint against Pasquale Magri, a Maltese-British subject who was resident in Cairo: she too accused him of living from the proceeds of her prostitution.[83] Pasquale was an unskilled labourer surviving on temporary jobs around the Azbakiyyah – he had worked as a waiter at the Semiramis, and as a mechanic at the Azbakiyyah Skating Rink for eight Egyptian pounds a month, but was unemployed for most of the time. Pasquale was known to the Secret Police, because in 1911 he had served a sentence for owning a hashish den in the 'Abbasiyyah area.[84]

Alexandra's testimony gives us a glimpse of the features of an ordinary life as a prostitute: a high degree of instability and violence. Alexandra regularly moved between Cairo and Alexandria for the purpose of prostitution, promptly followed by Pasquale. Back in Cairo the couple had rented a room in Bab-al-Sha'riyyah, where Alexandra earned money prostituting herself under the professional name of Luisa Marianucci in the Luxembourg, a brothel managed by the Italian Grazia Pastore, in Darb Ducal. Alexandra went to the Luxembourg on a daily basis and was paid in tokens. She would give the tokens to Pasquale, and he would return them to the *padrona* in exchange for cash (usually two or three tokens per day, the equivalent of four dollars). He administered all her money, constantly urging her to work harder, occasionally beating her and threatening to leave her in a brothel if she didn't make more money. When she was hospitalised for postpartum complications, he abandoned her and left for Alexandria on his own.[85] A similar case is that of Amalia Vescovo, an Italian national who in 1919 filed a report against her pimp, James Kelly, alias James Hughes, a 25-year-old Irishman and a deserter after the Battle of Gallipoli.[86] Amalia and James had lived together for four years, first in Alexandria (where she had worked in the notorious al-Ginaynah prostitution district), and then also in Cairo. During that period, James did not work and they lived from the proceeds of Amalia's prostitution. They lived together in the different brothels that she worked at in the Wagh-al-Birkah district, as well as in private houses; on one occasion, they were evicted from a furnished room in the Coptic Bazaar, due to their relentless fighting and brawls. James regularly battered Amalia and once even threatened to burn the brothel she worked at if the owner did not give him more money.

Amalia attempted to escape from him five times, while she was in Alexandria and Cairo. On her last attempted flight from her pimp, to Suez, she was caught by the police and brought back to Cairo, where she denounced her pimp.

Unsurprisingly, relationships between pimps and prostitutes involved a great deal of physical and psychological violence. A case I found significant in this regard is that of Caterina Mikha'il, a 45-year-old Egyptian subject (originally from Rhodes), and Antonio Romeo, a Sicilian chauffeur.[87] On 16 July 1932, Antonio Romeo was taken to the police station of Bab-al-Sha'riyyah and accused of stabbing Caterina Mikha'il during a fight. He maintained that she had accidentally hurt herself while trying to assault him in a fit of jealousy. According to Romeo, on taking off his clothes in bed, Caterina questioned him about his clean underwear, and accused him of having met his second mistress. He replied that he could do whatever pleased him, upon which she allegedly drew a razor and attempted to stab him, accidentally harming herself. The story told by Caterina, however, is quite different. According to her testimony, Romeo had stabbed her when she refused to give him money, as she did each evening. Caterina told him that she had not earned any money that day, but Romeo did not believe her and attacked her. She claimed that Romeo was unemployed and lived from the profits of her prostitution. He had been Caterina's pimp ever since they had met three months earlier, upon her arrival in Cairo. On a previous occasion, he had called for her at one of the pensions where she had worked, in the area of Shaykh Hammad, hitting her for having stayed too long with her customers. As some witnesses stated, Romeo was a notorious pimp in Darb-al-Hatta and he was known for his ruthlessness; he had already attacked a woman he was exploiting by stabbing her legs, and had disfigured another one. Romeo was eventually sentenced to 18 months of imprisonment in Rhodes. After being released, he returned to Italy where he served in the army for 16 months, before making a formal request to the Italian consular authorities to reenter Egypt.

Disfigurement, either by using a razorblade or vitriol, seemed to be the pimps' most common type of assault on their women. A typical case in this instance is that of Gino Biffi, which made the headlines of the *Egyptian Gazette* in 1913.[88] An Italian woman – whose surname was Tedesco – had nearly been killed by an Italian man named Gino Biffi, in Tawfiqiyyah. A few months before, he had been expelled from the country for attempting to force the same woman into prostitution, with the aim of living off her earnings. Once back in Cairo he attempted to persuade her again. Since she refused to prostitute herself, he disfigured her with a razor blade.

Another interesting case that sheds light on transactional sex between men and women in Cairo is that of the 26-year-old Italian Antonino Rizzo, and a 23-year-old Greek woman from Smyrna, Maritza Vladi.[89] In 1920 Rizzo had migrated to Egypt from Sicily, and had been working as a warehouseman at the electricity company Giacomo Cohenca and Sons of Shari' Qasr-al-Nil, until he met Vladi. They lived together for a while before she decided to leave him and move to a place of her own. On 28 February 1926, while Vladi and her new flatmate, Jerusalimite Nazzarina Naser, were returning home from the movies, Rizzo ambushed the women at the house door, throwing vitriol in their faces and stabbing them with a knife. According to his testimony, Rizzo had met Vladi in a brothel. Having fallen in love with her, he claimed that he had wanted to save her from the sordid life she was leading. They next moved in together and lived as a couple. However, he soon realised that 'the leopard cannot change his spots'. In a plea sent to the Italian Consul on 17 April 1926, he wrote:

She kept on plying that vile trade when I was not around [...] I suffered! I wanted to forget, to get away and escape from her, but passion enslaved me. I cried as a baby, praying her to give up those dreams her mother had inculcated in her young head: you are young and beautiful, she would tell her, you could find a bey or a pasha to maintain you, instead of 'this Italian pederast', words I heard myself, without rebelling because I was too in love with her. But Maritza followed her advice and she evicted me from our house. She said we would remain friends, until her husband, as she was not legally divorced, would return to her. It was not true: she just wanted to keep me quiet, while she was opening her arms to his new lover, experience new embraces, satisfy her lust and destroy another man. Eventually I resigned myself, tried to forget by drinking, getting drunk to ease my pain: this was not a life, I felt doomed, I felt the dishonour I was bringing to my family. Maritza would keep on coming and see me from time to time:

I was the object of her voluble pleasures, driven by the artificial
dreams the injections of morphine and ether procured her.[90]

On the night of the incident, Rizzo claimed he had come to talk to her,
although he was heavily intoxicated by alcohol. According to his
testimony, Vladi drew a kitchen knife and stabbed him in the leg. At that
point, Rizzo lost his temper and threw vitriol in the women's faces while
also taking hold of the knife and stabbing them. The letter he wrote to his
consul, from the European penitentiary in which he was being held, was a
desperate attempt to invoke passion, as an extenuating circumstance for
the crime he had committed; he depicted himself as the innocent victim of
a ruthless she-devil. However, too many elements did not corroborate his
version. Interestingly, Rizzo had resigned from his job precisely at
the time he had met Maritza, a strange move for an individual starting a
happy marital life with a woman. Moreover, the fact he had a bottle of
vitriol on his person, on the night of the incident, clearly undermined the
hypothesis of a lack of intent to commit the crime.

Perhaps more interesting than Rizzo's staged persona, that is, the
broken-hearted and distraught lover, was Maritza Vladi's version of
the events. The tone and language used to explain the nature of her
relationship with Rizzo were very different from the sentimentalism
evoked in Rizzo's letter. In contrast, her account was more akin to a
pragmatic estimation of gain versus loss. Vladi confirmed she had met
Rizzo at the Pension Di Milano, the brothel he used to frequent as a
client. She accepted his courtship as he made her a lot of promises:

He told me he was working at Cohenca's and that he earned 15
liras a month. He said he could have paid for any sort of luxury and
that he would have married me. I trusted him and welcomed him
in my house. Time passed and he did not do anything of what he
had promised me.

They lived *more uxorio* for 18 months, during which she paid the rent and
all other expenses. Maritza continues her story:

Since living in that way was not convenient in any way to me, and
I clearly realized he just wanted to have fun and exploit me, I drove
him out. He protested and did not want to leave me. I explained to

him that I had to pay the rent for the flat and many other expenses, and since he was not in a position to help me, as he was unemployed, I could not keep him living with me any longer. I moved to my new flat in 3 Sharia Daramanli, 'Abdeen, where I rent out two rooms. I use the money I get from the rent to sustain myself.[91]

Coerced prostitution in clandestine brothels figured as a trope in coeval sources: local press and pamphlets of abolitionist movements were rife with sensationalist stories about naive working-class girls, seduced and ensnared by ruthless men and vicious procuresses. Once again reality was more complex and nuanced than allowed for by bourgeois narratives of coercion. In May 1925, a young man came across an 18-year-old Egyptian girl in a clandestine house, and later contacted the American Mission and the IBS in Cairo in order to help her. According to the records, the girl was shopping when she met a woman who invited her for a coffee in her home. Once there, the girl was kept in the house against her will for the purpose of prostitution. The young man offered to take her home but she refused, replying that she was too scared for the reaction of her parents. Police authorities, who were called to respond on the case, pointed to the fact that the house was being watched by the police and that young girls living there were not captives. This example shows that fabricated narratives of coercion often disguised a voluntary, albeit often temporary, entry into the world of prostitution for the purpose of accruing greater material wealth.[92] A similar case is that of a 16-year-old Cairene girl of Greek origins, who was reported missing by her parents, a stonecutter and a housewife. The fourth of five children, she had been working as a buttonholer for one year at Bonne Marché, before leaving her job for unknown reasons. According to the girl, she had been invited to the movies by a Greek man she had recently met. When she realised it was very late and became afraid of going home alone, the man proposed to host her at his house, a Greek pension which doubled as a brothel; the girl was found there one week later.[93]

Another interesting case shows how nominal record-linkage methodology in archival research can be used to shed light on real historical encounters between individual lives and disciplinary systems, and on the subversive quality of clandestine prostitution, more specifically. In 1914, the 21-year-old Alexandro Tanti from Malta was tried by the Supreme Court for managing a house in Shari' al-Sahhah, in the district of 'Abdin. According to multiple witnesses the house, which was leased to Tanti by its legal owner, 'Abdul Latif Fahmi, was a clandestine brothel (*bayt-lil-'ahirat fi-manzil*), attended by 'respectable looking' men and women. Alexander Tanti would stand at the door or walk in front of it, with the aim of recruiting women for his business. As Muhammad Shakib, *Ma'amur* of the 'Abdin Police, stated: 'some of the women used to enter the house, some just passed by. He also spoke to me, not recognizing me, and told me: 'There are nice women upstairs!' No exterior sign qualified the house as a brothel, where women sold themselves to men for one dollar, keeping half the sum and giving the rest to Tanti, who denied that he was the manager. He claimed to have been tricked by his maid Hanim Bint Rizq, who he had met while he was sitting in a café along the road one night as she approached him, wrapped in a black long robe, a *milayyah*. She had supposedly told him that she knew a way for him to make some easy money, explaining that she was trying to avoid creditors and required someone to sign a new lease contract for her house, so that her name could be struck off the papers. Tanti agreed and received one pound for drawing up the new contract in his name. It is hard to determine precisely what happened next: apparently, as soon as Tanti came to know that Rizq was running a clandestine brothel in the house, he attempted to evict her. Resisting his attempt, she allegedly beat him and he subsequently sued her for assault. From the minutes of the hearing, it seems more likely that Rizq was actually co-managing the brothel with Tanti, who had signed the leasing contract due to his privileged legal status under Capitulary provisions. Their judicial feud probably resulted from Tanti's attempt to take advantage of the circumstances.[94] By the same token, Alexander Tanti used to exploit his Capitulary protection at least in one more case. On 4 April 1914 Tanti, by then already in prison, was tried for allowing a house he legally leased at 8 Harat-al-Fiddah, in the 'Abdin district, to be used as a hashish den. The premises were occupied by a coffee shop run by a native, Hassan 'Ali Guda. The man claimed that Alexander Tanti had been hired twice to prevent police from closing down the hashish den. Tanti eventually took up the place's lease and became the manager, while Guda stayed on as a keeper, employed by the Maltese for 24 piastres a day. Hussein Muhammad, Marshal of the Native Summary Court, and Hassanayn Hassan, acting as a Shaykh al-Harah, went to close down Guda's café, after it had been reported that hashish was smoked on the premises. Upon their arrival, they were stopped by Tanti, claiming to be the owner of the place and denying access as granted by Capitulary rights. The case was finally passed to the Parquet and the aforementioned Muhammad Shakib summoned the Maltese to give evidence before transferring the case to the British Consulate.[95]

These cases are particularly enlightening because they are able to reveal the contours of a certain form of subaltern agency, challenging – while at the same time appropriating and remaking – hegemonic structures of power and control based on racial hierarchies. Local subaltern groups were not simply subjected to discriminatory legal provisions, which established a dual standard for native and foreigners: they actually appropriated and turned them into self-empowering tools, through a strategic alliance with foreign subaltern groups. Natives would thus form mixed enterprises with foreign subalterns, who were sheltered by the Capitulation system, for mutual economic interests. The racial, hegemonic discourse of the elites, maintaining a careful as well as fictional separation between Europeans and natives, was thus challenged 'from below', by occasional class-based cooperation between native and 'white' subalterns.[96]

Conclusion

The introduction of licensed prostitution in Cairo, with its local and global dimensions, marked a clear departure from previous types of sex work: it was dramatically characterised by the wider colonial political order, in the emergence of a discursive hierarchy of sexual workers based on race and ethnic affiliation. One one hand, sex work diversified due to the emergence of new consumption practices among a newly arisen local bourgeoisie, and as a result of the conspicuous presence of international travellers and businessmen in the nighlife area of the Azbakiyyah, where both local and foreign, complacent artistes populated ballrooms, bars or in clandestine houses. On the other, native and foreign licensed prostitutes catering for local and white subalterns, rural migrants and imperial soldiers could be found in the Wass'ah and the Wish-el-Birkah respectively. My emphasis on the diversity of working arrangements serves to take us beyond the essentialist representations of prostitution generally offered by hegemonic accounts. A similar focus on material conditions, strategies, aims and the actual agency of sex workers is likely to give us a better understanding of commercial sex. It overcomes the simple reproduction of the hierarchy of the trade, which was constructed by colonial authorities indicating foreign, 'enclosed' (i.e., taking place in licensed brothels) prostitution as the more advantaged form of sex work. The adoption of this approach thus aims to go beyond nominalism: it deconstructs the un-nuanced 'prostitute' stereotype and stresses the notion of agency instead, clearly showing that no unified category of sex workers existed in Cairo. On the contrary, women actually plied the trade under dramatically different working conditions, with different aims and with varying degrees of autonomy. Moreover, coeval sources routinely described the Cairene sex trade as marked by racial hierarchy, juxtaposing European and native, commercial sex. As this chapter has tried to reveal, a close study of archival data challenges the colonial language of racial superiority, showing how native and foreign sex workers shared an experience of economic vulnerability due to a structural violence and feminisation of poverty, which prevented women from accessing wealth through other, potential strategies of accumulation. Local women mostly resisted state supervision and practised clandestine prostitution as casual labourers who integrated other economic activities, enjoying more autonomy compared to foreign brothel residents. Without overemphasising the autonomy of women in a trade that was ultimately dependent on a male-controlled sex/gender system, my analysis stresses the fact that a different story can nonetheless be told. Sex work constituted for many women, both European and native, a strategy for coping with economic and social vulnerability, and a way of fulfilling their goals. One question remains unaddressed, though: what kind of meaning can or should be assigned to this type of agency? In other words, should these actions be interpreted as women consciously resisting patriarchal practices, possibly an embryo of feminist consciousness? In this book, I adopt a non-reductionist understanding of agency, one which breaks with the liberal subject's rhetorical dichotomy between resistance andsubmission. Prostitution was not a 'liberating' activity, something it could only be in a context where sex work was free from third-party control and not culturally and socially stigmatised. Instead, it provided prostitutes, especially native and unregistered ones, with a viable alternative means of earning a living for themselves and their families, even if it reproduced a male-dominated repressive sex/gender system. While moving into prostitution will certainly have been the result of disadvantaged social and economic circumstances, particularly for women, rather than an uncoerced and deliberate decision, a history of how women coped with these circumstances and recouped a level of agency needs to be told.

CHAPTER 5

IMPERIAL WAR, VENEREAL DISEASE AND SEX WORK

This chapter will investigate the relationship between imperial warfare and sex work in Cairo. Whereas the role played by war and militarism in nation-making processes has been widely recognised, together with the function fulfilled by sex work regulation in safeguarding the efficiency of the military apparatus, less attention has been devoted so far to the integration of imperial and military perspectives in the study of sex work regulation.[1] If we consider the genesis of imperialism as the deployment on a global scale of the centralising disciplinary techniques at the core of modern state-making, it will appear clear how the regulation of sex work in the colonies was vital in maintaining a viable model of 'garrison state' overseas, especially in times of warfare and threat to imperial security and power. Chacko Jacob Wilson wrote:

> By the end of the century, an important perspective emerged that regarded the empire as being in a state of decline. The evidence had been building from the Indian rebellions in 1857, to the Afghan Wars, the successes of the Mahdi's army in Sudan, and the Boer War.[2]

These imperial setbacks, the 1857 Sepoy Mutinee in India more pointedly, led to the introduction of contagious diseases laws in England and the Empire. The Sepoy Mutinee seemed to confirm the need for preserving the health and strength of imperial troops by closely supervising sexual contacts between prostitutes and soldiers. However, due to the energetic campaign of a vast abolitionist front of social purity movements, libertarian feminists and religious movements, the closest to sex work regulation in England ever introduced – the Contagious Diseases Acts – were abolished in 1888, at a time when regulation came to be vigorously debated as a necessary tenet of colonial disciplinary politics. Ten years later, the Boer war (1899–1901) made the physical degeneration of British recruits apparent and spurred the imperial dimension of abolitionism.[3] New ideas about soldiers' body management and restrictive views of individual freedom extending to the corporeal practices and pleasures were introduced among the troops. Nevertheless, keeping soldiers chaste and sober seemed to prove a titanic task.

The presence of imperial troops in Cairo during World War I had a dramatic impact not only on public security but on public health as well. During the war, contagion from venereal diseases seemed to be out of control. Imperial warfare can thus be argued to have played a major role not only on the making of the relationship of colonisers and colonised but also as a testing ground for British conceptions of moral and civilizational superiority. It also had a lasting impact on bringing about abolitionist policies to be enforced at a later stage by Egyptian authorities.

Men in Town

The outbreak of World War I created the conditions for the imposition of a far more direct form of colonial rule on Egypt. The vital importance of the Suez Canal as a communication line granting access to the Indian subcontinent turned Egypt into a huge imperial barrack. British, Indian, Australian and New Zealander troops (ANZAC)[4] were deployed to the Canal zone in order to protect it from possible Ottoman attacks from Palestine. By January 1915, 84,000 imperial troops were stationed in the country, 70,000 of whom were based in the Canal area. As Mario M. Ruiz noted, 'within a few weeks from their arrival' imperial soldiers 'flooded the city of Cairo', where the British General Headquarter was located.[5]

World War I played rather an important role in shaping both colonial and local perceptions of the desirability of regulated prostitution in the Egyptian capital. While the unruly behaviour of imperial soldiers posed a direct threat to both the efficacy of military operations and the prestige of the Empire, Cairenes highly resented the presence of foreign troops in town and the disruptive effect it had on local morals and public order. At the same time imperial troops, the ANZAC in particular, fueled a whole new economy in Cairo. Australian soldiers were on the highest pay in the allied forces and Egyptian business people took stock of it immediately. Private Ernest Charles Tubbenhauer was garrisoned at Mena Camp with the 1st Division Engineers. In one of his letters home, on 14 December 1915, he recounts:

> It was pay day today amongst the troops and the men have been paid right up to date. A big majority of men in our company are drawing their full money and drew from £8 to £14 a man and will spend every penny of it, so you can imagine the difference it makes to this place. However, I understand that the military authorities are only going to pay 2/ [shillings] a day limit while we are in Egypt. That means a lot of the men's money will be kept in Australia as the men will only be able to draw 14 a week instead of 35/...We are getting a holiday on Xmas day, so after dinner I am going to do a bit of exploring in the native quarters of Cairo. There is a party of ten of us going to Cairo on donkeys. We have our promised leave till 11.15 pm so are looking forward to a good time [...].[6]

Private J.C. Egan, from the same division, wrote that Cairo traders, especially Greek canteen keepers, knew how to attract the Australians:

> All the restaurants and saloons have been renamed in Cairo, such as the Triple Entente Dining Room, the Allies Cafe. But the Australians seem to take precedence also, for everywhere you will see the names such as The Australian Bar, the Kangaroo Cafe, and the New Zealand Bar, and they have special prices for the Australians and the New Zealanders. If you happen to stop to look at anything displayed for sale, the shopkeeper will come out and say 'Come Inside Australia, for Australia very Good'.[7]

On 30 October 1916, H.R. Williams, an Australian who had just disembarked in Suez, and his regiment set foot in Cairo, their final destination being the battlefront in Gallipoli:

Our train pulled into a siding about 11 pm. We scrambled into our equipment, and fell in under floodlights. We marched off under the directions of guides along a good road, on both sides of which were military depots and headquarters [...] we found ourselves before our quarters, large huts made of reed matting. We were in the Zeytoun Camps, outside Cairo [...] Our first work was that of erecting tents for ourselves – with a promise to leave to Cairo in the afternoon [...] We caught a train in the nerby station and where in the city in fifteen minutes. From the station we came out into a large square with flower-beds; on the city side many fine buildings could be seen. Hardly we had appeared in the square when from a cafè across the way a flying cloud of 'Boot-clean' boys made for us [...] Our first purchases were canes. Every soldier carried one mainly for the purpose of beating away persistent street sellers.[8]

Williams and his companions crossed the Azbakiyyah, and entered the Wass'ah:

Our guide led us to the largest house in the street, where in a large room a penny-in-the-slot piano shrieked tunes to a great muster of soldiers: Australians, New Zealanders, Jocks and Tommies. The crowd was laced with women of many nationalities: coal-black Nubians, slim copper-coloured Arabs, a few Frenchwomen, fair-headed Russians, but low-browed, black headed Greeks predominated.[9]

Sapper Harry Bonser of the Royal Engineers wrote in his diary that the girls seated on chairs outside, waiting for hire: 'one of their tricks was to snatch a soldier's hat and run into their room with it, in the hope that he would follow.'[10]

The Battle of the Wass'ah

In 1915 and 1916, serious riots took place in the Wass'ah district, signalling the mounting tension existing between local population and imperial troops. On 2 April 1916, Good Friday, what later became known as the 'Battle of the Wassa' took place in the red-light district of Cairo.[11] The ANZAC looted a brothel in response to rumours concerning the infection of some comrades by prostitutes working in the area. Once they were told that a group of ANZAC troops in turn had been assailed and stabbed in a house of ill-fame nearby, highly intoxicated Australian soldiers (according to some estimates 2,000 ANZAC troops were in the area, out of 20,000 on Easter leave, and about 500 took part in the fracas) assaulted the brothels, set fire to mattresses, threw women and their pimps out of windows together with the brothel's furniture. The situation was exacerbated by the arrival of the Red Caps, the military police, who shot warning signals in the air; the Australians responded by throwing stones and bottles. In the Azbakiyyah, shops were ransacked and a Greek tavern was burnt down. Eventually the Lancashire Territorial Corps intervened and succeeded in bringing the riot to an end. Some photographs, now kept in the Australian War Memorial, show the Wass'ah after the battle, ravaged and depredated.[12] A second riot followed at the end of July. According to historian Suzanne Brugger,[13] the Wass'ah riots constituted the epilogue of a protracted period of hostility between the ANZAC, frequenting the red-light districts, and the local population of prostitutes, pimps and petty thieves: brawls were frequent between Australian customers, brothel owners, pimps and sex workers, particularly as soldiers often refused to pay on leaving the brothels. It is likely that rumours played a vital role in the Wass'ah riots. From mid-December a number of stories had been circulating in the Hilmiyyah camp, concerning ANZAC troops who had been attacked or killed in the quarter of ill-fame. Other rumors were about barkeepers defiling beverages sold to the ANZAC soldiers by urinating into them, surely reflecting the fact that the quality of alcohol sold in town was certainly not of the highest type. For the accident that caused the first Wass'ah riot someone talked of a British soldier from Manchester who happened to find his long-time disappeared sister stripping in a bar. The story has it that the girl had left England for Egypt in service of a lady who then fired her. She ended up prostituting herself in the Wass'ah, where her brother found her. He tried to get her put out of the house but was attacked by a group of bouncers. He then went back to the camp to get the help from his fellow soldiers, and the riots ensued. Although these rumours were denied by the press, they may have played a relevant role in exacerbating the ANZAC's behaviour.[14]

Martial Men, Venereal Women

During World War I, the spread of venereal diseases among imperial troops garrisoned in town reached unprecedented, worrying proportions. According to Australian historian Alistair Thomson, by February 1916 almost 6,000 men from the Australian Imperial Force (AIF) were treated for venereal diseases in Cairo. In addition, over 1,000 diseased soldiers were sent back home.[15] British army officer Lieutenant-Colonel Elgood stated that 'in April 1916, in one formation of the Army, admission from venereal disease into hospital had risen to the annual ratio of 25 per cent, and the average annual rate throughout the whole expeditionary force during that month was 12 per cent approximately'.[16]

Military authorities were obviously concerned with how to guarantee men's efficiency by preserving them from venereal diseases and physical decay. Top-brass anxieties centred on homosexuality among troops, and the danger of miscegenation proceeding from sexual relationships with local women, primarily through prostitution. Before 1916, when the rank-and-file were permitted to frequent brothels, soldiers were only allowed to consort with European prostitutes. In contrast, local brothels were out of bounds; native women were considered to be ridden with disease and prone to criminality on an unprecedented scale. Martial law, which had been introduced by Sir General John Maxwell in November 1914, shortly before the declaration of war against the Ottoman Empire, changed the privileged status of European sex workers. Foreign consuls met on 23 December 1914 at the request of Cairo Police Commandant Harvey Pasha, and adopted a number of temporary measures to control foreign prostitution more effectively 'with consideration given to the differences of habit and mode of life'.[17] European women now had to register and undergo medical examinations, although they attended a separate 35-bed lock hospital in Shubra where they were checked by European doctors only. In this way, the war also brought about a restrictive understanding of the extent to which sexually active unattached working-class white women in the Colonies could claim to be part of the colonisers' dominant class: in other words, a question of citizenship and racial prestige. Philippa Levine has observed that

> the war brought about an increasingly alarmist link between racial
> mistrust and a vision of 'sexual disorder' in which 'unruly' women

and potentially disloyal colonials were subject to far more rigorous controls than other groups. Sexual politics could not escape the tight bounds of race given Britain's imperial pre-eminence at this juncture, nor could the politics of race exist except as marked by sexuality [...] and just as the colour of citizenship remained firmly white during and especially after the war, so too did it remain predominantly masculine.[18]

This is evident also in the remaking of rank-and-file masculinity during the war. Since the mid-nineteenth century, soldiers had been considered by their senior officers a target for moral regeneration, something they would not have been deemed before. From the 1860s onwards, on the contrary, military manuals spread the notion of a masculine 'muscular Christianity' made of sexual restraint, fitness and chivalry.[19] Moral rectitude and temperance become a national patriotic duty:

As opposition to the CD Acts mounted [in the UK], more emphasis was placed on morality and uplifting recreation for soldiers. Army camps were provided with skittle alleys, workshops, libraries and gymnasia, and the soldiers' entitlement to alcohol was reduced. At the same time, a more tolerant attitude towards the marriage of soldiers was emerging, for it was hoped that marriage would discourage casual sexual liaisons.[20]

The strategy for combating the spread of syphilis and other sexually transmitted pathologies among troops coupled prophylaxis with discourse on countenance, chastity and physical exercise to release and neutralise the dangerous effects of sexual drive: two different approaches, one evangelical-abolitionist and one regulationist-disciplinarian, coexisted. Religious indoctrination came to play a relevant role in Cairo as well. Guy Thornton, Chaplain-Captain of the New Zealand Expeditionary Force in Cairo, discussed in his book *With the ANZACs in Cairo, the Tale of a Great Fight* (1917) the attempt by military authorities and religious men to contain the spread of vice and immorality among the troops. Thornton, an evangelical leader, believed that England – as a civilising power – had the duty to inculcate locals with morality and 'correct' their 'innate' lustfulness so as 'to make an end of the existing flaunting, bare-faced immorality', while simultaneously trying to defend imperial troops from degradation and corruption.[21] A cultural programme was organised in the Hilmiyyah Camp for the troops to keep them away from the 'terrible temptations of Cairo',[22] such as a weekly concert, lectures on Egyptian history and archaeology, Islam, Masses for moral edification and 'all the things they needed for writing home was [sic.] sold in the Camp so that they didn't need to go to the city centre and be exposed to temptations'.[23] Preventing soldiers who had just returned from the front from frequenting the red-light district proved to be an arduous task, though, even for a champion of religious zeal like Thornton. He started following intoxicated soldiers inside the brothels, urging them to repent and refrain from the evil deeds they were about to commit. Describing an episode when a young soldier was being enticed by a big Berber pimp to enter a house of ill-fame, Thornton narrates how he got into a brothel room in order to impede the New Zealander from consorting with the prostitute: 'the women, of whom there were two in the room, broke out into voluble entreaties, but a sharp word and threatening gesture would quickly reduce them to frightened silence.'[24] Thornton frequently came into contact with touts and *madames*, with whom he often clashed in his attempt to disrupt their business. In one instance, he preached to 100 New Zealanders queuing in front of a brothel:

> As soon as my work began to tell, the women came down from the rooms about and [. . .] cursed me [. . .] in so many tongues, in many languages of the Levant, in French, in Arabic, in Italian, Greek and broken English [. . .] at last, enraged by the fact that not a single man was entering their house, their madam (the woman who hold [sic.] the place), as they generally did on similar occasions, tried to stir up a riot.[25]

The 1916 Purification

Public security and the spread of venereal diseases appeared to be out of control during the war. Vice and immorality were perceived to be rampant by local and imperials authorities alike, while many British residents and locals were vehemently opposed to state-regulated prostitution. In 1916 a joint military-civilian commission known as the Purification Committee was set up with the aim of assessing the efficacy of existing sanitary policies to curtail the diffusion of venereal diseases among troops. The committee was chaired by Lieutenant-Colonel E.A. Altham and was composed of important military and religious personalities and medical experts.[26] They concluded that the existing system of medical check-ups was not a guarantee against the spread of venereal diseases and, as far as the impact of licensed prostitution was concerned, they pointed out that regulationism was detrimental to the containment of venereal pathologies; it created a deceptive feeling of security in customers while augmenting their exposition to contagion.[27] Since regulated prostitution did not constitute a deterrent to the spread of sexually transmitted diseases and sanitary measures were easily being circumvented by sex workers, the correct strategy, according to the commission, was an emphasis on moral regeneration. This would be achieved through the adoption of strict prohibitionist policies. Cairo's purification policy consisted in the intensification of moral reform and religious indoctrination among troops and the repression of any form of vice. Under martial law, it was stipulated that all women suspected of being diseased with venereal diseases should be examined and confined to the lock hospital if found infected; knowingly transmitting syphilis by consorting with men was also made an offence. Many prostitutes tried to escape from supervision by pretending to be artistes and frequenting the music halls.[28] As a result, the aforementioned *Miralai* Harvey Pasha ordered that only certified artistes could drink with the audience according to the *fath* custom but, as the press prophesied, 'no doubt some way of evading this rule will be discovered, and all these women will soon obtain apparently genuine contracts to the effect that they are artistes'.[29] Associated forms of 'vice' conducive to sexual promiscuity were also outlawed. In June 1916 Harvey Pasha banned belly dancing (*danse du ventre*) from coffee houses, music halls as well as any other public places as he 'came to the conclusion that the dance is suggestive and immoral in its tendencies, and therefore should not be permitted in the capital of a city which is now a British Protectorate'.[30] Another moralising measure taken by military authorities was the arrest and detention of transvestites, 'the corrupt male of Cairo [...] the males of lewd character, who abandon the characteristics of manhood and assume the appearances of females in dress and toilette'.[31] As the selling of spirits was considered to play an important role in the flourishing of vice, alcohol was prohibited in the Azbakiyyah between 5 p.m. and 8 a.m.[32]

Morally suspect professionals such as actresses and artistes were also barred from frequenting public cafés in the theatre district.[33]

The Debate about Prophylaxis

While moral edification was emphasised and appeals to sexual abstinence reiterated among the troops, very pragmatic considerations about the ongoing consorting of soldiers with sex workers and the major threat posed by sexually transmitted diseases to military efficiency called for medical prophylaxis more than the stigmatisation of soldiers, an approach I call regulationist-disciplinarian. Military authorities believed that as moral edification and the elimination of troops' deviant behavior were not goals in short sight, some form of medical prophylaxis ought to be enforced. The Purification Commission, which included a number of abolition enthusiasts from the religious and military establishment, as well as several medical officers inclined to prevention policies, was mild in its statements about prophylaxis. For instance, the Bishop of Jerusalem, Major General Watson and Colonel T.W. Gibbard disagreed with the dominant resolution according to which, while compulsory prophylaxis should be considered unacceptable on the moral grounds, prophylactics should be sold to soldiers on demand. In particular, the clash between moralist and sanitarian attitudes revolved around the issue of the distribution of prophylactic packets to men taking military leave. New Zealander activist Ettie A. Rout (1877–1936) distinguished herself as one of the most vocal supporters of VD prophylaxis, and methods of early treatment in Egypt during World War I. 'A curious brew of libertarian and disciplinarian', she actively campaigned for the distribution of prophylactic kits among the troops in Egypt first, then in London and eventually in Paris, where she was famous for awaiting troops who arrived from the front at the Gare du Nord and distributing business cards where she advertised the services of 'safe' brothels. Founder of the New Zealand Volunteer Sisterhood, in 1916 Rout opened the Tel-al-Kabir Soldiers' Club, and a canteen in al-Qantara, to provide troops with better food and recreation. Highly despised by the religious establishment for her anti-moralistic stance, her concern for sanitation and hygiene was in fact rooted in eugenics and racism. In her view, prophylaxis was required to defend the purity of Australian breed. As Philippa Levine has pointed out, in her writings she contrasted time and again the 'vigour of young Australia with Britain as old, decrepit, and potentially dangerous'.[34]

The kit consisted of calomel ointment against syphilis and permanganate potassium tablets for gonorrhoea. Dominion military authorities began distributing prophylactic kits to their men from 1916. This provision encountered strong opposition from metropolitan social purity movements; the British Association for Moral and Social Hygiene (AMSH) sent a missive to the War Office requiring the public to be informed about whether this practice had also been covertly adopted among British troops.[35] Opponents maintained that troops should in no way be explicitly encouraged to use prophylactic measures as this would be tantamount to condoning vice. In practice, however, military authorities both made the kits available to soldiers and lectured about the virtues of chastity. This same controversial approach regarded the establishment of lavage rooms, that is, clinics for post-coital disinfection. Opened in Egypt in 1916, lavage rooms offered soldiers confidential treatment when they returned to the barracks after leave. Methods used to eradicate possible venereal infections included penile irrigations and prostate massage. The treatments in the lavage rooms were not compulsory and understandably unpopular with troops. Indeed, the soldiers, despite restrictive regulations, kept frequenting brothels without adopting any prophylactic measures or having recourse to post-coital disinfection.

Imperial Troops and Brothels

The enthusiasm with which imperial soldiers frequented licensed and unlicensed brothels in Cairo is well documented by a wealth of historical sources. In March 1916, Harvey Pasha wrote a thorough report about the purification measures taken to combat the spread of both local and European prostitution, pimping and traffic of adulterated alcoholics in Cairo which circulated among British and Dominions' military authorities.[36] In 1921, A.T. Upson, Publishing Superintendent of the *Nile Mission Press* (a British missionary publishing company active in Cairo since 1905), published an alarmist article about the moral degradation of imperial troops in Cairo. Since 1918, the *Nile Mission Press* had been agitating against in-bound brothels, that is, brothels that could be used by imperial troops, and had welcomed the decision of the colonial authorities to close 20 brothels in the Wass'ah. However, as Mr Upson hastened to remark, the ordinance failed to curb the link between British soldiers and prostitution as 'some of these brothels were small and there was nothing like the traffic there that there was in the Azbakiyyah district of Cairo. These five or six streets contained a number of European women but an overwhelming majority of native ones'.[37] Upson denounced the fact that military authorities were taking no effective measures to protect the 'youth of the Nation' against the sins of Cairo. To substantiate his point, he recalled the exemplary story of a British soldier he had rescued in the red-light district:

> Last Saturday night, while distributing some tracts in a street called 'Atfat Shalaby (Out of Bounds) I came across a poor depraved-looking specimen of a British soldier, too drunk to stand. A chum was ineffectively trying to get him out. Now, this is a notoriously bad street for [...] it is inhabited by notorious criminals and vagabonds, who are in league with, if not organically linked to, with [sic.[the painted women who occupy the houses. I urged one friend to get out, as he was liable to be apprehended by the military police at any time and, if he escaped their notice, the women would get him inside, and drug him, after which they would rob him of everything he possessed, and, if nothing worst happened, he might wake up next morning upon a dunghill. He expostulated and tried to get away from me, but as it was quite hopeless to walk along, his chum and I propped him up under the arm-pits and propelled him forward. Even then we had two spills going down the steps [...] This is merely one incident of an evening's work. I know not his name but, wonder what, his mother would say thanks to me for having rescued him, for, after all, he is somebody's boy.[38]

In 1921, all brothels were designated as out-of-bounds for imperial troops. Venereal contagion was also experimentally made into a military offence, and was liable to martial court. However, regulation was enforced for only six months. Such an ambiguous approach – officially prohibiting the troops to frequent brothels while in fact tolerating this activity – prevailed through the years. In the 1930s a new polemic was initiated by the AMSH. In 1934 Miss Florence Wakefield, an activist of the AMSH in Cairo, submitted to the association's Central Bureau in London an extensive report about the link between British troops and regulationism in the city. She denounced that segregated districts in Egypt were not completely out-of-bounds, as military authorities allowed their men to make use of some brothels:

> In Cairo they are ns. 8, 9, 23, 27, 33 in Sharia Birka, and men are severely dealt with as they visit any others as the ones selected are considered to be better class houses with less risk of contagion. One of the selected houses contains far more women than the others and there are certain rooms in some of the houses that the men are not supposed to enter.[39]

On asking Colonel Barnes, the officer responsible for organisation in the Army, about the reason why anti-regulationist measures had been successful in India but failed in Cairo, she was told that

> women in Egypt were so much more attractive than women in India, and also more in evidence whereas in India they do not appear in the streets during the day and have to be sought for indoor even in the evening [...] So, the temptation for British soldiers is even greater [...] For these reasons the military authorities in Egypt feel that they cannot expect the soldiers to exercise continual self-control and that 'the men must be allowed to blow off steam sometimes'. Therefor permission is given through a 'verbal quibble' to visit certain houses in one of the segregated districts. I asked the colonel how the men knew which houses to go to. After a moment's reflection, he said he did not know. I obtained the information later from a young British Police Officer who had been in the Army in Egypt until 1929 and whose duties still take him occasionally to the barracks.[40]

Following the publication of this report, the matter was immediately brought to the attention of the War Office. Miss Wakefield, among others, hoped that the British Army in Egypt would adopt an abolitionist stance once and for all, so as to put an end to regulatonism, 'a slur on the British reputation'.[41] In April 1934, Miss Neilans, the General Secretary of the AMSH, wrote a letter to the War Office informing them of the situation in Cairo with regard to British troops and their use of brothels. The reply from the War Office confirmed that the practice described in Miss Neilans' letter was absolutely contrary to the policy of the British Army Headquarters in Egypt, and to that of the War Office. Troops were specifically warned by a notice issued in 1925 and regularly re-published, that no brothels were under the control of military authorities and that soldiers frequenting houses of ill-fame were liable to contract venereal diseases. As an informer of AMSH from the King George Soldier's Home in 'Abbasiyyah, later remarked, the War Office was trying to conceal the actual state of things: 'If the War Office did not encourage the whole business [...] how did special dressing rooms [the lavage room] ever come to be opened in every British Barracks?'[42]

Conclusion

Because of Egypt's strategic importance within the system of communication of the Empire, thousands of British, Dominion and Indian Troops were deployed in the country during World War I. Other than in the Canal zone, the greatest concentration of soldiers was in Cairo. Despite the imposition of martial law since the beginning of the conflict, wartime Cairo witnessed increasing lawlessness and disorders. The influx of imperial troops was connected to the burgeoning consumption of alcohol, drugs and the flourishing of prostitution. Riots erupting in the Wass'ah area, where Australian troops destroyed and set fire to a number of buildings, exacerbated the hostility of the locals against colonial soldiers and the occupation regime. The unruly behaviour of the troops not only posed serious threats to the very image of colonial racial superiority in terms of values of self-discipline and moderation, but it also undermined their offensive potential. Military authorities attempted to contain the spread of venereal disease among the troops by using a complex discursive strategy. What prevailed, in fact, was a mixture of moralistic repression, championed by the abolitionist evangelic leaders aiming at uplifting soldiers by strengthening their ethic qualities through spiritual and physical exercises, regulationism and prophylaxis cautiously supported by the military establishments and medical experts.

CHAPTER 6

POLICING 'SUSPECT' FEMININITIES: THE WORK OF BRITISH PURITY MOVEMENTS IN CAIRO

In Egypt, Capitulary privileges and a bustling speculative economy attracted increasing numbers of subsistence migrants from Europe, Eastern and Southern Europe in particular. This trans-Mediterranean migration meant an increasing stratification of foreign communities, growing polarisation between European propertied residents and proletarian ones, and a waning class difference between the lower segments of the foreign communities and the colonised local population. European subsistence migrants were considered detrimental to the colonial rhetoric of European racial superiority in general, but white freewheeling women were particulary problematic. Discourses about European domesticity and national motherhood were called into question by such liminal characters, unaccompanied women roaming the world in search of a life unhindered by the trappings of bourgeois respectability and unrestrained by any sort of patriarchal supervision. The presence of European women selling themselves in Egyptian brothels, as elsewhere in the Empire, forced British colonial authorities to face the thorny question of the presence of 'white subalterns' who challenged, by dint of their very existence, hegemonic racial and civilisational hierarchies.[1] As Anne McClintock expounded in her magisterial *Imperial Leather*, by the late Empire 'the analogy between gender and race degeneration came to serve a specifically modern form of social domination, as an intricate dialectic emerged between the domestication of the colonies and racializing of the metropolis'.[2] At the centre of the Empire, the 'degenerate classes', that is, 'the militant working class, the Irish, Jews, criminal, alcoholics, the insane' and prostitutes, were to be seen as anachronistic remains of the past that could not find a place in the modern world. In the colonies, promiscuous contacts and bodily exchanges between locals and low Europeans were sources of contagion and racial degeneration, calling for strict supervision on those gendered categories which, McClintock argued, 'were ambiguously placed on the imperial divide, nurses, nannies, governesses, prostitutes and servants. Tasked with the purification and maintenance of boundaries, they were especially fetishized as dangerously ambiguous and contaminating'.[3] Bourgeois animosity towards these gendered subalterns, under the guise of paternalistic social reform, was but the imperial dimension of the veritable social hysteria which created the so-called 'White Slave Trade' media sensation, the symptom of a more profound social and political crisis in the metropolis and extending into the colonies.[4] The 'white slavery' question spread like a moral panic, bringing together two powerful themes, that of prostitution and slavery. The perception of civic disorder and societal collapse was expressed through images of subjugation and victimisation of the female body, most specifically that of young girls allegedly trafficked and exploited as sexual slaves in European and overseas brothels. After a brief analysis of the emergence of metropolitan obsession with the 'White Slave Trade', this chapter will explore the colonial dimension of social purity, showing how a specific category of subaltern social actors, in Cairo, foreign prostitutes and 'fallen' women, came to play a very important role in the preservation of the besieged category of colonisers' racial and civilisational superiority through the creation of a specific apparatus of coercion, control and, possibly, regeneration managed by British purity and feminist movements in Cairo, from the beginning of the twentieth century until World War II.

The 'Maiden Tribute of Modern Babylon':
Brief History of a Moral Panic

In 1880, revelations about young British girls being trafficked to Belgian brothels were published by Alfred Dyer, a journalist and prominent purity activist.[5] It had the effect of galvanising a heterogeneous front made up by Christian fanatic moral reformers and libertarian feminists. The idea of 'white slavery' was not new in fact. Used in the early nineteeth century to critique the blatant exploitation of the working classes under capitalism, the concept increasingly assumed a clear gendered and sexual connotation, identifying the body of the prostitute as the ultimate site of oppression.[6] In a letter to British social reformer Josephine Butler (1828–1906), French writer Victor Hugo firstly narrowed the term down to the plight of professional prostitutes in brothels under regulationist regimes across Europe.[7] In England, the passing of the Contagious Diseases Acts in 1864, which stipulated the compulsory identification and registration of sex workers in specific military depots in Southern England and in Ireland, introduced *de facto* regulation in the country and was fiercely opposed by a pro-repeal campaign; one of the more prominent organisations that was active in the campaign was the Ladies' National Association (LNA) guided by Butler. The powerful recombination of reformist idioms moulded during the repealers' battle, until their eventual success in 1886, was at the core of the new 'white slavery' sensation spreading in the 1880s. In 1885, W.T. Stead, a *Pall Mall Gazette* editorialist and a leading figure in the purity movement, succeeded in instigating public outrage by orchestrating the famous 'Maiden Tribute of Modern Babylon' case.[8] Rebecca Jarrett, a 36-year-old regenerated prostitute, was hired to procure a minor virgin so that Stead could demonstrate that a 13-year-old girl in London could be easily bought and initiated into a career in vice. Young Eliza Armstrong was thus purchased from her mother for five British pounds, on the arrangement of going into service, and then brought to a low boarding house where Stead pretended to be a customer willing to take advantage of her, before revealing his real identity. Starting on 6 July 1885, he published a series of articles that focussed on stories of children being lured into prostitution. As Edward J. Bristow puts it, the series 'was a prurient hash which centred on the disguised Eliza Armstrong story. Some of the horrifying descriptions of child rape in fashionable brothels may well have reflected a shocking reality; but the accounts of international and local white slavery were exaggerated'.[9] The police, accused of being acquiescent to the moral carnage, easily confuted most of the charges. Nonetheless, the staged scoop was exactly what was needed to inflame the public opinion. The 'Maiden Tribute of Modern Babylon' case effectively compelled the Government to pass specific restrictive legislations such as the Criminal Law Amendment Act, which raised the age of consent to 16 and fuelled a number of national and international civil society groups lobbying for moral regeneration and correction of vice. On 22 August 1885, a large rally at Hyde Park marked the apex of the purity campaign and the founding of the Nation Vigilance Association (NVA), which was to become the main agent for moral reform campaign in the years to come, targeting prostitution, homosexuality, obscene publications and vice. W.T. Stead is credited for having conceived the Association and laid down its basic principles, but the first secretary was William Alexander Coote, a compositor of *The Standard*, imbued with fervent religious zeal and puritanism. Initially, repealers of different orientations collaborated and joined the NVA organising committee, despite the profound divergences among them. Nevertheless, the clash between the libertarian, constitutionalist, pro-individual rights vision of groups such as the feminist Ladies' National Association on the one hand, and the coercive, repressive and religionist outlook of the NVA on the other, soon became evident, to the effect that the feminist and constitutionalist goals of the repeal movement – from which the NVA had derived its impetus originally – were totally neglected in the newly developed version of priggish reform.

The NVA aspired to a supranational operative dimension, its goal being an international crusade against the globally organised exploitation of women and children.[10] National committees were first established in a number of countries, with volunteers willing to gather information, work toward the suppression of the racket and promote abolitionist policies in their respective countries. One of the main instruments for the consolidation of the association was the organisation of a series of international conferences, which stressed the need for intergovernmental coordination. The first conference was held in London in 1899, when the International Bureau for the Suppression of the Traffic in Women and Children (IBS) was officially set up under the aegis of the British National

Vigilance Association.[11] The main goal of the IBS was the incorporation of the theme of traffic in women and children in the international legal corpus, something which, in turn, required local governments to adopt specific abolitionist measures. Despite growing tensions between regulationist and abolitionalist national committees, a first international convention was signed in 1910, which ruled that significant measures should be undertaken by the signatory states to adjust domestic laws, if necessary; to punish the procuring of girls under the age of 20, even if the victims gave consent; and the procuring of any women by force or fraud. These acts would be considered criminal offences even if committed across national borders, and could therefore be extraditable. After World War I, the lead of the battle against the international traffic in women and children was taken up by the League of Nations.[12]

Social Purity in Egypt: The IBS Committee

At the turn of the twentieth century, a number of British purity movements, charity associations and religious groups were active in Cairo, the most prominent of which was the Egyptian branch of the International Bureau for the Suppression of the Traffic in Women and Children, led by the NVA. The Egyptian Committee of the IBS was made up of three sub-branches: Alexandria, Cairo and Port Said. The first was established in Alexandria in 1904, when William Coote (Secretary of the British NVA) founded the Alexandria Committee for the Suppression of the Traffic in Women in collaboration with Baron Jacques de Menasce, a prominent member of the local Jewish community. Government authorities granted annual subsidies to Alexandria's IBS Committee, which was formed by members of the foreign communities, but featured no Egyptians. Donations were nonetheless vital. In time, the differences in approaches and methods between the NVA and feminist groups active in the country resulted in growing tensions. Groups such as the Association for Moral and Social Hygiene (AMSH), the new denomination of the LNA after 1915, which was concerned with the existence of a double standard of morality granting men freedom of agency while degrading and repressing women, advocated more radical change and social criticism, and promoted clear abolitionist goals; purity groups, by contrast, were primarily concerned with the enforcement of more rigorous standards of morality and decency, to be implemented through repression and coercion if necessary.[13] Purity activists from the NVA thought that abolitionism should be brought about very gradually in a colonial setting such as Egypt, given that the country was not advanced enough to apply successful abolitionist policies. This shows the inherent contradiction between their anti-racket agenda and the existence of a regulationist system ordinarily supplied by the international traffic.

Purity movements played a vital role in buttressing the colonial enterprise. As Margot Badran rightly observed, hindered as they were by the Capitulations, British enforcement law authorities 'welcomed cooperation with private anti-white slavery organizations',[14] and were much more benevolent toward them than abolitionist feminist groups calling for legal deregulation of prostitution. The hard abolitionist front was composed of international and local feminists and evangelical groups – such as the American United Presbyterian Mission, the Scotch Mission, the Church Missionary Society, the British and Foreign Bible Society and the American Bible Society. Missionary groups in particular were active on the ground and devoted their efforts not only to the evangelisation of the Muslims and Copts, but also to the moral edification and uplifting of imperial troops stationed in Cairo: they did so by organising musical evenings, lectures, readings of the Gospels and by distributing religious tracts.[15] Such divisiveness within the reformist front is well illustrated by the polemic that was ignited when Miss Higson, an activist from the NVA with Butlerian leanings, arrived in Cairo in 1930, for a lecture on abolitionism in the country.[16] Mr Sempkins, at that time General Secretary of the British NVA, was greatly alarmed. According to him, a too-aggressive abolitionist stance could well lead to rapid disruption of all the work being done in Egypt. If the closing down of regulated brothels in the country was certainly the desired, final aim of their campaign, NVA members maintained, such an objective had to be pursued gradually and with caution.[17] In other words, while every effort had to be undertaken to fight the international traffic and influx of European sex workers in the country, Egyptian sex work should have been regulated by the State for sanitary and public order considerations, provided that all brothels should be declared out of bounds for British and Imperial troops, so as to ensure complete segregation and lack of contact between the military and prostitutes, at least on an official level. This view clearly rested on the racist assumption that prostitution, sexual looseness and vice were natural traits of uncivilised native societies. As Philippa Levine points out, 'shame was allegedly absent in colonial cultures, normalizing prostitution in "degraded" society'. This notion was essential to the way British colonial authorities commented on native sex work, seen as an evidence of the natural inferiority of colonised people, thus legitimising regulationist legislation that would not be condoned in the domestic context.[18]

In 1925, the IBS branches of Alexandria, Cairo and Port Said were organised into a joint national committee in order to strengthen the association's propaganda efforts, enhance the staff and facilitate communication with local authorities and the public at large. In 1928, Miss Cecily McCall was hired as the Organising Secretary for the IBS Egyptian Federation. Later to become famous as the first female psychiatric social worker in Britain and author of a number of tracts on social work with female convicts (based on her experience in the Holloway prison of London), McCall was a graduate of St Hughes' College, Oxford, with secretarial training. She had worked for 18 months in Poland, as the English tutor and lady companion of the wife and children of a Polish prince, and had spent some time in India, being 'therefore used to those climates and to the difficulties of a non-European population'.[19] After lengthy discussions about her salary and the training she wanted to pursue at the Josephine Butler Memorial House of Liverpool, something which Mr Sempkins – then Secretary of the British NVA – decidedly opposed to because of the 'excessive feminism' of the institution, she eventually left for Egypt, reaching Alexandria towards the end of January 1928. McCall took on her tasks with the outmost enthusiasm and dedication, doing her best to reorganise the activities of the Egyptian committee. Miss McCall's secretariat marked the period of the most fervent NVA activism in Cairo, and indeed in the whole country. Thus she visited the philanthropic organisations specialised in rescue work with street women, gathering more information about their activities in Alexandria, Port Said and Isma'iliyyah. She also visited the Cairo Lock Hospital, the venereal wards where registered prostitutes were examined weekly and the female penitentiary in order to spread information about the IBS among sex-workers. Other than this she collaborated with British law enforcement authorities, worked on the project for the appointment of female police officers in duty in the Alexandria port, and she reorganised the refuge the IBS ran in Cairo, the Beyt 'Arabi. She also made frequent visits to the red-light district of Cairo, leaving vivid descriptions of the prostitution milieu:

> I took up work in the night in order to get a better knowledge of the places where these *wretched creatures* [my emphasis] are taken [...] There are also some men working as acrobats who make ten or twelve-year-old children going around begging in bars. I stopped one in front of the Eden Palace Hotel thirty minutes past midnight and I told her that, had she been found in a public place again, she would be arrested. In the same street, I came across a nine-year-old child who gave me her servant license (roska) [Arabic *rukhsah*], but she was in the street bawling out to passer-byes [...] One night we made all the girls of the Manchester Bar, who were out in the streets calling out at customers, go inside. Next to the bar, there's a public brothel, in front of which four women were seated. We asked them to go inside, and they did so, except the brothel keeper's sister, who refused and would shamelessly grab the passer-byes by their arms. I called an agent in and the woman was taken to the Police Station where she spent the night and paid a 50-pt. fine. We visited the brothel-district as well, but all the women seemed to be of age [...] Visiting Giza and Gezirah, on the shores of the Nile, I saw that the task is hard, as difficulties are plenty. In front of the Semiramis, small boats have to be carefully watched over, as it often happens that isolated couples haul offshore and many of these girls are very very young.[20]

Growing tensions within the Egyptian IBS, due in particular to the conservatism of the Alexandrian Committee, its regulationist stance and its overt hostility towards the young and energetic Miss McCall, eventually led her to resign at the end of 1930, in deep frustration and resentment. As she explained in words imbued with racism and contempt:

> And so I have come to the conclusion they better get someone else out whose enthusiasm is not in the battered condition as mine is in, and if they keep on getting out new secretaries every two years

or so, they may be able to keep the thing going. More than two years turns you either into a passive cynic or a lunatic. The practical work is bad enough in a country like this where you are dealing largely with the *dregs of the Levant- girls who should have been drowned at birth and men whose mothers should have been drowned not to speak of their fathers* [my emphasis].[21]

After Miss McCall's resignation, NVA President Sempkins made a trip to Egypt in order to ascertain the moribund situation of the Egyptian Committee, take stock of the advancement of pro-abolitionist propaganda in the country and see to the reorganisation of preventive and rescue work. Despite McCall's efforts, the situation in Alexandria was highly problematic. A newly founded Ladies' Committee had opened a refuge with no clear operative strategy or organisation. As to the Cairo Refuge, the place struck Sempkins as being utterly mismanaged. As he explained, the main reason for the success of the refuge in previous years was the strong support of Cairo's police *Bimbashi*, Major Tegg, who had provided many of the prostitute inmates:

> His methods are perhaps unorthodox but are decidedly helpful. Since the squabbles started in the Committee in Cairo, the Police have ceased to interest themselves greatly in the Refuge, and without the assistance of the police only an exceptional worker would ever get girls as inmates. Major Tegg, out of sheer kindness, had put in a number of more or less respectably married women with their children pending their deportation to England, but when I was there the Refuge was not doing what it was designed to.[22]

Sempkins meant to say that, while the Cairo Refuge was specifically designed to 'reform' sex workers and convert them to 'decent' 'honest' women, almost the totality of inmates were in fact destitute women with children, not professional prostitutes. Most of the time sex workers deliberately avoided reformist institutions, and more in general any external intervention in their business, choosing instead to avoid registration and practise the trade clandestinely and temporarily.

The IBS Refuge in Cairo was reorganised in May 1935 and reopened at 36 Shari'a Madbuli, in the district of 'Abdin. It was overseen by a matron and contained 18 beds. The purpose of the institution was twofold: helping needy girls by preventing them from falling into bad ways and rescuing those who had been forced into a life of vice. Girls were taught domestic chores such as cooking and sewing, and work was found for them whenever possible. As shown by the IBS Report of 1937,[23] 109 women had been helped by the Refuge during that year, the majority of them local Jews (with no definite nationality), Egyptian and foreign subjects: British, Austrian, Swiss, Armenian, Greek, French, Italian, Syrian, Russian, Yugoslavian and Czechoslovakian. Boarders were almost without exception adolescent, single mothers who were taken to the Refuge with their children, for safety. They would normally stay until some kind of income-generating activity could be found for them, so that they could provide for themselves and their babies, and they were given medical assistance if necessary. Despite the initial optimism, the management of the Refuge did not achieve any significant results with regard to the fight against licensed and clandestine sex work. Sex workers kept avoiding voluntary entry into the Refuge and showed no interest in being reformed. With the advent of World War II, the whole abolitionist campaign in Egypt came to a halt: as Miss Devonshire, then outside worker of the IBS Refuge in Cairo, wrote in a confidential letter to Mr Sempkins on 8 March 1939:

> The Government can think of nothing but Defence and it is quite possible that the grant may be cut down this year. Bribery and corruption are rapidly getting worse and the new *Bureau Des Moeurs* leads the way in this respect. So what can be the use of passing resolutions or discussing methods of dealing with these ghastly problems? The women here are little better than animals and will certainly not avail themselves of free V.D. clinics even if these are provided. Our present Committee is so disinterested or perhaps I should say so engrossed in A.R.P. that no meeting was held before the Annual Meeting!! Only immediately after it, Matron and I asked for six weeks what precautions the Committee wished us to take for the safety of the girls in the Hostel and were told that we should probably close down altogether, and that in any case the girls would have to be evacuated!! We were not told what place we should take them![24]

Beyt 'Arabi

Despite the enormous organisational problems, from 1920 to 1939 the IBS Refuge was the sole institution of its kind in Cairo. It collaborated with foreign consulates, religious authorities and other philanthropic and charitable associations, who reported cases for potential internment in the Refuge. The institution was presided over by an organising committee, made up of prominent members of the British expatriate community alone. They relied mainly on subscriptions and donations by individuals. The centre was staffed by an organising secretary and an external worker who did the administrative work, conducted fund-raising, liaised with local Egyptian and British authorities and monitored the situation on the ground. The staff members also included a matron, who worked inside the house and supervised the girls in their daily chores.

From 1920 to 1929, the Refuge was situated in an old house called Beyt 'Arabi. Following the creation of the joint committee in 1929, it was transferred to an old Turkish house opening into a *salamlik* in 3 'Atfet Fayruz, with airy rooms, painted ceilings and a shuttered veranda serving as the former *harim*, on the first floor. It could accommodate 20 to 30 girls. In this section I will draw on existing reports by the IBS Refuge in order to study not only the sociological profiles of the inmates, but also their daily regimes, the relation between moral reform and the material realities of the Refuge, and the impact of moral discipline on the inmates. Their responses were far from unified: some of them, in fact, decided to conform to the ideology of moral regeneration they were subjected to, while others did not, claiming – occasionally in radical ways – their right to alternative and autonomous choices. As previously mentioned, collaboration with local law enforcement authorities was essential for the process of recruiting inmates for the Refuge. Thus the external worker attended medical inspection rooms where professional prostitutes were periodically screened, so that the girls knew of the existence of this institution, in case they wished to change their life and apply voluntarily for entry into the Refuge. Thanks to an agreement with Cairo police, a licensed prostitute could voluntarily enter the Refuge and stay there for a probation period of three months. If she 'repented' at the end of this period, and proved to be ready to lead a 'decent' life, her name would be removed from the registration list.[25]

An interesting case is that of a 32-year-old Greek woman, who migrated to Egypt as a family servant. Some time later, she found herself alone and with no means of subsistence, and started working as a licensed prostitute. She plied the trade for 12 years and gave birth to four children, of which only one survived. As a result of the life she led, she got seriously ill and had to undergo a number of operations. Upon being discharged from the hospital she heard of the Refuge and applied for admission: 'She seems to be very determined to change her life and she makes a very good example for the other inmates.'[26]

The mission of the Refuge was rescue and reform. Reintegration of sex workers into society under the guise of decent and morally uplifted, industrious women reflected the first aim of the institution, namely to restore 'fallen women' to conformist notions of femininity. Purity activists considered prostitutes to be idle and indolent. As we read in a report of the Refuge's activities for the year 1929:

> *Three months, of course can't change a prostitute which has led an idle, sordid life of abjection into a hardworking independent woman* [my emphasis]. They lack self-reliance and self-respect, apart very often from complete lack of training or education. Three months is the minimum time limit in such cases, but as a rule they stay longer, sometimes leaving to go back to their relations, sometimes getting married, and sometimes taking posts as servants, dress-makers or shop girls. We keep in touch with them as far as possible, and, in spite of the disheartening and inevitable failures, we have had enough success to prove it is well worth the constant effect and patience involved.[27]

Attracting professional prostitutes proved to be no easy task, though, as the vast majority of them had no interest in middle-class, authoritarian moral reform. Most inmates were therefore not professional sex workers,

> but women in distress, unmarried mothers who stay a few nights or a few weeks until better accommodation can be found for the baby and work for the mother; and we have destitute women whom, owing to their character or for some other reason, no other charitable institution will take in and who, but for us, would die in the gutter. Some can pay a few piasters, but the great majority

are housed and fed free, and employment found for them as soon as they are fit.[28]

Some were widows with no source of income, such as Mrs Foley, a Maltese woman whose husband died in the collapse of their house in Bulaq and was left with two children, no job and very poor health.[29] An even more dramatic case was that of Mrs Phillippine Borrell, a 50-year-old Greek refugee from Smyrne and widow of an Englishman, who was disabled and lived with her sister on a very poor allowance paid by the Ottoman bank, the former employer of her husband.[30] Other cases involved girls coming from disrupted families. Thus Miss Walker was a British girl of 15, whose mother had divorced from her father. After her father left for the Sinai, she ran away as she no longer wanted to live with her legitimate mother.[31] A similar case regarded an Irish-Egyptian girl of 14, whose parents divorced when she was seven years old. At the age of nine, her father wanted her to get married. The mother then arranged for her to flee to England, where she spent 18 months in a convent. Once she returned to Cairo, she was shunted from one place to another until she escaped from her mother's custody and took refuge at the home of her father's Syrian mistress. Eventually she was found in the Bezenzan convent, before being taken to the IBS Refuge. After medical examination, it turned out that the father had abused her. He was found and arrested in Alexandria.[32] Many inmates were abandoned women with children: Mary Williams, for instance, was a Greek milliner who had married to an Englishman. She had been abandoned, in very bad financial conditions, with her 5-year-old child.[33] Similarly, Deborah Perlmann was a 28-year-old Palestinian Jew, married to an Alexandrian dragoman working for Thomas Cook. She had already stayed once at the Refuge, with a child she had from a previous relationship. In 1925 she was taken in again as her husband, a drug addict, sold all her belongings. She left him and, along with their 18-month-old child (later to be entrusted to a family), asked the Refuge for help. The refuge staff tried to find her a job as a healthcare worker, given that she had some experience in this sector.[34] In some cases, the Refuge staff also provided tricked women with legal advice. An exemplary case is that of Rifka Friedmann and her little daughter Bertha. Rifka, 'extremely ugly and very sickly', married Friedmann with a dowry of 300 British pounds. Her husband spent all the money and left her, but she followed him to Cairo with the baby, where he threatened to leave her again. The woman turned to the IBS Refuge for help and Mrs Altman, then matron in charge, reported the case to the Rabbinate: the latter, in turn, asked the Permit Office and Cairo police not to issue the man a passport.[35] Where possible, foreign women were repatriated. Typical was the case, among many others, of an English girl of 21 who had been forced into prostitution by her Egyptian husband. He had deceived her by pretending to be a wealthy aristocrat, but things turned out to be quite different once they arrived in Cairo. She was forced to prostitute herself, battered and threatened. One day she went to the hospital for medication and there she met a policeman, to whom she appealed for help. He took her to the Caracol (the local police station), from where she was transferred to the Refuge. Here the necessary steps were taken for her repatriation.[36]

A specific action taken by the IBS Refuge was that of preventing young girls from entering in or returning to prostitution. Delicate cases were specifically monitored by the Refuge's social workers, in collaboration with police authorities, as the following examples demonstrate. Rose and Ida Artiniou, two Armenian cousins aged 20 and 16 respectively who both worked as waitresses in the Devonshire Bar, were hosted at Beyt 'Arabi; they were assisted in finding a job outside the nightclubs of the Azbakiyyah.[37] Elene Cassarou also worked as a waitress in a bar, to support her crippled father. The Refuge staff tried to help the father so that the girl could move to Beyt 'Arabi and be trained into some kind of 'respectable' income-generating activity.[38] An 11-year-old British girl had been reported singing and dancing for the troops in various bars of the Azbakiyyah. Investigations revealed that the child was the daughter of an Englishman who had left his family, and a Russian Jew. Her mother was terminally ill and the children were entrusted to her maternal aunt, a dubious character rumored to have been the owner of a brothel in her native Salonica. The consulate eventually took steps to remove the child from her aunt's custody. When the girl was finally taken to the refuge by the police, it turned out that her passport had been tampered with by her aunt, in order to transfer her to Greece.[39] Julia was a 19-year-old Syrian Jew who had left her home country with her *souteneur*, an Egyptian: he kept her in one of his two *dahabiyyas* on the Nile. The man was wanted by the police, because he was living on the prostitution of a number of girls, including minors. Julia's mother, an artist, sought the help of the Refuge in order to find her daughter. The police found her in her pimp's company and placed her in the Refuge until the trial began. As an X-ray examination ordered by the police demonstrated that the she was not a minor, contrary to what her mother said, she was released and went back to her pimp.[40] Another 19-year-old Jew, from Rumenia, was found in a house of ill-fame managed by a woman who claimed to be her half-sister. The girl asked to be helped and was taken to the Refuge, but her so-called sister was determined to get her back, as there was no consular ordinance for keeping the girl on the premises of the Refuge.[41] Finally, an Italian mother of two asked to be taken into the Refuge together with her daughters of 21 and 18 respectively. She was married to an unemployed cabdriver, who regularly beat her and the girls. One daughter had already left the family to go into prostitution, while the other was about to do so.[42] The woman asked the refuge to host her and her daughters until they would be able to find an occupation.

Some women were reported to the institution by the police, if they were known for offences not related to sexual matters. This was the case of Helen Frankfurter, a 24-year-old Swiss national married to a local; she had relations with other men and eventually threw vitriol in her husband's face. She was in prison when she was brought to the attention of the Refuge's staff.[43] Another typical case was that of Dawlet Ahmed Yusuf, a ten-year-old Egyptian child from Alexandria living with a male cousin in Bab Sha'riyyah. Placed in service, she had been accused of theft and sent by the Caracol to the Juvenile Court in 'Abdin. The Parquet declassified her case but decided for her admission in an orphanage. Refused by several institutions, she entered the IBS Refuge, where she stayed 20 days before escaping with the house key, several garments and 140 Egyptian pounds.[44]

In the Refuge, the daily routine was relentless and purposefully designed to keep girls ever busy. The institution was completely dependent on the inmates' work: they cleaned, washed, cooked and did needlework. Inmates were given classes by voluntary, external teachers in handicrafts, physical exercise, dancing, writing and French, the language spoken in the Refuge in addition to colloquial Arabic. This schedule applied to younger inmates only: unlike older women they were never allowed out alone, and it was therefore assumed they needed no spare time. Immorality was equated to laziness; hard work was thought to be uplifting and purifying. In other words, women could expiate their previous misdeeds by turning into efficient workers. Immorality was considered a function of sin, not poverty, as implied in the following statements by Cecily McCall, Organizing Secretary from 1928 to 1930, which accurately reveal the punitive disposition behind the rhetoric of female solidarity:

> First, about Margaret Nassoughli. I don't think there is anything at present that you can do in the matter, thanks very much. We have no funds to send her to England. It is a very curious case because the girl persists in wanting to go back to her father, sometimes saying so openly, sometimes objecting to every other plan. I think myself there is a young man somewhere in the offing too. Your idea of marrying her off strikes me as flippant in the extreme, and callous of the welfare of your sex! The girl is barely 16, *very lazy, and unwilling, untrained, and apparently incapable of doing needlework, housework, cooking or looking after children. She has no other gifts, or more accurately, no gifts. Her one desire is to spend money on clothes, whose money does not interest her* [my emphasis].[45]

Lives of resident women were carefully organised and cadenced, the underlying principle being that of domesticating and civilising 'idle' women and transforming them into submissive and obedient servants. Once inmates proved to have thoroughly interiorised the discipline and had effectively been reeducated, they were reintegrated into society: they were given an occupation (milliner, shop assistant, embroiderer, cook, maid) and in some cases marriages were arranged. The Refuge developed a system of strategies of moral regulation that ranged from incarceration to training and education. Emphasis was placed on the concept of 'gentility', defined as those qualities connoting a refined and appropriate middle-class femininity. French and dance classes were not aimed at turning inmates into 'ladies', though, something that was completely at odds with the institution's purposes, but at training them in the values associated with being a lady, in order to make them disciplined and reliable servants. The Refuge thus engineered a class-specific definition of working-class femininity, based on hard work and deference to middle-class authority. Philanthropy was not an innocuous project: on the contrary, it was inherently authoritarian and conservative, as it reinforced and reproduced a social hierarchy based on the subordination of working women. The desire to 'save' and protect working-class women betrayed a deeper will of controlling them, by correcting what was perceived as subversive sexual and vocational behaviour.

Coercion was thus an integral part of the strategy of moral regulation that was put in place in the Refuge. It was hoped that inmates actively cooperated and conformed to the requested disciplinary standards, but confinement was enforced on rebellious girls when necessary. In some extreme cases girls were sent back to their families. The Jewish Marie Cohen had been taken into the Refuge after five weeks in the lock hospital. She was found a job, but she left it after only five days. She was forced to go back to Alexandria after the matron had to guard her for a whole night in a locked room, and the police formally restrained her from going back to Cairo.[46] Overt rebellion was not unusual as inmates did not necessarily agree with the project of reform to which they were subjected. Two Armenian girls of 16 and 17 years old, for example, had been taken from the red-light district to the Refuge; one of them was two-months pregnant. They stayed in the Refuge for one night, but tried to leave the hostel during the night by climbing the walls. They were locked up and guarded until the arrival of a police officer, who succeeded in calming them down. They were then transferred to a pension owned by a Syrian, and kept under strict surveillance.[47] A similar case regards a 25-year-old Palestinian Jew married to an Egyptian subject, who was brought in by the police but did not want to stay. She threatened to kill herself and was released, eventually going back to her husband and pimp.[48] Sometimes the epilogue was more dramatic, though. In January 1928, a Greek inmate of the Refuge, 14-year-old Irene Capsis, committed suicide by throwing herself out of the window. According to the matron, she could not live with the moral stigma of her own past and with that of her sisters: they were all prostitutes. She was so weak and spiritless that she could not see any way out. The matron's lapidary comment on the case was that 'they were very sorry for her. The only consolation was that the post-mortem examination had ascertained that her internal organs were almost completely destroyed by the kind of life that her father had forced her to lead', and so she would not have survived long anyway.[49]

Competing Approaches: The AMSH

Another important movement campaigning for sex workers' reform in Egypt was the Association for Moral and Social Hygiene (AMSH). An outcome of the merger of the Ladies' National Association, founded by Josephine Butler, and the Internationalist Abolitionist Federation in 1915, the AMSH was a gender equality pressure group whose objectives included the promotion in public opinion, in the legislative corpus and in social practice of a high standard of morality and sexual responsibility in women *and* men. The ultimate goals of the Association were the promotion of administrative, sanitary and educational reforms bringing about the highest individual and collective morality. The AMSH vision was based on social justice, equality of all classes before the law and a single moral standard for men and women. Feminists were obviously against state regulation of prostitution, which they saw as a blatant violation of women's rights: according to them, disadvantaged women were turned into social outcasts whose bodies were accessible to male control and harassment, whether by clients, magistrates, police officials or medical practitioners. Differently from purity movements, feminists linked poverty to prostitution, and sex work was seen as a function of economics more than of sin and amorality. After the repeal of the Contagious Diseases Acts in 1864, the AMSH focussed more on Continental Europe and the Colonies, places where state regulation of prostitution was still in place. By the 1920s it developed a radical stance against VD prophylaxis as a manifestation of prolonged state condoning of prostitution; this, according to Philippa Levine, accounts for their marginalisation within much more pragmatical, imperial debates.[50] Although informed by what Julia Laite calls a 'libertarian feminist perspective',[51] in which the civil rights of prostitutes took centre stage the AMSH work in Egypt was based on that same fundamental belief in the imperial civilisational mission, and eventually did not hesitate to show its authoritarian face.

In 1931, Louise Dorothy Potter was sent to Egypt by the AMSH to perform educational work and work toward the abolition of licensed prostitution. Potter was in fact the most radical and daring abolitionist social worker in the country. As was mentioned earlier, she published a small booklet entitled *Egypt awakening! Is it true?*, which featured on the front page a picture of the famous statue by Mahmud Mukhtar, entitled

'Egypt's Awakening': it represented an Egyptian peasant woman standing on top of a sphinx, a plastic rendition of the formulation of Egyptian national identity by local modernist, nationalist elites. The leaflet tackled the issue of Egyptian prostitution and called for its abolition, as a much needed measure to safeguard civic order and public health and, more broadly, as an integral part of the Egyptian process of modernisation and civilisation.[52] Potter summarised the arguments in favour of regulationism, that is, public order (concentrated vice is more easy to control) and sanitary inspections (spread of venereal disease can be checked where prostitutes are registered and subjected to medical examinations), showing how they were in reality false and provided evidence for this. She stated that, on the contrary, regulationism was harmful as it stood 'in the way of the provisions of efficient centres for the treatment of venereal disease'; that it legally sanctioned corruption and vice, encouraging debauchery among the population; and that it actually supported the international traffic in women and children.[53] Instead, Potter proposed a number of potential solutions: the education of the public on matters of sex and morality, propaganda on venereal diseases, the creation of a network of up-to-date clinics that would provide free and confidential treatment for both sexes, and a strong legislation against third-party profiteering and exploitation of immorality by others.[54] The abolition of prostitution being the ultimate goal, this approach entailed a more thorough medical supervision of the entire population, concerted efforts to implement moral and sanitary education as a civic duty, making national culture more scientific, a new regulationist philosophy or, perhaps better, a new regulationism, and the substitution of notions of moral stigma with medical imperatives.[55]

These proposals were put into practice by an experimental project for the abolition of licensed prostitution that the AMSH carried through under Potter's supervision in 1932, in Damanhur.[56] There were 55 registered women in town, all Egyptians, the majority coming from the Alexandria area. They worked in 18 licensed brothels, two or three of the better kind, the rest very squalid, although according to local police, there were probably two to three times as many secret houses. Abolition was not expected to eliminate prostitution altogether, but to pave the way for correct educational, social and legal measures, encouraging a better moral standard for men and women. The closing down of town brothels was thus accompanied by educational institutions, and the expansion of existing facilities, for the treatment of venereal diseases. Propaganda activities included the printing of posters and pamphlets alerting to the dangers of venereal diseases, which were disseminated in all hospitals, clinics, chemists, shops, lecture halls and outside police stations. Such an educational effort, it was argued, would provoke an increase in the number of people going to the clinics voluntarily to seek treatment for VDs. A fundamental issue was, nonetheless, that of the rehabilitation of former sex workers, as one of the key elements of the abolitionist doctrine was that of the unjust gender- and class-based marginalisation and victimisation of this specific group of women. According to Louise Potter, in fact, economic reasons were at the core of prostitution:

> Some women were obviously too lazy to work, but many others would, I believe, have taken work in the first place, if they could have found any sufficiently well paid. Women are therefore driven into prostitution to keep themselves and their families. It is almost impossible to find work for women when one wants to help them. A few years of the life of a prostitute usually render such a woman flabby and unfit for work, though earlier she might have been *saved* [my emphasis].[57]

After the houses were closed down, a large number of prostitutes moved to brothels in other towns or entered the clandestine sector, that is, they remained in the trade. This was partly due to the fact that the abolitionist project was only local, but it also reflected the reluctance of women to abandon the trade for lack of occupational alternatives. Women were offered a refuge but the majority decided not to avail themselves of it. This led Potter to specifically address the issue of a comprehensive scheme for former sex workers. Although she stated that prostitutes could not be forced to accept help, she devised a very strict rehabilitative programme where all women had to be interviewed and classified before being divided into three categories: young, fit and attractive women could go in a refuge, be taught some form of work and eventually re-marry; other young girls should be placed in training houses or given industrial training; older women, finally, should relocate to a refuge to end their days there. Although the sociological analysis of economically vulnerable, female roles did constitute an integral part of feminists' elaboration of the problem of prostitution, and they were genuinely concerned with the women they wanted to 'save', they struggled to acknowledge the full rationality and agency of those women who did not want to conform to their project. In other words, a custodial approach nevertheless prevailed.

Egyptian Feminism and the Struggle against Prostitution

The last section of this chapter deals with the complex and increasingly antagonistic relationship between imperial reformers and local Egyptian feminists. In the 1902s, Egyptian advocates of women's rights – organised in the Egyptian Feminist Union (EFU), founded by Hudá Sha'rawi in 1923 – engaged in a (feminist and nationalist) battle against state-licensed prostitution. In May 1923, an EFU delegation comprised of Hudá Sha'rawi, Nabawiyyah Musà and Saiza Nabarawi attended the International Women Suffrage Alliance (IWSA) congress in Rome, where abolition of state-licensed prostitution and suppression of the international sex trade were high on the agenda.[58] The core contradiction in which Egyptian feminists found themselves caught was the struggle for social equality between men and women, all the while being clearly relegated to a marginal and subaltern position by an international feminist movement that was part and parcel of the colonial project. This explains why Egyptian feminists worked both toward the creation of a variegated abolitionist front within Egyptian civil society – for example, by networking with al-Azhar religious authorities, who were deemed important for the mobilisation of public opinion – and for a nationalist campaign to end the Capitulations. As Margot Badran explains, 'Egyptian feminists abhorred Capitulations, not only for "protecting" foreign prostitution but also as an odious infringement upon Egyptian sovereignty sustaining inequalities between citizens and Westerners'.[59] It was not possible, they argued, to combat double sexual standards and class inequalities if the Egyptian people were subjected to a discriminating corpus of law, allowing female exploitation and every kind of dubious business. Hudá Sha'rawi first denounced the role Capitulations played in regulated vice and international women's trafficking, in a 1924 IBS conference in Graz, Austria, where she asked Capitulary powers to abdicate their powers and allow local authorities to close down establishments run by foreign nationals. Egyptian feminists were isolated not only in the IBS conferences, though, but also in the International Alliance of Women (IAW) forum, where they were the only feminist delegation to come from a country with extraterritorial laws. During the IAW congress in Paris in 1926, Saiza Nabarawi asked to pass a resolution that would require Capitulary powers to give Egyptian authorities legal competence over their nationals, so as to facilitate prosecution of foreign traffickers and brothel owners. The resolution remained a dead letter. Egyptian feminists cooperated with the British Police Chief Russell Pasha, who furnished them with fresh data about thriving foreign sex work, and who was opposed to Capitulations from a strictly technocratic, public order point of view. He did not get so far as openly lobbying in favour of their repeal, though, as this would have meant a diminishing of British influence in the country. In 1929, during the International Alliance of Women for Suffrage and Equal Citizenship congress in Berlin, thanks to the vigorous pleading of Hudá Sha'rawi, Saiza Nabarawi and Mary Kahil, the assembly passed a resolution stating that Capitulary powers should pave the way for the Egyptian government to control morality and public health, thus implicitly acknowledging an interference with Capitulations. In 1930, Miss Higson from the British NVA (who, as we have seen, had a pronounced Butlerian outlook), toured the country to campaign for abolitionism. She met with government officials, doctors, social workers, feminists, etc., and came to the conclusion that

> the time has come when a definite step should be taken by the people of Egypt to convince the Government that they demand the abolition of the State regulation of vice, by the closing of all licensed houses and the removal of the registration and medical examination of prostitutes.[60]

She eventually made a number of recommendations to the International Bureau for the Suppression of Traffic in Women and Children central committee, including the drafting of a bill to abolish all licensed houses, register and perform sanitary inspections of prostitutes; the reform of the Criminal Code to include severe punishment of third parties of either sex who exploit the immorality of others; protection of minors (of both sexes); a general law protecting passers-by from aggressive soliciting;

and punishment of sodomy. Miss Higson also hoped for the organisation of a major educational programme, along three main lines:

> education in simple social hygiene and an equal moral standard for men and women, education in social responsibility and the need for effective free treatment of VD combined with lectures on the same, education in the need for remedial work, to raise funds for the work of the Refuges, etc.[61]

The response from Egyptian feminists was twofold: while Sha'rawi signed Higson's petition, Nabarawi took the opportunity to stress how, once again, the basic problem of Capitulations had not been addressed, thus making any effort to combat regulated prostitution in the country meaningless. It is possible to conclude that, in subordinating their feminist goals to nationalist ones, Egyptian feminists were a typical product of their times: before formulating any radical critique of unequal gender and class relations, they pressed for recognition as legitimate actors in the construction of an Egyptian sovereign bourgeois order. A turning point was constituted by the IWA congress of 1935 in Istanbul, on the topic of dialogue and cooperation between East and West, that is, between colonised and imperial countries. In acknowledgement of the fact that international feminism had so far been very much a Western discourse, international committees were ready to sign a declaration that, for the first time, clearly individuated in Capitulary legislation a limitation to national sovereignty and a permanent mark of inequality, calling for its outright abolition. Margot Badran explains, nonetheless, how such a position was once again the product of Western ethnocentrism: 'it was around the issue of a wife's nationality',[62] in fact, 'and not the issue of prostitution that after years of Egyptian persistence and IAW resistance, the international feminist body finally took a resolution against the Capitulations'.[63] In other words, the repeal of Capitulations rested on the acknowledgement of a typical bourgeois issue, as is that of nationality, and not on the protection of civic rights of subaltern working-class women engaged in prostitution. In 1937, the Capitulations were finally abolished with a 'transition period' of 12 years, until 14 October 1949. Egyptian feminists were now confident that the national government, free from foreign influence, would hasten to abolish prostitution. Their hopes were soon to be frustrated, though. Egyptian authorities temporised, and political and police authorities were unwilling to take active measures to combat prostitution. Egyptian feminists therefore became particularly prone to collaboration with pro-abolitionist British activists. When in the early 1940s the idea of organising an IBS congress in Egypt started to circulate, as a way to advance the cause of abolitionism in the country, Egyptian feminists were eager to give their support, as shown by the contacts taken up by Hudá Sha'rawi, Saiza Nabarawi and Muniah Sabet with Lady Nunburnholme of the British NVA during the IAW congress of 1939 in Copenhagen.[64] The proposal did not come forward as a result of the increasing disarray within the Egyptian IBS committee, and the deterioration of the general political situation due to the beginning of World War II. Even more so than colonialism and neo-colonialism, class and gendered prejudice, the resilience of sexist and patriarchal mentality, and sexual double standards proved to be the real cause for the persisting of licensed regulation. In 1949 brothels were eventually closed down by military decree, but state-regulated prostitution wasn't outlawed until 1953, as part of the comprehensive Nasserist reform to break with the liberal *ancien régime*.

Conclusion

This chapter has shed light on the ways in which a specific group of marginal social actors in early twentieth-century Cairo, mostly European prostitutes and destitute working-class women, were managed and contained by imperial social purity and feminist groups. Starting as a metropolitan cultural paranoia in the 1870s, the notion of 'white slavery' came to play an important role in the political economy of the Empire. European prostitutes plying their trade in the colony and, more generally, women not subjected to moral supervision, represented the fear of the possible erosion of the 'natural' coloniser-colonised divide and of racial degeneration. Metropolitan purity movements and feminists active in the colony became vital allies of the colonial administration in trying to reinforce imperial bourgeois categories of morality, decorum and domesticity, through the articulation of a whole discourse and practice of fallen women's social and ethic regeneration. Such an attempt at 'moralising' the Empire was not critical of the imperial power structure: on the contrary, both the puritan discourse and the more libertarian feminist one tried to revive and implement the 'civilising mission' that was at the core of the imperial enterprise. Local feminist activists on their part found themselves caught between the contradictions of internationalist feminism, on the one hand, and their capacity to advance a political critique of class and gender inequalities which were diluting social and economic justice in a gender-blind nationalist struggle, on the other.

CHAPTER 7

ABOLITIONISM ON THE POLITICAL AGENDA

The late Egyptian historian Yunan Labib Rizq remarked how, in the 40 years between the British occupation of 1882 – when sex work was legalised for the first time in Egyptian history – and 1922, when Britain recognised Egypt's *formal* but fictitious independence, prostitution never came under attack by proponents of the nationalist movement: 'prostitution tended to be viewed as one of those bitter facts of life that only occasionally surfaced in the context of discussions of the social ills that befell Egypt under the British occupation.'[1] However, after World War I, and increasingly during the period leading up to the 1919 Revolution and the seizure of national independence, realms of sexuality and morality were tackled by Egyptian nationalists as discursive areas to be conquered, in order to define archetypical notions of Egyptian community and family. Local nationalists struggling for Egyptian independence and sovereignty felt the urge to legitimise their project and define 'their' modern national identity vis-à-vis colonial influence by formulating gendered definitions of normative citizenship. The process of sex workers' social marginalisation, which had been at the core of regulationism, became central to a much wider debate on local identity and political sovereignty. Licensed prostitution was widely discussed in the local press and unanimously condemned by local actors, whose political sensibilities were in fact quite different. While secular, liberal nationalists and feminists rejected licensed prostitution on the basis of Western standards of civic progress or universalist discourses on human rights, religious leaders were concerned with the regeneration of correct Muslim practices as a tool of resistance to Westernisation and the degeneration of the believers' community.

The sexualisation of the Nation, that is, the process by which a gendered female character was assigned to the emerging idea of a national community, was evident in a number of different, discursive motifs: on one side the victimised female body of the prostitute – often a minor or a girl – was seen as the metaphor of the very subaltern status of the colonised nation, who was abused and transacted by or who sold herself to foreign powers. On the other side, wanton and rowdy – often foreign – sex workers incarnated the corruption of local morals by excessive Westernisation. Some renowned underworld figures such as former prostitutes and brothel owners, sisters Raya and Sakinah and Ibrahim al-Gharbi, a transvestite and notorious 'trader of virtues' in Cairo's Wass'ah, were made into national 'villains' by the reiteration of discreet heteronormative, discursive tropes in the local press. As examples of social and sexual 'abnormality', they constituted metaphors of social uneasiness as much as they were functional in defining normative canons of moral behaviours. This last chapter will elucidate on the role of gender and sex in the history of the emerging Egyptian nation by providing a close reading of some discursive tropes about gender and social danger in general, sex and prostitution in particular, as they appeared on the interwar Egyptian press. By mapping out the tropes of Egyptian public discourse on prostitution in nationalist press during the 1920s, I will expand our knowledge on how femininity was debated in a modernising country under colonial control, and how this crucially contributed to the definition of normative notions of virtuous gendered citizenship. While Shaykh Mahmud Abu al-'Uyun fulminated against the danger of public vice from the pages of *al-Ahram*, state authorities eventually put abolitionism on the political agenda. Abolitionism was surely part and parcel of the cosmopolitan discourse of moral purity and eugenics,[2] and as such it was accepted by Egyptian decision-makers and social activists as a benchmark of civic and cultural maturity; however, it was forged by creatively using local, cultural-specific materials and acquired a distinctly local, anti-colonialist twist in the Egyptian context. The shift from regulationism to abolitionism, I believe, illuminates some interesting implications for the study of the interaction between the metropolis and the colonies. The study of the trajectory from regulation to abolition in the Egyptian colonial-national context allows us to complicate traditional centre-periphery models, particularly in illustrating processes of cultural communication and the circulation of different types of disciplinary apparatuses within the Empire. Egyptian abolitionist discourse, gaining momentum from the 1920s onwards and eventually prevailing in the 1940s, in the context of the radicalisation of anti-British sentiments in the country, was vernacularised and inflected with local meanings in the process. In her study on the regulation of obscene publications in the Empire, Deana Heath observed how this regulatory project, although 'initially exported from the metropole to the colonies, it assumed new life in the process, becoming appropriated, distorted, and resisted in ways that not only served colonial interests but that were antithetical to, and undermined, the interests of the metropolis'.[3] Egyptian abolitionism furthermore constitutes a case study useful to the decentring of imperial histories. On one hand, subaltern actors resisted the introduction of the biopolitical, either evading or carving new spaces of agency into the interstices of domination and control, thus 'indigenising' and 'vernacularising' these normative systems based on difference and exclusion and inflected with racial meanings. Local disorder thus became instrumental to the imperial power as it stood to legitimise the European civilising mission. On the other hand, the emerging nationalist middle class championing the values of Egyptian modernism co-opted discourses of social hygiene as important elements in the definition of a vernacular, modernist identity. Britain came to be perceived not only as 'anti-modern', but as constraining the very same production of the modern Egyptian citizen. Examining the trajectory from regulationism to abolitionism, I argue, shows how governmentality was not a unitary project but became a contested terrain between colonisers, colonised and diverse subgroups within these categories, in order to affirm their visions of modern rule through the regulation of gendered and racialised bodies.

Nationalism and the Rise of an Imagined Egyptian Nation in the Press

The 1920s, characterised by the introduction of constitutionalism and pluralism in Egyptian political practices, are often deemed to signal 'the apogee of political consensus upon liberal nationalism before the emergence of Islamism and Arab Nationalism in the 1930s and the 1940s'.[4] In fact, far from establishing a shared ideological consensus on the emerging national political community, the aftermath of the 1919 Revolution saw intense debates and the ensuing inability to reach an agreement on a shared political identity among political forces. Class, gender, secularism, religion, democracy and authoritarianism were extensively debated across the political body, and from such contestations a number of competing discourses on 'Egyptian-ness' began to take form.

Nationalist Wafdists and more moderate Liberal Costitutionalists (*Hizb al-Ahrar al Dusturiyyin*, 1921) shared in fact a Westernising, evolutionary discourse on social change. Strongly identifying with modern Western culture, they were both concerned with progress and advancement. Despite their common modernist outlook, they clashed about strategic issues: according to the former group, complete independence and sovereignty were necessary prerequisites for modernisation, while the former thought Egypt's development could be obtained only with British assistance and cooperation. However, Wafdist and Liberal Constitutionalists adopted a similar stance on cultural questions such as the role of women in society: they both campaigned for the improvement of women's status in words, but were much milder in practice, careful as they were not to subvert the patriarchal foundations of society. Islam was brought into formal party politics by the *Ittihad* Party, a filo-monarchist religious group formed by al-Azhar *ulamas* and supported by the ruling dynasty. Outside the formal political environment, the emergence in 1928 of the *Ikhwan al Muslimun*, the Muslim Brotherhood, marked the advent of contemporary Islamist mass politics. Aiming at the re-Islamisation of Egyptian society from below and the restoration of the Islamic ethos of social justice within the Egyptian community, the *Ikhwan* initially concentrated on educational and charitable work, soon to become a chief anti-hegemonic and anti-colonial political force in the country.

In this context, the Egyptian press played a fundamental role in articulating the concept of a national imagined community, as so aptly described by Benedict Anderson.[5] Since the middle of the nineteenth century, Egypt saw the rise of new educational opportunities in state-funded schools, more occasions for travelling and direct cultural contact with the West, the strong contribution of Levantine publicists and the so-called *ruwwad* (or pioneers, as they are referred to in Arab cultural history); all these factors led to the emergence of a local educated intelligentsia, a new audience of readers interested in innovative ideas and concepts expressed through books, periodicals and newspapers, and in the sharing of a common national identity. The moment a public of receptive and educated Egyptian readers was established, towards the end of the nineteenth century, the private press became the first outlet for criticism of the country's social and political situation and for the articulation of an Egyptian identity through the characterisation of local socio-types in fiction and vignettes. The press thus became the public arena for debates about national identity, modernisation and tradition.

As Shaun T. Lopez rightly pointed out in his work on crime press coverage (*akhbar al-hawadith*) and the 1920 Raya and Sakinah case,[6] expansion and changes in the Egyptian press after 1918 resulted in the development of modern mass culture in Egypt. Although only literate groups, elites and *effendiyyah* (middle-class) Egyptians constituted the main reading public of the press, news coverage transformed local matters involving Egyptians from all classes, religions and genders into matters of public and national concern. Individual tales of immoral lives made public by this new mass medium thus became shared experiences among those who consumed the news circulated by the press. Thus commentators and politicians often referenced the lives of Raya, Sakinah and their victims as they constructed their versions of what Egyptian identity really was, and therefore played an important part in the formation of elite discourses about Egyptian identity and gender.[7] Moreover, for the first time characters, locales and situations belonging to the lived experience of the lower classes were incorporated into and played a vital role in the making of Egyptian collective imagination, by exemplifying the modern and civilised citizen's 'other'.

Gender and Danger in Cairo

Gender was situated at the centre of competing discourses about citizenship and national identity.[8] The 'woman's question' (*Qadiyyat al-Mar'ah*), that is, the debate about the status of women in society and the qualities they should possess to contribute to the construction of modern, independent Egypt, became prominent in public discourse. Religious and secular elites were divided over their conceptions of ideal femininity. Employing an evolutionary approach influenced by social Darwinism, secular nationalists considered cultural formations such as segregation and veiling symbols of Oriental backwardness, to be actively fought against in order to promote modernity and progress. Egyptian feminists accepted this formulation, while drawing on a universalist discourse of individual political rights to legitimise their specific struggle for women's emancipation, which bourgeois nationalists did not subscribe to; this revealed the patriarchal foundations and exclusionary practices at the core of modern liberalism. On the other side, Muslim activists saw traditional and religiously sanctioned, gendered practices as the cornerstone of a harmonious society, to be preserved in order to affirm Islamic and Oriental cultural authenticity in the face of Westernisation. Despite differences in the ways gendered roles were constructed, it is important to note how gender and gender-related biopolitical discourses about sex and the family constituted a formidable medium for expressing ideas about the rising Egyptian civic and political community. Correct social development was seen as based on hierarchical sex and gender relations: as Selma Botman wrote, 'liberalism's advocates successfully posited the ideological dichotomy between the private/personal and the public/political whereby a hierarchy of power assigned a subordinate place to women based on their natural role as child-bearers'.[9] The maintenance of carefully patrolled and hierarchically constructed, gendered spaces depended on notions of family honour and shame, which in turn were based on women's modesty and propriety. If the Egyptian nation came to be imagined as a family, Egyptian women, although politically marginalised, were to be the very repositories of national honour.[10]

In fact, an important dimension of the widely perceived social crisis in Egypt, during the 1920s, was expressed through the association of sex and gender with danger. According to coeval commentators, one of the main features of the moral crisis was the increased presence of women, especially working-class females, in public space. The dominant narrative of gendered peril was that, under the pressure of economic necessity, increasing numbers of women had entered the labour market, unencumbered from family supervision, free to wander around the city and unleash their sexual appetites out of greed or lust, and easy preys to evil procurers. Abolitionists blamed the Egyptian government not only for being incapable of taking steps towards the elimination of licensed prostitution, but also for failing to deploy effective policies in support of disadvantaged and economically vulnerable social categories such as working-class women: 'the Government should act as first point of reference for those women who are likely to fall [*suqut*, in the original], unemployed women, vagrants, and force them to find respectable occupations, whether their husbands were unable to support them', wrote a fervent abolitionist Azharite on the pages of the *al-Ahram* daily in 1923.[11]

In the press, flourishing prostitution in Cairo was described as the ultimate menace to the very survival of the Egyptian nation, a dense referent in opposition to which the idea of a homogeneous and virtuous Egyptian national community was constructed and diffused. It could well be argued that the idea of strict and pristine gender segregation, or the stigmatisation of sex workers, in Egyptian popular neighbourhood life was highly fictional and did not reflect everyday social practices on the ground,[12] but for the purpose of my analysis here, I deliberately decided to focus on the process by which the very reiteration of a number of discursive tropes on sex work and its dangers for the collective social body was transformed into an ontological truth. The pathologisation of prostitution was used as a strategy to enforce a disciplinary project over society.

'When Virtue Screams': The 'Fight against Prostitution'[13]

Press campaigns against licensed prostitution started to be waged as early as 1893, by the pen of 'Abdallah al-Nadim, the so-called 'orator of the 'Urabi revolution'. In accusing the West of exerting a bad influence over Egyptian society and corrupting Islamic morals, he was the first champion of Islamo-nationalism to campaign for the abolition of regulated vice. In his *Majallat-al-Ustadh*, al-Nadim often talked of the state of moral standards in the country, especially in a series of articles for the edification of girls entitled *Madrasat-al-Banat* (Girls' School) where a number of female characters expressed (in Egyptian vernacular) their concerns for the spreading of vice in society and the corruption of their husbands' morals.[14] The association between nationalism and abolitionism was thus inaugurated. The prominent nationalist leader Muhammad Farid (1868–1919)[15] too was a fervent abolitionist. In his memoirs, he wrote that the reason why vice had invaded the country had to do with its state of colonial subordination: foreign consuls, in his view, had become the 'guardians of immorality' in Egypt, thanks to the Capitulations.[16]

A number of positions were articulated by the press regarding the debate on regulationism. While publications such as *al-Siyyasah* or *Ruz-al-Yusuf* were decidedly in favour of regulationism, *al-Ahram*, the main Egyptian daily, constituted the vanguard of the abolitionist wave. The newspaper editor-in-chief Dawud Barakat, in fact, had been a convinced abolitionist since 1907, when he had translated Dr Burtuqalis Bey's epidemiologic study on venereal disease in Egypt. In November 1923, a press campaign against state-licensed prostitution was inaugurated on the pages of *al-Ahram* through the letter of a Shubrah female resident, Fawqiyyah Kamil.[17] In her letter, Kamil talked about an article she had read in the newspaper, regarding a New York businessman who had been fined 5,000 dollars for kissing a girl against her will. The reader asked how this could possibly happen: in Egypt, she remarked, the current state of affairs was such that no one, not even among the intellectuals (*qadat-al-afkar*), was raising their voice against the thriving traffic in sex and vice. Fawqiyyah Kamil called upon Fikri Abazah to invite their co-nationals to sobriety and moderation.[18] Long before nationalist liberal elites eventually put abolitionism on their agenda, Kamil's complaints only captured the interest of an al-Azhar *shaykh* in the first place, Mahmud Abu al-'Uyun (1882–1951).

Born in the Asyut province in 1882, from a distinguished sharifian family, he graduated from al-Azhar in 1908. Known for his heated anti-colonial sermons during the 1919 Revolution, Abu al-'Uyun was accused of being a member of the so-called 'Black Hand Society', a secret association founded with the purpose of threatening and killing Egyptians who would not take part in the General Strike. In May 1919, he was imprisoned in a German-Turkish prisoner camp in Rafah for three months. After being released, he resumed his activism against the British and was therefore imprisoned again. In February 1920, he was released for medical reasons. Back in Cairo, he had eye surgery and remained under arrest until November 1920, when he was made to sign a statement according to which he would refrain from playing any active role in nationalist propaganda. After the 1922 Treaty, he decided to abstain from party politics and devote himself to social reforms and moral purity campaigns. The first and most prominent of these was his crusade against state-licensed prostitution, soon followed by campaigns against alcohol consumption and undressing on Egyptian public beaches, when he was in charge of the al-Azhar institute in Alexandria, in 1938.[19] He subsequently moved back to Cairo where he was appointed as secretary at al-Azhar, the post he retained until he passed away in 1951.

Shaykh Mahmud Abu-al-'Uyun was the veritable torchbearer of abolitionism and social purity, who chose journalism as a medium to sensitise public opinion to the need for Egypt's moral purification in two main *al-Ahram* series: 'Slaughterhouses of virtues' of 1923, and 'Licensed prostitution' of 1926. This second series was published after the creation of a Special Commission of Inquiry on Licensed Prostitution and Traffic of Women and Children, set up by the Ministry of Interior in response to the League of Nations' anti-abolitionist pressures.

On 20 November 1923, Shaykh Mahmud Abu al-'Uyun published the first instalment of the series *Madhabih al-A'rad* ('Slaughterhouses of virtues'), entitled *'Ala Mar'ah min al-Hukumah wa Misma'* ('In the face and the ears of the Government'), where he painted a black picture of Egyptian morals:

> In Egypt the market of vice [*suq al fujur*] thrives under the eyes and the ears of the government [...] and virtues are sacrificed to greed and lust [*shahawat and atma'*] without restraint and control [*raqabah*]. Clandestine organisations of white slave traders organise themselves under the nose of the government.[20]

Shaykh Abu al-'Uyun blamed Egyptian political elites for their acquiescence and went so far as to repeatedly denounce the collusion between traffickers, brothel owners and the police.[21] Reproducing a deep-seated biological metaphor, he likened prostitution to a lethal disease, conducive to the Death of the Nation (*mawt al-ummah*), because of the corruption of morals (*fasad al-akhlaq*), dilapidation of wealth (*diya' al-amwal*) and national honour (*diya' al-sharf*), and the degeneration of the race because of the spread of venereal disease. The annihilation of the community was primarily imputed to the venereal peril, but in fact prostitution was considered to be antisocial not only because of public health considerations, but because of its impact on the institution in charge of social reproduction par excellence: marriage.

While secular nationalists saw prostitution as a waste of economic and reproductive capacities, the cultural question was central to the Islamists' view of sex work; prostitution as *zina'*, extramarital sex, was first and foremost *haram*, contrary to the Islamic law and the traditions of the Oriental Muslim community (*ummah sharqiyyah muslimah*). On 12 December 1923, in the eighth instalment of his 'Slaughterhouse of Virtues' entitled *'Fada'ih la hadd laha'*, 'Endless Shame', Abu al-'Uyun reported a letter sent to the newspaper by a reader under the pseudonym of Ghazal bi-Misr, *Egypt's Gazelle*, who lamented the dangers of prostitution by using a religiously connoted language:

> I know of many boys who don't think of getting married [...] to the effect that many girls end up without a husband. And I am sure it won't escape His Gracefulness' notice that this state of affairs is bad for both parties [*firqatayn*, i.e., boys and girls] and it is conducive to the spread of prostitution, vice among the sexes [*fasiq jins*] and the unprecedented incidence of venereal diseases.[22]

The reader asked how the Egyptian government, as a Muslim government, could tolerate prostitution, while the British themselves did not condone sex work in their own homeland. Furthermore, Ghazal bi-Misr urged the national community to face the situation in all its abject squalor and to stop behaving as those men who, while being infected with syphilis, tried to conceal it out of shame, ignorance and stupidity.

According to such a view, the weakening of social cohesion and the 'marriage crisis' were by-products of prostitution, state regulation and lack of control over public morality. While in the eyes of state officials regulation served as a means of controlling the trade and safeguarding public order and health, in the reader's opinion regulation did not achieve its objectives, as clandestine sex work flourished undisturbed and the spread of venereal diseases was far from being under control: on the contrary, 'every day we witness endless shameful acts taking place everywhere, even in coaches, cabs and boathouses berthed on the Nile'. The letter ended with a desperate cry: 'Egypt, poor Egypt, how can you bear these wounds, wounds in your soul, wounds in your virtue, in your wealth?'[23]

Themes of diffused vice, both overt and undercover, and contamination spreading like an epidemic across the social fabric were recurrent. A main concern was that of the potential contact between 'marginals' such as prostitutes, criminals and homosexuals, and 'respectable' citizens, families and young generations. In particular, commentators felt the urge to protect the latter from vice and debauchery, as the future of the Nation was considered to depend on their sound moral and physical constitution. On 28 November 1913, Abu al-'Uyun quoted in his column a letter from a certain 'shaykh haram', who pointed out the physical proximity between state-licensed vice in the Azbakiyyah area and religious schools' pupils.[24] Some days later, on 8 December, the topic was touched upon again with extreme alarmism in an article called 'Chastity screams!', where Shaykh Mahmud Abu al-'Uyun decried the fact that decent, honest people (al-ahrar, literally free people, as individual freedom is seen as the first prerogative of citizenship) had to mingle with those who traded in vice (tijarah al-a'rad).[25]

Although quite reluctantly, state officials eventually addressed the problem and took action: while the Minister of Communication stated that public health, wealth and young generations had to be effectively protected and safeguarded by the government as they were the foundations of the State's power, the Minister of Public Works declared that the insalubrious houses nearby the Patriarchate would soon be demolished,

> to make space for a wide thoroughfare where decent people and family can live, instead of those wretched creatures [hasharat, literally 'insects', referring to prostitutes and pimps]. At the same time, al-Khalig street will be widened by forty metres, in order to purify it from the filth it is notorious for, and to restore it to its original dignity.[26]

The Making of a 'National Villain': Ibrahim al Gharbi

In his work on the 1920s Alexandria murders, Shaun T. Lopez aptly described how media sensations such as that of the Rayya and Sakinah case contributed to the making of an imagined national, 'virtuous' community of Egyptians who subscribed to a certain moral code.[27] Religious piety and morality served as criteria for the determination of normative discourses on citizenship largely constructed by difference, that is, by the creation – together with moral standards – of stereotypes of blatant immorality, iconic embodiments of widespread social unrest. A group of criminals rose to the status of 'villains', as norms were established through emphasis being placed on their transgression. As shown by Lopez, the sisters Raya and Sakinah, ex-prostitutes and brothel owners who robbed and killed 17 women whose bodies were found buried under their houses in the al-Laban neighbourhood in Alexandria, exemplified the dangers of increased female mobility and disrespect for gendered roles. Daily reports from their trial attracted people attention considerably, while a vast number of vignettes in the illustrated press enabled illiterate Egyptians to follow the development of the case as well, which in fact resounded nationally and in an unprecedented way.[28] Raya and Sakinah were certainly the most famous, but not the only phenomena of this kind. The well-known Ibrahim al-Gharbi, for example, constituted another emblematic case, the protagonist of another media sensation known as 'Qadiyyat-al-Raqiq-al-Abyad', the 'White Slavery Case'.

Ibrahim al-Gharbi had long been known to the general public as the 'King of the Underworld': born in the Aswan area and son of a slave merchant, he came to Cairo in 1890, opening a brothel in Bulaq, in Shari' al-Mayyah. In 1896 he rented a brothel in the Wass'ah and a *baladi* coffee shop. In 1912, just before the crackdown on prostitution under the martial law of 1916, al-Gharbi managed 15 houses of ill-fame in the Azbakiyyah, which employed 150 women. In 1916, Ibrahim al-Gharbi was arrested together with other transvestites and confined to the Hilmiyyah camp. In order to be released he bribed the *Ma'amur* of Cairo police, the Greek George Filippidis; Mahmud Muhammad, *Musa'id hikimdar* of Cairo; Muhammad Shakib, *Ma'amur Shurtat 'Abdin* (Chief of the Abdeen police); and Ahmad Kamil, *Ma'amur Shurtat Masr al-Qadimah* (Chief of the old Cairo police). According to Alifah Bint 'Abdallah, a sex worker employed by Ibrahim al-Gharbi, he paid 300 Egyptian pounds to Filippidis, but the *hikimdar* of Cairo police did not agree on al-Gharbi's release and Filippidis was forced to give him the money back, although he retained 20 Egyptian pounds of interest.[29]

While the demonisation of non-conforming femininity and its perceived threat for the social order was essential in the construction of Raya and Sakinah's public image, in Ibrahim al-Gharbi's case it was his homosexuality and transvestism, together with his infamous career in vice and debauchery, that made him outrageous in the public eye.

Ibrahim al-Gharbi's appearance and attitude were described with remarkable uniformity in contemporary narratives and journalistic accounts, often in hyperbolic terms. The 'devil-man', as he was dubbed, and 'one of the most abominable sights of Egypt', could be found – according to a contemporary observer – seated in front of one of his many houses in the Wass'ah,

> dressed as a woman, painted and glazed as though he were a black statue. This fellow has a shining skin, large black eyes and even features. Across his forehead, running past his temples and hooked at the back of his head, was a large solid gold band studded with precious stones. His arms were naked to the shoulder but for the gold bracelets which adorned them. On one arm, I counted fourteen differently shaped bejewelled arm-clasps or bracelets. The other arm was covered with a gaudy network of gold spangles and beads, and around his neck he wore a collar of welded gold, gold, it was said, which had come as presents from his admirers in Abyssinia. On his fingers were several valuable rings, his ankles were protected by gold clasps, and his body was enveloped in a light gauzy material covered with gold and silver spangles which glittered in the light. Thus arrayed the fellow had the appearance of some pagan demi-god or devil.[30]

In 1923, Ibrahim al-Gharbi was involved in a famous judicial case which, starting on 4 December 1923, was covered by daily updates in Egyptian newspapers while also reverberating in the foreign press.[31] Known as the 'White Slavery Case', although no foreign prostitutes were actually involved, the trial reflected the considerable amount of social hysteria about the dangers young girls were exposed to because of lewd and ruthless 'traders of virtues'. On 16 September 1923, a 14-year-old girl by the name of Ihsan Hassan Mustafà went to Sayyidah Zaynab police station and denounced that, in the preceding month of February, she had been raped by a certain Muhammad Higazi. According to her testimony, she had been approached by a woman called Fatimah Muhammad al-Fayyumiyyah, nearby the mausoleum of Sayyidah Zaynab: the girl would accept Fatima's invitation home 'to meet her son', and would be kept against her will and drugged for three days, before being deflowered by the man, with the help of Fatimah

Muhammad al-Fayyumiyyah and her daughter Nafidah Farag, a prostitute in the Zayn 'Abdin area. Once deflowered, the young girl would then have been exploited as a prostitute in a brothel. Further investigations in the al-Hod al-Marsud lock hospital, in the Zaynhum area and in the Wass'ah disclosed a ring of prostitution behind which the investigators detected the presence of the notorious Ibrahim al-Gharbi. Press coverage emphasised al-Gharbi's sexuality as an evidence of his abnormal, devilish nature: he was forced to wear male garments in prison and detailed information was given about the examination he was subjected to by the *niyabah*, in order to verify his masculinity and see whether he was chargeable of sexual assault (which he was not as he resulted impotent, *ghayr kamil al-rajulah*). Asked about his cross-dressing, he defiantly stated that he dressed as a woman as a 'hobby'.

The 'White Slavery' (*Raqiq al-Abiad*) trial opened officially on 2 December 1923, and involved a number of Egyptian subjects. Muhammad Hijazi, a cabdriver, was accused of raping young Fatimah Hussayn Hassan, known as Ihsan Hassan Mustafâ, with the help of the prostitute Nafidah Farag and her mother Fatimah Muhammad al-Fayyumiyyah. Nafidah Farag was also accused of helping in the rape (*hatk 'ird*) of another young woman, named Zaynab 'Abd-al-Khaliq, by pinioning her on the ground so that they could commit immoral acts on her (*bi-an masakat bi-ha rijlayha ala al-Ard kay yatamakkanuna min al fasiq biha*). Fatimah al-Shabiniyyah, a brothel owner, and Hashim Ahmad were accused of forcing into prostitution another young girl, named Fahimah 'Uthman. Fatimah al-Shabiniyyah had arranged a marriage between Fahimah and her associate Hashim, who then forced his wife to prostitute herself in Fatimah's brothel. Finally, Zabidah Ahmad 'Awf, Zaynab 'Ali and Hanim Muhammad al-Jazzarah were all charged with exploiting young 'Aliah Bint Mursi. Ibrahim al-Gharbi was indicted and eventually condemned for corruption of morals and instigation to prostitution of seven minor girls.[32] As Judge Hughes, Chief Inspector of the Native Parquet, noted in a report that was sent to a British moral purity association in Cairo, only in the case of two girls had actual violence been used. According to Hughes, there was enough evidence to claim that most of the girls involved in the case had been volunteers, albeit minors, to the effect that the case could not be related to the international traffic in women and children known as the 'White Slave Trade':[33] this term identified the abduction and exploitation of foreign women and girls against their will. Not only did the case concern local girls, but it was proven that they mostly took up sex trade voluntarily and were not coerced.

Bringing in Abolitionism

After Egypt's independence, nationalist elites took possession of marriage and 'nationalised' it, formulating normative definitions of correct matrimonial conduct and family models, in order to create 'adult, permanent, preferably monogamous families, that, in turn, would serve as the foundation' for a modern nation free of social illness'.[34] As Hanan Kholoussy rightly pointed out, this was not unique to post-independence times, as 'marriage figured at the centre of the processes through which the modern, nationalist experience was learned and practiced in modern Egypt' even before independence.[35] Nonetheless, the articulation of such a pervasive and vibrant debate on the 'marriage crisis', an expression which served to indicate the perceived spread of bachelorhood and increase in the number of marriages with female minors,[36] a phenomenon which many observers deemed conducive to the collapse of social order in Egyptian press before 1919, was in many ways unprecedented.

Since the 1890s, the women's press had depicted men as 'fleeing from marriage', while in 1913 a 'letter to the Editor' – penned by Muhammad al-Bardisi – appeared in *al-Ahram* under the title 'Young Men and their Aversion to Marriage'.[37] In this letter, al-Bardisi expressed his concern for the dreadful state of the matrimonial institution, 'the fundamental cornerstone in the development of a civilization'. In his eyes not only economic stagnation was to blame for this,[38] but also greedy parents requesting exorbitant dowries and uncultivated, uneducated women who were incapable of exciting enduring love and affection from men. A more radically nationalist view was articulated by another reader, Ibrahim Ahmad Fathi, who saw the marriage crisis as strictly linked with foreign economic power and competition, although Egyptian men were certainly to blame for their lack of initiative:

> If Egyptians applied themselves seriously and intensively, they could establish their presence in commerce and accumulate vast wealth. The young men of today spend their time in coffee shops

and in places of entertainment [. . .] having squandered whatever money they had with them, whereas if they economized, they could have saved great sums from the money they spent on coffee, water-pipes, drink, and games.[39]

And we could, of course, add to this, prostitution.

Egyptian licensed prostitution, exclusively targeting native women, came to be seen as increasingly intolerable for its racist connotations and, of course, its blatant incompatibility with Islamic laws. In April 1926, the Law Department (*qism al lawa'ih*) published a memorandum containing the views of local authorities on licensed prostitution.[40] It reported that no justification was to be found for the preservation of such legislation as countless studies had demonstrated that, due to the lack of adequate sanitary structures and juridical barriers, legalisation of sex work had in the past not succeeded to curb venereal diseases. The section recommended a repeal instead of a modification of the existing law on prostitutes: 'the Egyptian government should follow in the steps of those Nations who led the struggle against licensed prostitution and in defence of public health.'[41] In 1932, a mixed Anglo-Egyptian commission was formed with the precise task of investigating all the circumstances relevant to licensed prostitution in the country, and its impact on public health and security, in order to establish once and for all whether the system was desirable or not. The commission worked for three years and the final report came out in 1935.[42] In the text, a very precise definition of abolitionism can be found. Abolitionists agreed on the mischief caused by prostitution; the impossibility of extirpating it; the difficulty of repressing it; and the unwisdom of allowing it to flourish rampantly. They insisted, however, that regulation fails to achieve its purpose; worse still, the moment prostitution is accepted, provided it submits to certain rules, the State is placed in the position of authorising, legalising or privileging the practice of vice.[43] The correct stance that the State should adopt, hence, was considered to be abolitionism, that is, not the abolition of transactional sex in itself, something impossible to achieve if not through moral reform, but abolition of any legislation condoning the existence of brothels and the trade plied by their inmates.

Next, the report lists a number of domestic and international factors that caused the failure of regulationism in Egypt, and led to the formation of a vocal abolitionist front: the scarcity of financial resources to ameliorate the system of sanitary checks and prophylactic measures; the peculiarities of the Egyptian legal system; the inadequateness of sanctions against clandestine brothels; and the existence of a dual, indigenous and foreign, legislation. In the report, the undesirability of regulation in Egypt is studied and analysed under three main headings: public health, public order and human traffic. In doing so it explicitly – and for the first time – refers to the emerging discourse of humanitarianism. Sanitary checks were found absolutely unsatisfactory. The main goal to be attained in this case was to make medical treatment of syphilis widespread. To this effect, it was stated, venereal clinics had to be free and confidential. Compulsory medical inspection of prostitutes, an essential part of the regulationist system, should therefore be abandoned. On the public security side, it was stated that while increased severity of punishment should be enforced for third parties exploiting prostitutes, and entry of traffickers and sex workers in the country should be prevented at any cost, mere repression of prostitution was not conducive to any result, if not that of increased soliciting in the street and under the public eye:

> The ideal policy therefore would appear to be gradual and discreet suppression of prostitution, without taking such drastic action in the suppression of 'clandestine' houses, as would necessarily drive immorality into other channels, which might prove to be in some respect more dangerous to society, especially in its home life.[44]

As long as the traffic in women and children was allowed, the existence of regulated brothels with their steady demand for manpower was seen as the natural cause of the trade in human beings. Abolition was therefore advisable for the eradication of the traffic by targeting the mechanism of supply and demand. A draft law was proposed; it stipulated the arrest and detention of all third parties involved in debauchery, either in brothels or clandestine houses, for no more than 15 years, or for a fine of 500 Egyptian pounds. Those who aided prostitution by knowingly renting out rooms or flats used for debauchery, and those who earned their leaving by prostituting themselves, were liable to detention for up to two years and a fine up to 50 Egyptian pounds. On 26 March 1938 the Ministry of Health issued a decree forbidding the licensing of new prostitutes and the opening of new brothels. One year later, a new commission of enquiry was appointed under the auspices of the Ministry of Health, to reassert the conclusion reached by the previous one. The topic of the fate of sex workers was also tackled by the aforementioned commission: four refuges for 'fallen women' were opened in Cairo, Alexandria, Tanta and Asiut, where they would be trained in marketable skills such as cooking and sewing. Regulationism was progressively restricted, without the implementation of any significant policy aimed at preparing the ground for the correct application of abolitionism. By incorporating the recommendations of a series of international conventions against human trafficking under the aegis of the International Bureau for the Suppression of Traffic of Women and Children (1904, 1910, 1921 and 1933), Egyptian abolitionism became grounded, for the first time, in the international human rights agenda, a move that clearly showed Egypt's will to become fully integrated within the international community. This approach centred on the decriminalisation of sex workers, while putting the onus on those who exploit the prostitution of other persons, both female and male, even with their consensus. As the Egyptian Penal Code was still based on the French Code of 1810, a new committee gathered in 1937 to revise it in light of the principles contained in the international anti-human racket Egypt had recently signed.

While Egyptian legal experts tried to find a way to reconcile local and international law, regulationism was brought back for very pragmatic reasons during World War II. A rampant increase in VD rates among troops implied a wartime expansion of commercial sex. Despite the emphasis military authorities placed on continence, they thought better to establish seven VD centres, specialised in the treatment of venereal patients. According to military sources, in 1941–2, of the 127,000 Allied troops stationed in Cairo, 954 were hospitalised in a venereal ward.[45] Military medical officials established an interesting link between the unprecedented spread of venereal disease in Cairo and the arrival of the 7th Armoured Division from Cyrenaica. Despite the predominance of abolitionism in public discourse, regulationism was reintroduced during the War in order to cope with increased demand by 'sex-starved' troopers: some brothels were officially declared 'in bounds' and amenable to soldiers.[46] While most of the Birkah remained formally off-limits to foreign troops, a strong demand for sexual services was quickly met by generous supply, as many Cairene women turned to sex work and entertainment to cope with economic anxieties: the cost of living, since the beginning of World War II, had risen by 45 per cent. While the British Army in Cairo was spending about 4.5 million pounds a month, prices of basic foodstuff such as beans, oil and flour, had been pushed up by foreign presence, with an increase of 94 per cent since 1939.[47] Thus during the war female rural migrants and domestic servants became cabaret artistes and bargirls. A contemporary observer, Pennethorne Hughes, accurately described how these girls, 15,000 according to the figures he reported,

> sat at the bars, or at tables with the customers, having drinks and cigarettes bought for them at specially high prices and, in most cases, reporting back at intervals to the proprietor or their own particular protector, one of the thick-necked, scar-faced full-lipped pimps who scowled from seats at the back. How far the money girls made was supposed to be, and was, augmented by prostitution no doubt varied.[48]

He referred to them as a veritable 'sociological problem', since in his view bargirls were likely to be doomed to a slow descent in permanent prostitution, eventually becoming social outcasts.[49] In the provinces outside Cairo, though, abolitionist policies were applied also during World War II: the military decree 384 of 1943, in fact, gave municipalities and provinces the right to close down brothels under their jurisdiction.

Paternalist Humanitarianism and the Repeal of Licensed Prostitution

At a time of social and political unrest, marked by the ascendancy of the Muslim Brotherhood and a rampant dissent from Western influence and imperial presence on Egyptian soil, hopes of sound political development, social justice and full self-determination – the same hopes that had inspired the 1919 Revolution – were fading. Several aspects of social unrest swept Egypt in the late 1940s: the Wafd's inability to offer a credible alternative to Egyptian political fragmentation; the increasing frustration of educated young generations for whom business and governmental job opportunities dramatically contracted compared to preceding *effendiyyah* generations; prolonged economic challenges brought about by the Great Depression, followed by World War II; the lack of political credibility of King Faruq; and the poor performance in the First Arab War against Israel. Images of domesticity, marriage, gender and relation between sexes were used as a microcosm expressing the state of the Nation in its various circumstances:[50] just as in 1919 cartoons from the urban, middle-class press represented the National Home, 'Bayt al-Ummah', as 'a site of promise, in which monogamous husbands and their educated (house)wives presaged the nation's potential', the 1940s press was dominated by images of houses as sites of 'treachery and deceit, where men were suckers and women lost their virtues'.[51] Houses were in disarray and men were victimised by wanton and greedy, dangerous femininities. As Pollard has demonstrated, cartoons were populated by lousy wives, fiancées and prostitutes (*ghaniyyat*, sing. *ghaniyah*). The main message these cartoons wanted to deliver was that men had been 'feminised' by women who placed way too much importance on material consumption, and thus the men escaped from monogamous marriages. Paid sex with prostitutes could not make up for the loss of harmony within the conjugal relationship, as it would fail to produce a sound, healthy and legitimate new generation.[52] As a last expedient to stop social derangement, abolitionism was eventually implemented in 1949, when Ibrahim 'Abd-al-Hadi Basha, Prime Minister and Commander-in-Chief, promulgated the special military decree 76 of 1949. It called for the closure of all brothels where more than one woman worked as a prostitute, within two months from the decree's issuance (Art. 1). As it becomes evident from this Article, prostitution per se constituted no criminal offence, but third-party exploitation came to be prosecuted by law, unlike what happened under regulationism. All those found to manage houses of ill-fame or living on the proceeds of female prostitution became liable, after two months, to arrest and detention for one to three years (two to four years if the *souteneur* was a relative of the exploited woman). If a woman suffering from VDs was found to practise prostitution in a house of ill-fame, she incurred arrest and detention for three to five years and a fine of 100 Egyptian pounds (Art. 5). In 1951, a comprehensive law still in force today, Law 68 of 1951 against debauchery, was passed. In the spirit of international human rights legislation, it called for the punishment of all those involved in the procurement of other people for prostitution, management of brothels or any type of support for the exploitation of other people for prostitution. While the principle of non-exploitation was strongly reaffirmed, the text unambiguously lapsed back to the die-hard criminalisation of sex workers: the legislator, in fact, found any person – male or female – who engaged in paid sex liable to imprisonment for at least three months, and to a fine of 250–300 Egyptian pounds. Law 68 of 1951 on Combatting Prostitution, moreover, defined prostitution as 'the practice of vice with others with no distinction'. While the transactional or monetary nature of sex work was not recognised, consensual sexual activity outside marriage was equated with prostitution. Sex workers were subjected to the usual type of discrimination, but such a heightened emphasis on the regulation of sex, and on its lawful practice only within the framework of a religiously sanctioned conjugal contract, accounts for the central importance of sexuality in the state's disciplinary project: as Scott Long aptly observed, 'lawmakers may have wished to make it easier for vice squad officers to arrest prostitutes even without witnessing money being exchanged. However the desire to make a sweeping moral statement was also clearly evident'.[53]

Conclusion

In many ways, the final repeal of regulated prostitution in Cairo and elsewhere in the country, at the end of the 1940s, was not due to public health and moral concerns, although these featured as fundamental themes of the abolitionist campaign and in public discourse from the 1920s onwards. It was mostly a political move, in response to the decisive turn to radicalisation of Egyptian politics preceding the collapse of the *ancien régime* and the eventual success of the 1952 July Revolution. The Egyptian State ultimately banned prostitution partly in the attempt to appease a burgeoning nationalist, religiously conservative wave following the disgraceful defeat in the First Arab-Israeli War, and after the assassination of Prime Minister al-Nuqrashi in 1948 by affiliates of the Muslim Brethren. At the end of the 1940s, the Egyptian government tried to stem the tide of anti-imperialist demonstrations by eventually suppressing a business, prostitution, which was considered to be a blatant feature of colonial oppression, both because of the imperial troops' patronage of brothels and the privileged legal status of European sex workers.[54] Law 68 of 1951 was subsequently amended with minor changes and changed, during the Revolutionary Period, into Law 10 of 1961 on Combatting Prostitution, when it was extended to Syria, recently united with Egypt in the United Arab Republic, to fit within the programme of postcolonial moral regeneration as championed by the Nasserist regime.

CONCLUSION

In this book I have tried to tell a story of global modernity as far as it endeavoured to show how the 'power to colonize',[1] of which the regulation of sex work constituted an important facet, travelled from the metropolis to the colony and, more importantly, how it was locally inflected and manipulated. The specific Egyptian trajectory from prostitution regulation to abolitionism is explored here as one of the multiple dimensions of the colonial encounter, the process by which the experience of Europe-driven capitalist modernity, with its associated microphysics of power, increasingly extended to non-metropolitan spaces through the acceleration of imperialist expansion in the long nineteenth century. I have tried to offer a rich and detailed treatment of the history of sex work regulation in colonial Cairo, my main objective being that of deepening the knowledge of a space of 'marginal' agency, namely that of prostitutes' agency, whose constitutive role in the deployment of a new type of modernist political rationality in Egypt has long been overlooked. Postmodern historiographic trends influenced by the so-called 'cultural turn' have brought about a dramatic reconsideration of the concept of 'social marginality', by advancing a more subtle, dynamic and productive understanding than the one conventionally accepted by orthodox 'history from below'. Not only has marginality been understood as a positional, shifting construct, but the normalisation of marginal subjectivities has been acknowledged as a constitutive element in the making and remaking of hegemonic power structures through disciplinary projects of various types. This work subscribes to the view, dominant in socio-historical studies on sex work since the 1980s, that prostitution is far from being a salacious topic or a minor area of academic enquiry. On the contrary, I have argued that the study of the construction of prostitutes' social *persona*, and their management through regulatory or repressive practices, have held important implications for the conceptualisation of both the colonial and the nationalist political order. More specifically, this work has attempted to demonstrate the integral link between the management of sex workers by colonial officials and local elites, and the making of Egypt as a colonial and, subsequently, independent State. The 'invention' of prostitutes as a specific sociological category of women identified with their peculiar type of sexuality, that is, promiscuous sex in exchange for money, can thus be understood as a distinct disciplinary project among the various ones that Michel Foucalt has studied in relation to the emerging notions and techniques of modern governmentality. In this regard, I have extended Foucaulds' theory of governmentality beyond its Eurocentric blind spot. This study is based on the assumption that modern governmentality practices were not simply transplanted into the colony. Colonies were not just sites of coercion and exploitation, but veritable 'laboratories of modernity' where the bourgeois foundations of colonial regimes appear simultaneously strong and contested, and the self-celebratory rhetoric of European civilisational efforts less unassailable than often maintained. The construction of race and sex as discourses of societal regulation expressed their productive power to the fullest in the colonies. Racial, gendered and sexual hierarchies were an integral part of the colonial and metropolitan order of thought, not because of their ontological fixity, but because they continuously needed to be remade and reinforced, embodied and practised. Nowhere more than in the colony, the realm of 'difference', this occurred in everyday social practices. As we have seen, in Cairo race, class and gender interacted in complex ways in the definition of sex workers' subjectivities. Both colonial and local middle-class reformers saw working-class female sexualities as something to be controlled, regulated and eventually reformed into submissive and subordinated domesticity.

Race was an important facet of the discourse on prostitution. While British authorities were reluctant to approach the problem of European, migrant sex work on Egyptian soil in order to maintain the fiction of racial and civilisational superiority on which the colonial enterprise was based, race played an important role in the way both local sex workers and foreign prostitutes were represented by colonial authorities and Egyptian nationalists, respectively. Once again, prostitutes were not 'marginal' to the functioning of the colonial State and expanding local state power, as they constituted a dense discursive referent in the articulation both of imperial identity and of an autonomous and virtuous, Egyptian national community. In fact, what is at stake is a dramatic reappraisal of received understandings of cultural genealogies, which see the colony primarily as the passive receiver of universalist discourses proceeding from the metropolis to the periphery.

While pre-modern sex work was a highly informal sector, conspicuous for the very limited extent to which patchy labelling or supervision practices were applied to sex workers by the central government, prostitution in colonial times fell under the rational scrutiny of British and Egyptian authorities. Thus, after the British occupation of Egypt in 1882, sex work was dramatically restructured. In this regard, my reconstruction of the sex market in fin-de-siècle Cairo mostly focussed on structural factors: urbanisation, proletarianisation and pauperisation; gendered segregation in the 'regular' job market; and migration (domestic and international), which in the context of a financially booming, cosmopolitan and rapidly modernising urban space shaped modern Cairene prostitution, both as an actual occupation and as a metaphor expressing the many ambiguities of urban change. Next, I devoted my attention to the actual organisation of the trade. In order to deconstruct the dominant, essentialised representation of prostitutes, chiefly the mantra of victimisation versus criminality, I looked at prostitution as a form of labour, the most available form of labour to unskilled female workers. I have shown how sex work in Cairo was performed by women coming from different backgrounds, with different working arrangements, ranging from prostitution in state-licensed brothels through clandestine houses to disguised sex work in bars and night clubs, and for different reasons, whether this be their or their family's survival, the lure of easy earnings or the desire for greater purchasing power. Earning a living was certainly difficult for all sorts of working-class women in colonial Cairo: prostitution was a choice among the few choices that were available to unskilled female labourers and migrants, and one which, in some cases, paid better than other service activities. Also, in the case of foreign girls being trafficked into the country, coercion was not in any way the norm, in contrast to what is maintained by much contemporary, cautionary literature. Prostitution could thus be a free choice, but this does not mean that sex workers were not exploited by their *madames* and pimps. At the same time, a number of micro-histories I have presented here stand as a demonstration of the fact that in spite of their heavily subordinated position, women could make independent, if limited, choices: for instance, by switching from registration to underground work, as the majority of sex workers in Cairo actually did, or by using the judicial system to sue their lover pimps in order to administer autonomously the money they earned through their work. In other words, it is possible to write a story which does not speak only of women's victimisation or 'fallenness', one which shifts the focus of analysis to the contours of a form of prostitutes' agency. At the same time, this type of agency was still located within male-dominated power structures; I believe it would therefore be a gross exageration to advance a sort of empowering reading of sex work in this case. What we can, however, trace is the outline of agency within constraints.

Regulationism amounted to a failed policy which did not bring about any of the expected results. This situation was exacerbated by the events of World War I and the impact of warfare on Cairenes' lives. The presence of thousands of imperial soldiers garrisoned in town caused an upsurge in the demand for sexual services. Wartime public disorders and cultural crises were fundamental in reorienting the ideas of local authorities' about licensed prostitution, and bringing into being abolitionist policies with a clear local nationalist and anti-colonial twist. In the abolitionist discourse, which prevailed from the 1920s until the final repeal of licensed prostitution in 1949, sex work was no longer to be compartmentalised or marginalised but simply erased from society. Sex workers became targets for programmes of regeneration and social rehabilitation, which aimed at reintegrating them into the social order. The shift from regulationism to abolitionism in Egypt can be understood as the reconfiguration of a metropolitan discourse that Egyptian nationalists appropriated in order to legitimise their own nationalist project. Marginalisation of sex workers, as of other subaltern subjectivities, was part and parcel of the process of Egyptian modernisation. Indigenous abolitionism certainly reproduced all the tropes of the metropolitan abolitionist discourse. It was based on the positivist belief in the possibility of engineering a fit nation of Egyptian citizens by combatting venereal disease. Yet, Egyptian abolitionism was also a reconfiguration of the metropolitan discourse from which it derived and constituted a response to Western cultural and political domination. Prostitution came to be seen as intolerable, not only because it conflicted with modern understanding of civilisation and progress, but also because it stood against locally specific understandings of morality as rooted in Islam. The reason why sex work was so pervasive in Cairo was not because of the inherent bestiality and irrationality of Oriental people, as the colonisers sustained; in nationalist discourse it was seen, rather, as a blatant instance of the corrupting influence of the immoral West on Oriental and Islamic morals. Indigenous social reformers thus surely accepted and internalised the ideological premises on which abolitionism was based, but they rearticulated and added a distinct anti-colonial tone. The extent of corruption of local morals was an instance of the pernicious influence of the West and its threat to local cultural authenticity: the preservation, or better, the restoration of correct, Oriental and Islamic, practices and values was an integral part of abolitionism, and added a culturalist and religious nuance to which even the secular-oriented and middle-class *effendiyyah* subscribed to, influenced as these were by the ideas of Islamic modernism. Local nationalists based their modernist project on a belief in the existence of a common bond between the Egyptian people and their educability into a cohesive national community, free from colonial tutelage or interference. Egyptian abolitionism thus constituted a specific type of modernist project whereby the struggle against the social dangers of commercial sex and the purification of Egyptian society from vice was considered a precondition for obtaining political autonomy. As I have shown in this work, the transition from regulationism to abolitionism, a theme which became increasingly conspicuous in public discourse with the coming of age of Egyptian nationalism after the 1919 Revolution and the Independence of 1922, well exemplifies the way in which gender and class were used to mould local concepts of political community and citizenship, evoking the need to rule over dissident and antisocial, embodied 'otherness'. The process by which metropolitan biopolitics were vernacularised is not unique to Egypt, but it was certainly context-specific, and the 'thickness' of the historical narrative I have presented in this book is instrumental in re-writing the history of sex work management into the history of the Egyptian Nation in all its complexity.

GLOSSARY

'ahirah	prostitute
'alimah, 'awalim (pl.)	'learned woman', a female trained in poetry and singing, performing for an all-female audience
'awamah	houseboat moored along the Nile
badrona	brothel owner, from the Italian 'padrona' meaning 'mistress'
Bimbashi	rank of Major in the Egyptian army
Capitulations	commercial treaties originally established in the sixteenth century and granting nationals of Western countries on Ottoman soil favourable tariffs and extraterritorial judicial rights
Caracol	police station
fath	practice of sitting and drinking with customers
fatihah, fatihat (pl.)	a girl perfoming fath in a club or a bar
garsunah, garsunat (pl.)	waitress
ghaziyyah, ghawazi (pl.)	dancers from the lower classes performing at folk festivals
harim	in a traditional Arab house, this is the part reserved to women
hikimdar	Ottoman title, Governor-General
karakhanah	brothel

kavass	Ottoman title for an armed police officer, also used in terms of a courier
Ma'amur	chief
maqturah, maqturat (pl.)	licensed prostitute resident in a brothel
Miralai	Turkish title, a colonel
Parquet	native judicial court
qism	police section
salah, salat (pl.)	ballroom, from the Italian 'sala da ballo'
salamlik	men's apartment and greeting area in a traditional Arab house
shaykh al-harah	among the most distinguished residents in the neighbourhood, acts as an overseer
souteneur	French for pimp

NOTES

Introduction   The Making of Modern Prostitution in Egypt

1. Here I am using the second English translation, Vivant Denon, *Travels in Upper and Lower Egypt in Company with Several divisions of the French Army, during the Campaign of General Bonaparte in that Country and published under his Immediate Patronage by Vivant Denon. Embellished with Numerous Engravings, translated by Arthur Aikin in 3 vols*, Vol. I (London: Longman and Rees, 1803).
2. Ibid., p. 223.
3. For an analysis of the interplay between power, colonialism, gender and representation see Malek Alloula, *The Colonial Harem*, translated by Myrna Goldzich and Wlad Goldzych, with an introduction by Barbara Harlow (Minneapolis: University of Minnesota Press, 1987).
4. Denon, *Travels in Upper and Lower Egypt*, p. 223.
5. For a definition of transactional sex and the vital role of gifts, both in cash or in nature, in driving everyday sexual relations in a context characterised by gendered economic inequality, see Mark Hunter, 'The materiality of eveyday sex: Thinking beyond "Prostitution"', *African Studies* 61/1 (2002), pp. 99–120. My thanks to Professor Sharad Chari for this reading suggestion.
6. Cited in Louis Awad, *The Literature of Ideas in Egypt* (Atlanta, GA: Scholar Press, 1986), pp. 22–3. Shayhk al-Jabartis' chronicles of the first seven month of the French Occupation from June to December 1798 have been edited and translated into English by Shmuel Moreh in *Napoleon in Egypt. Al-Jabarti's chronicle of the French Occupation, 1798* (Princeton, NJ: Markus Wiener Publishers, 2003).
7. *A Non-Military Journal or Observations Made in Egypt, by an Officer upon the Staff of the British Army* (London: T. Cadell and W. Davies, 1803). James Aldridge in *Cairo* (London: McMillan, 1969) identifies Carlos Bey with Major General Sirc Charles Holloway (1749–1827).
8. Awad, *Literature of Ideas*, p. 24.

9. *A Non-Military Journal*, p. 33.

10. Awad, *Literature of Ideas*, p. 24.

11. Edward William Lane, *An Account of the Manners and Customs of the Modern Egyptians, written in Egypt during the Years 1833, 34 and 35*, Vol I (London: Charles Knights & Co., 1836), p. 99; p. 377; Denon, *Travels in Upper and Lower Egypt*, pp. 77–8; *A Non-Military Journal*, p. 98. About the *ghawazi* see also John Lewis Burckhardt, *Arabic Proverbs: Or the Manners and Customs of the Modern Egyptians Illustrated from Their Proverbial Sayings Current at Cairo* (London: Curzon Press, 1984), pp. 173–9; Bayle St John, *Village Life in Egypt*, Vol. I (New York: Arno Press, 1973), pp. 23–8. Learned and artistically skilled female performers entertaining women's audiences in wealthy *harims* were called *'awalim*. In time the term *'almah* lost its specificity and was used for performes of the lower class too. See Lane, *An Account*, Vol. II, pp. 61–2; Gustave Flaubert, *Flaubert in Egypt, a Sensibility on Tour* (London: Bodley Head 1992), p. 110; pp. 113–20; Auriant (pseudo), *Koutchouk-Hanem, l'almée de Flaubert* (Paris: Mercure de France, 1949), pp. 10–38. For a thorough, albeit quite pedantic, genealogy of the term *'almah* see John Rodembeck, 'Awalim, or the persistence of error', in J. Edwards (ed.), *Historians in Cairo, Essays in Honour of John Scallon* (Cairo: American University in Cairo Press, 2002).

12. Judith Tucker, *Women in Nineteenth Century Egypt* (Cambridge: Cambridge University Press, 1995), pp. 77–104; pp. 150–6. See also Khaled Fahmy, 'Prostitution in Egypt in the Nineteenth Century', in E. Rogan (ed.), *Outside In: On the Margins of the Modern Middle East* (London: I.B.Tauris, 2002), pp. 77–104.

13. Flaubert, *Flaubert in Egypt*, p. 39. See also Auriant (pseudo), *Koutchouk-Hanem*, pp. 10–38.

14. Flaubert, *Flaubert in Egypt*, pp. 113–20.

15. Naguib Mahfuz, *The Cairo Trilogy*, translated by William Maynard Hutchins et al. (London, New York and Toronto: Everyman's Library, 1990), p. 912.

16. E. Rogan (ed.), *Outside In: On the Margins of the Modern Middle East* (London: I.B.Tauris, 2002), p. 2.

17. This work is clearly influenced by Foucauldian scholarship insofar as it explores the theme of the construction of prostitutes' social marginality, as part of a mode of domination based on the production and disciplinarisation of various types of normative and heteronormative subjectivities. Classic points of reference are *Madness and Civilization* (1967), *The Birth of the Clinic* (1973), *Discipline and Punish: The Birth of the Prison* (1977) and *The Will to Knowledge – The History of Sexuality* (1979).

18. Michel Foucault, *Aesthetics, Method, and Epistemology*. Edited by J. Faubion (Harmondsworth: Penguin Books, 2000), p. 336.

19. Michel Foucault, *History of Sexuality*, Vol. I (New York: Vintage Books, 1980), p. 4.

20. Ibid., pp. 140–1, 143–4, 229; Michel Foucault, *The Birth of Biopolitics: Lectures at the Collège de France 1978–1979*. Edited by M. Sennelert (Basingstoke:

Palgrave Macmillan, 2008). For a thorough conceptualisation of 'power to colonize' see also Timothy Mitchell, *Colonizing Egypt* (Berkeley: University of California Press, 2002), p. IX.

21. Timothy J. Gilfoyle, 'Prostitutes in history: From parables of pornography to metaphors of modernity', *The American Historical Review* 104/1 (1999), pp. 117–41.

22. Judith R. Walkowitz, *Prostitution and Victorian Society: Women, Class and the State* (Cambridge: Cambridge University Press, 1982) and *City of Dreadful Delights: Narratives of Sexual Danger in Late Victorian London* (Chicago: Chicago University Press, 1992); Alain Corbain, *Women for Hire: Prostitution and Sexuality in France after 1850* (Cambridge: Cambridge University Press, 1990); Jill Harsin, *Policing Prostitution in 19th Century Paris* (Princeton, NJ: Princeton University Press, 1985); Linda Mahood, *The Magdalenes, Prostitution in the Nineteenth Century* (London: Routledge, 1900); Mary Gibson, *Prostitution and the State in Italy, 1860–1915* (Columbus: Ohio State University, 1999); Laurie Bernstein, *Sonia's Daughters: Prostitutes and their Regulation in Imperial Russia* (Berkeley: University of California Press, 1991); Sumanta Banerjee, *Dangerous Outcasts: Prostitutes in Nineteenth Century Bengal* (New York: Monthly Review Press, 1998); Donna J. Guy, *Sex and Danger in Buenos Aires: Prostitution, Family and Nation in Argentina* (Lincoln and London: University of Nebraska Press, 1990); 'Imad Hilal, *al-Baghaya fi Misr. Dirasah Tarikhiyyah wa Igtima'iyyah, 1834–1949* (al-Qahirah: al-'Arabi, 2001); Gail Hershatter, *Dangerous Pleasures, Prostitution and Modernity in Twentieth Century Shanghai* (Berkeley: University of California Press, 1997); Christian Henriot, *Prostitution and Sexuality in Shanghai: A Social History, 1849–1949* (Cambridge: Cambridge University Press, 2001); Luise White, *Comforts of Home: Prostitution in Colonial Nairobi* (Chicago: University of Chicago Press, 1990).

23. On this the most complete comparative work to to date is Magaly Rodríguez García, Lex Heerma van Voss and Elise van Nederveen Meerkerk (eds), *Selling Sex in the City: A Global History of Prostitution, 1600s–2000s* (Leiden: Brill, 2017).

24. Philip Howell, *Geographies of Regulation, Policing Prostitution in Nineteenth-Century Britain and the Empire* (Cambridge: Cambridge University Press, 2009).

25. Stephen Legg, 'Beyond the European province: Foucault and postcolonialism', in J.W. Crampton and S. Elden (eds), *Space, Knowledge and Power. Foucault and Geography* (Aldershot: Ashgate, 2007), pp. 265–88.

26. See Stephen Legg, *Prostitution and the Ends of Empire. Scales, Governmentalities, and Interwar India* (Durham: Duke University Press, 2014), p. 6.

27. See Corbain, *Women for Hire*; Walkowitz, *Prostitution and Victorian Society*; Frances Finnegan, *Poverty and Prostitution: A Study of Victorian Prostitution in York* (Cambridge: Cambridge University Press, 1979); Mahood, *The Magdalenes*; Gibson, *Prostitution and the State*; Guy, *Sex and Danger in Buenos Aires*; Ruth Rosen, *The Lost Sisterhood, Prostitution in America 1900–1918* (Baltimore, MD: John Hopkins University, 1982).

28. White, *Comforts of Home*.
29. Timothy J. Gilfoyle, 'Prostitutes in the archives: Problems and possibilities in documenting the history of sexuality', *American Archivist* 57/2 (1994), pp. 514–27.
30. Hershatter, *Dangerous Pleasures*, p. 4.
31. Gail Hershatter, 'Courtesans and streetwalkers: The changing discourses on Shangai prostitution, 1890–1949', *Journal of the History of Sexuality* 3/2 (1992), pp. 245–69, p. 267.
32. For a broad overview of the theoretical shifts within the Subaltern Studies Project see Vinayak Chaturvedi, *Mapping Subaltern Studies* (London: Verso Books, 2000).
33. Works like *Mudhakkirat Laqit* (Memoirs of a foundling, 1923), *Mudhakkirat 'arbagi* (Memoirs of a cabby-driver, 1923), *Mudhakkirat Futuwwa* (Memoirs of a Street Thug, second edition, 1923) and A. 'Atiya, *Mudhakkirat 'Amil fi biqa' al-'ahirat* (Memoirs of a worker in whores' whereabouts, 1927) fall within this category. Cited in Marilyn Booth, 'Between harem and houseboat, fallenness, gendered spaces and the female national subject in 1920s Egypt', in Marilyn Booth (ed.), *Harem Histories, Envisioning Spaces and Living Places* (Durham and London: Duke University Press, 2010), p. 348.
34. Hershatter, *Dangerous Pleasures*, p. 4.
35. Lila Abu Lughod, 'The romance of resistance: Tracing transformations of power through Bedouin women', *American Ethnologist* 17/1 (1990), pp. 41–55.
36. I thank Professor Marilyn Booth for the suggestion to elaborate on this point.
37. See Will Hanley, *Identifying with Nationality: Europeans, Ottomans, and Egyptians in Alexandria* (New York: Columbia University Press, 2017).
38. Julia A. Clancy Smith, *Mediterraneans, North Africa and Europe in an Age of Migration, c.1800–1900* (Berkeley: University of California Press, 2011).
39. A very similar and recent conceptualisation of the term 'sex worker' in a historical setting can be found in Joanne M. Ferraro, 'Making a living: The sex trade in early modern Venice', *American Historical Review* 123/1 (2018), pp. 30–59. In the same issue, see also Jocelyn Olcott, 'Public in a domestic sense: Sex work, nation-building, and class identification in modern Europe', pp. 124–31.

Chapter 1   Selling Sex in a Changing City

1. Amédée B. De Guerville, *New Egypt* (London: Walter Heinemann, 1906), p. 78.
2. See Janet Abu Lughod, *Cairo: 1001 Years of the City Victorious* (Princeton, NJ: Princeton University Press, 1971); Cynthia Mynti, *Paris along the Nile, Architecture in Cairo from the Belle Epoque* (Cairo: Cairo University Press, 2015); Trevor Mostyn, *Egypt's Belle Epoque Cairo, 1869–1952* (London: Quartet Books, 1989).
3. For a classic account of 'Ali Mubarak's work see Robert Hunter, 'Egypt's High Official in transition from a Turkish to a modern administrative elite, 1849–1879', *Middle Eastern Studies* 19/3 (1983), pp. 277–300.

4. Khaled Fahmy, 'Modernizing Cairo: A revisionist account', in N. al Sayyad, I.A. Bierman and N. Rabbat (eds), *Making Cairo Medieval* (Lanham, MD: Lexington Books, 2005), pp. 178–9.

5. Mitchell, *Colonizing Egypt*, p. 67.

6. Thomas S. Harrison, *The Homely Diary of a Diplomat in the East* (Boston: Houghton Miffin Co., 1917), p. 81. For a powerful critique of the 'dual city' trope, so relevant in both colonial and local sources and accepted rather unquestioningly by urban historians for quite a long time, see Nancy Y. Reynolds, *A City Consumed: Urban Commerce, the Cairo Fire, and the Politics of Decolonization in Egypt* (Stanford, CA: Stanford University Press, 2012), p. 19 et seq.

7. See Kenneth Cuno, *The Pasha's Peasants: Lands, Society, and the Economy in Lower Egypt, 1740–1858* (Cambridge: Cambridge University Press, 1992).

8. André Raymond, *Cairo* (Cambridge, MA: Harvard University Press, 2000), p. 319. See also Jean Luc Arnaud, *Le Caire: Mise en place d'une ville moderne* (Arles: Sindbad Acted Sud, 1998) and Nelly Hanna, 'The urban history of Cairo around 1900', in J. Edwards (ed.), *Historians in Cairo: Essays in Honor of George Scanlon* (Cairo: Cairo University Press, 2000), pp. 189–202.

9. Marcel Clerget, *Le Caire: Etudes de Géographie Urbaine et d'Histoire Économique* (Paris: Librairie Orientaliste Paul Geuthner, 1934), p. 242. According to Janet Abu Lughod, in 1917 25 per cent of Cairo's residents whose birthplace was known came from some other Egyptian area, while ten per cent were born abroad. In 1927 the percentage of Egyptian internal migrants was already 34 per cent as opposed to eight per cent of residents born abroad. Abu Lughod, *Cairo*, p. 174.

10. Raymond, *Cairo*, p. 320.

11. See Mak Lanver, *British in Egypt: Community, Crime and Crisis, 1919–1937* (London: I.B.Tauris, 2012).

12. Clerget, *Le Caire*, p. 222.

13. Ibid.

14. See Alexander Kitroeff, *The Greeks in Egypt 1919–1937, Ethnicity and Class* (London: Ithaca Press, 1989). For an extensive account of the history of the Italian community of Egypt see Marta Petricioli, *Oltre il mito: l'Egitto degli Italiani, 1917–1947* (Milan: Mondadori, 2007).

15. *Census of Egypt taken in 1927* (Cairo: Government Press, 1931), p. 216.

16. Clerget, *Le Caire*, p. 222.

17. Raymond, *Cairo*, p. 322.

18. Roger Owen, *The Middle East in the World Economy, 1800–1914* (London and New York: Methuen & Co., 1983), p. 235.

19. De Guerville, *New Egypt*, p. 27.

20. After 1896, public cabs faced increasing competition from the development of large-scale, Belgian-owned transport infrastructure in the form of electric tramlines. See John T. Chalcraft, *The Striking Cabbies of Cairo and Other Stories: Crafts and Guilds in Egypt, 1860–1914* (Albany: State University of New York Press), pp. 134–5.

21. Waterworks were taken over by the Suarès group and extended to new parts of the city. See Robert Vitalis, *When Capitalists Collide. Business Conflict and the End of Empire in Egypt* (Berkeley: University of California Press, 1995), pp. 32–6.

22. Clerget, *Le Caire*, pp. 242–4.

23. De Guerville, *New Egypt*, pp. 24–5.

24. On the origins of mass tourism in Egypt see Derek Gregory, 'Scripting Egypt, Orientalism and the cultures of travel', in J. Duncan and D. Gregory (eds), *Writes of Passage, Reading Travel Writing* (London: Routledge 1999), pp. 114–51; Waleed Hazbun, 'The East as an exhibit: Thomas Cook & Son and the origins of the international tourism industry in Egypt', in P. Scranton and J.F. Davidson (eds), *The Business of Tourism: Place, Faith and History* (Philadelphia: University of Philadelphia Press, 2006), pp. 3–33; Robert F. Hunter, 'Tourism and Empire: The Thomas Cook & Son Enterprise on the Nile, 1868–1914', *Middle Eastern Studies* 40/5 (2004), pp. 28–54. On the hotel industry in modern Egypt see Andrew Humphreys, *Grand Hotels of Egypt* (Cairo: American University in Cairo Press, 2012).

25. Elizabeth Cooper, *The Women of Egypt* (London: Hurst and Blackett, 1914), p. 32.

26. Numbers must be treated with caution as late nineteenth- and early twentieth-century Egyptian censuses are far from reliable. On some of the difficulties encountered in taking the 1917 census of Cairo, for example, see Timothy Mitchell, *Rule of Experts: Egypt, Techno-politics, Modernity* (Berkeley: University of California Press, 2002), pp. 111–12.

27. See Tucker, *Women*, p. 101.

28. White, *Comforts of Home*, p. 9.

29. See Liat Kozma, *Policing Egyptian Women: Sex, Law, and the Family in Khedivial Egypt* (Syracuse, NY: Syracuse University Press, 2011), p. 51. Kozma cites the seminal article by Eve Troutt Powell, 'Will that subaltern ever speak? Finding African slaves in the historiography of the Middle East', in I. Gershoni, A. Singer and Y. Hakan Erdem (eds), *Middle East Historiography: Narrating the Twentieth Century* (Seattle: University of Washington Press, 2006), pp. 242–61 which discusses the epistemological implications of recovering subalterns' lives and perceptions from dominant sources.

30. Diane Robinson Dunne, *The Harem Slavery and British Imperial Culture: Anglo-Muslim Relations in the Late Nineteenth Century* (Manchester: Manchester University Press, 2006), p. 43.

31. Tucker, *Women*, p. 190.

32. Robinson Dunne, *Harem Slavery*, p. 44.

33. Tucker, *Women*, p. 190.

34. The main references on the topic of slavery in the Islamic world and legal system are Imad Hilal, *al-Raqiq fi Misr fi al-Qarn al-Tasi' 'Ashar* (al-Qahirah: al-'Arabi, 1999); John Hunwick, 'The same but different: Africans in slavery in the Mediterranean Muslim world', in J. Hunwick and E. Troutt Powell (eds), *The African Diaspora in the Mediterranean Muslim World* (Princeton, NJ: Princeton

University Press, 2002), pp. ix–xvi; Ehud Toledano, *Slavery and Abolition in the Ottoman Middle East* (Seattle: University of Washington Press, 1998); Terence Walz, 'Black slavery in Egypt', in J.R. Willis (ed.), *Slaves and Slavery in Muslim Africa*, Vol. II (London: Frank Cass, 1985), pp. 137–60; Gabriel Baer, 'Slavery in nineteenth century Egypt', *Journal of African History* 8/3 (1967), pp. 417–41; Terence Walz and Kenneth M. Cuno, *Race and Slavery in the Middle East: Histories of Trans-Saharan Africans in 19th Century Egypt, Sudan, and the Ottoman Mediterranean* (Cairo: American University Press, 2011). For a lively account of similar transitional experiences see Eve M. Troutt Powell, *Tell This in Memory: Stories of Enslavement from Egypt, Sudan, and the Ottoman Empire* (Stanford, CA: Stanford University Press, 2012).

35. Walz and Cuno, *Race and Slavery*, p. 208.
36. Adam McKeown, 'Global migration, 1846–1940', *Journal of World History* 15 (2004), pp. 155–89.
37. Liat Kozma, *Global Women, Colonial Ports. Prostitution in Interwar Middle East* (Albany, NY: SUNY Press, 2017).
38. See Ronal Hyam, *Empire and Sexuality, the British Experience* (Manchester: Manchester University Press, 1990), p. 146 for a good map of trafficking routes. For a thorough discussion of women trafficking in a number of different locales based on primary sources see Jean Michel Chaumont, Magaly Rodriguez Garcia and Paul Servais (eds), *Trafficking in Women 1924–1926, The Paul Kinsie Report for the League of Nations* (Geneva: UN, 2017).
39. Central Office of the Italian Home Office, Report on the Repression of the Traffic in Women and Children, 1927. Italian National Archive (hereafter ACS), 13.180.3, folder 2.
40. Edward J. Bristow, *Prostitution and Prejudice: The Jewish Fight Against White Slavery, 1870–1939* (Oxford: Clarendon Press, 1982). With a specific reference to the Argentinian context see Guy, *Sex and Danger in Buenos Aires*, p. 8.
41. See Women's Library (hereafter WL), 4/IBS/5/2/040, Licensed Houses: Abstract of the Reports of the Governments on the System of Licensed Houses Related to the Traffic in Women and Children, Geneva, 28 February 1929.
42. The National Archives (hereafter NA), 4/IBS/6/033 FL 113, The International Bureau for the Suppression of Traffic in Women and Children, *Its Work in Egypt* (Cairo: Nile Mission Press, 1902), p. 3.
43. WL, 4/IBS/6/033, Report on Traffic in Women, 1905–1906, by Madame Tsykalas from Alexandria. With an abstract of a report by Lord Cromer. The Union Internationale des Amis de Jeunes Filles was among the purity associations active in Europe against the White Slave Trade at that time.
44. Thomas Russell Pasha, *Egyptian Service: 1902–1946* (London: J. Murray, 1949), p. 26. See also Laurence Grafftey-Smith, *Bright Levant* (London: John Murray, 1970), p. 12: 'In one notorious case in Cairo, two Italians, a Greek and a young Egyptian Jew called Jacoel were involved in a pocket-knife murder, unexpected when they broke in to steal. The Egyptian was the only one to be hanged. The others, after condemnation in their consular courts and release on appeal to

Athens and Ancona, were back in Cairo in less than three months, buying haberdashery from the Jacoel family shop'.

45. Ibid.

46. On the role of foreigners in Cairo's underworld see Abu Bakr 'Abd al-Wahhab, *Mujtama'at-Qahira al-Sirri, 1900–1952* (Cairo: Maktabah Madbuli, 1987).

47. WL, 4/IBS/6/034.

48. WL, 4/IBS/6/033, Report on Traffic in Women by Madame Tsykalas, 1905.

49. WL, 4/IBS/6/033, section taken from the 1927 Report of the Special Committee of the Experts on the Traffic in Women and Children.

50. ACS, 13.180.3, folder 30/3.

Chapter 2   The Geography of Sex Work

1. Thomas S. Harrison, *The Homely Diary of a Diplomat in the East* (Boston: Houghton Miffin Co., 1917), p. 81.

2. Douglas Sladen, *Oriental Cairo: The City of the Arabian Nights* (London: Hurst and Blackett, 1911), p. 55.

3. Joseph Ben Prestel, *Emotional Cities: Debates on Urban Change in Berlin and Cairo, 1860–1910* (Oxford: Oxford University Press, 2017), especially pp. 123–33.

4. Phil Hubbard, *Sex and the City: Geography of Prostitution in the Urban West* (London: Ashgate, 1999), p. 31.

5. Charles H. Nightingale, *Segregation: A Global History of Divided Cities* (Chicago: Chicago University Press, 2014); Philip Howell, 'Race, space and the regulation of prostitution in colonial Hong Kong', *Urban History* 31/2 (2004), pp. 229–48.

6. Legg, *Prostitution and the Ends of Empire*, p. 41.

7. Alexandria offers another example of this. See Nefertiti Takla, 'Murder in Alexandria: The gender, sexual and class politics of criminality in Egypt, 1914–1921' (Unpublished Ph.D. Thesis, UCLA, 2016).

8. The situation is in fact very close to that in semi-colonial Shanghai as analised by Gail Hershatter in *Dangerous Pleasures*.

9. On the concept of heterotopia with special reference to present-day Wust el Balad see Lucye Rizova, 'Strolling in enemy territory', proceedings of the conference *Divercities. Contested Space and Urban Identities in Beirut, Cairo and Tehran* (2013). Available at http://www.perspectivia.net/publikationen/orient-institut-studies/3-2015/ryzova_strolling (accessed 1 January 2018).

10. WL, 4/IBS/6/033, Cicely McCall, The International Bureau for the Suppression of Traffic in Women and Children, *Its Work in Egypt* (Cairo: Nile Mission Press, 1930), pp. 11–12.

11. Sladen, *Oriental Cairo*; Guy Thornton, *With the Anzacs in Cairo: The Tale of a Great Fight* (London: Allenson, 1916); Russell Pasha, *Egyptian Service* or op. cit.;

William Nicholas Willis, *Anti-Christ in Egypt* (London: Anglo-Eastern Publishing Company Co., 1914).

12. Muhammad al-Muwaylihi, *What 'Isa Ibn Hisham told us*, edited and translated by Roger Allen, 2 vols (New York and London: New York University Press, 2015); Naguib Mahfouz, *Cairo Trilogy* (New York, Toronto and London: Everyman's Library, 2001), p. 912; p. 1060 et seq.; pp. 1194–7; Naguib Mahfouz, *The Beginning and the End* (London: Anchor, 1989), p. 171; pp. 183–5. For the middle-class *flâneur* or *efendiyyah* as an emerging urban type in modern Egypt see Lucie Ryzova, *The Age of the Efendiyya, Passages to Modernity in National-Colonial Egypt* (Oxford: Oxford University Press, 2014), p. 209, and Marilyn Booth, 'From the horse's rump and the whorehouse keyhole: Ventriloquized memoirs as political voice in 1920s Egypt', *Maghreb Review* 32 (2007), pp. 233–61.

13. Willis, *Anti-Christ*, p. 28. Goshen is the Biblical name for Egypt.

14. Fillib Jallad, *Qamus al-Qada' wa al-Idarah*, Vol. 3 (al-Iskandariyyah: 1906), p. 240; p. 245.

15. Russell Pasha, *Egyptian Service*, p. 179. This image is in fact typical of the Orientalist iconography, clearly evoking women's seclusion and sexual enslavement in the *harim*. It can often be found in early twentieth-century pornographic postcards, studio portraits of female natives often active in prostitution. See Alloula, *The Colonial Harem*, p. 24.

16. Willis, *Anti-Christ*, p. 44.

17. WL, 3/AMSH/B/07/23.

18. WL, 3/AMSH/B/07/05.

19. Mahmud Abu-al-'Uyun, 'Chastity screams!', *al-Ahram*, 8 December 1923. This article opened a series devoted to the issue of licensed prostitution and the state of morals in Egypt, further discussed in Chapter 7.

20. 'Ba'd Sitt 'ashar Sa'ah', *al-Ahram*, 17 December 1932. The reader's list reads as follows: 'Tawfiqiyyah, near 'Ubur al-Mayyah (Aqueduct): 2 clandestine houses; al-Mawardi: 2; Dar al-'Awalim: many; Harat al-Tarabish and Shari' 'Abd al-'Aziz, 'Abdin: 1; Dar al-Muqattam al Qadim: 2; Shari' 'Abdin: 2; Shari' Tilifun: many; Shari' al-Qabbanah: 2; Hilmiyyah Gadidah: 5; Shari' al- Dawawin: 1; Shari' Khayrat: 2; Shari' al-Sahhah: 4; Shari' al-Baghghalah: 10; Shari' Zayn al-Abdin: 7; Shari' al-Khudari: 1; al-Qubisi wa Shari' al-'Abbasi: many; al-'Abbasiyyah: many; Misr Gadidah: 3; Ghamrah: 10; alleys behind Katbikhanah: 5; Bulaq: 5; Shari' al-Khalig: 5; Kum Umm Salamah: 10; Darb al-Junaynah: 5; Bab al-Bahr: 7; Awlad 'Anan: 4; Shari' Umm al-Ghulam: 1; Harat al-Zarabin: 1; Harat al-Gabbaruni: 1; Suq al-Zalat: 4; al-Faggalah: many; Shubrah: 4; Manshiyyat al-Sadr: 2; al-Dimardash: many; 'Izbat al-Zaytun: 3; Rawdat-al-Farag: 2; al-Zahir: 3; al-Sabtiyyah: 5; Darb al-Qittah: 7; Shari' 'Ashara-al-'Abbasiyyah: 4; Clot Bey: many; Suq al-Tha'ban: 1; Bab al-Luq: 1; Bab al-Shari'yyah: 12; Behind the Muhafazah: 3; Kubri al-Qubbah: 2; Citadel: 7; Darb Riyyash: 2; Shari' Nubar: 1; Suq al-Nasari: 2.'

Chapter 3   Regulating Prostitution in Colonial Cairo

1. Gilfoyle, 'Prostitutes in history', p. 117.
2. See Ann L. Stoler, 'Making Empire respectable: The politics of race and sexual morality in the 20th century colonial culture', *American Ethnologist* 16/4 (1989), pp. 643–60.
3. Fahmy, 'Prostitution in Egypt', p. 77
4. The reasons for the ban have been extensively discussed in existing literature. See Fahmy, 'Prostitution in Egypt', p. 81; Tucker, *Women*, p. 151. Hanan Kholoussy in her article 'Monitoring and medicalising male sexuality in semi-colonial Egypt', *Gender & History* 22/3 (2010), p. 679 reconsidered the 'civil society' argument, according to which Muhammad Ali responded to popular distaste for foreign influence. Khaled Fahmy, in particular, reconsidered the 'public opinion argument' according to which the sex workers' ban was a response to people's dislike for the Pashas' Westernising reforms, or widespread protest against the power of such state officials like Copt Antum Tuma, who were in charge of the taxation of sex work.
5. Also known as the French System, sex work regulation was firstly theorised by the Parisian Doctor Parent in J.B. Parent-Duchâtelet, *De la prostitution dans la ville de Paris: considérée sous le rapport de l'hygiéne publique, de la morale et de l'administration*, 2 vols (Paris: J.B. Bailliére et fils, 1836). For essential references on the history and logic of regulation in France see Corbain, *Women for Hire*, and Harsin, *Policing Prostitution*.
6. Howell, *Geographies of Regulation*, p. 9, and Philip Howell, 'Historical geographies of the regulation of prostitution in Britain and the British Empire'. Available at http://www.geog.cam.ac.uk/research/projects/prostitutionregulati on/ (accessed 1 May 2017).
7. Hilal, *al-Baghayya*, p. 65. Hilal and Bruce W. Dunne, 'Sexuality and the civilizing process in modern Egypt' (Unpublished Ph.D. Thesis, Georgetown University, 1996), pp. 141–2, both agree on the fact that the first mention of this document, of which we no original version remains, is made in Fillib Jallad, *Qamus al-Qada' wa al-Idarah*, vol. III (al-Iskandariyyah: Lagoudakis, 1906), p. 240; p. 245. Here it is said that a Decree of the Ministry of Interiors dated 11 November 1882 referred that a previous 'law' had been promulgated by a British-appointed Sanitary Commission, with the task of addressing the most urgent matters of public health such as 'the medical examination of women prostitutes to prevent the spread of venereal disease'.
8. WL, 3/AMSH/B/07/05.
9. N.W. Willis, *Anti-Christ*, pp. 35–6.
10. Ibid., pp. 103–19.
11. Jallad, *Qamus*, p. 240; p. 245.
12. The concept of repentance (*tawbah*) seems to be connected to that of *islah-i-nefs*, self-reform, self-discipline, appearing in a number of Ottoman legal cases from the nineteenth century. According to Elyse Semerdjian, this practice was

established in court cases already in the seventeenth and eighteenth centuries, when prostitutes could express formal regret for their past misdeeds and promise not to engage in prostitution anymore. The practice had a religious undertone, symbolising a turn to the 'straight path'. A prostitute's repentance was registered in court and allowed reintegration into society. See Elise Semerdijan, *Off the Straight Path: Illicit Sex, Law, and Community in Ottoman Aleppo* (Syracuse, NY: Syracuse University Press, 2008), pp. 202–4. The language of religion seemed to give way to that of redemptive productive work in the ideology of modern reformist institutions such as the poorhouse and refuge in modert times (see Chapter 7).

13. *La'ihah Maktab al-Kashf 'ala al-Niswah al-'Ahirat*, article 14.
14. *La'ihah Maktab al-Kashf 'ala al-Niswah al-'Ahirat*, article 18.
15. *al-Qarrarat wa al Manshurat al-Sadirah sanat-1885*, al-Matba'ah al-Amiriyyah bi-Bulaq, 1886, pp. 153–7; *Nizarah al-Dakhiliyyah, Idarah 'Umum al-Sahhah, Dikritat wa Lawa'ih Sahhiyyah* (Cairo: al-Matba'ah al-Amiriyyah bi-Bulaq, 1895), pp. 54–6.
16. *Nizarah al-Dakhiliyyah, al-Qawanin al-Idariyyah wa al-Jina'iyyah, al-Juz' al-Rabi' al-Qawanin al-Khususiyyah* (Cairo: al-Matba'ah al-Amiriyyah bi-Bulaq, n.d.), pp. 430–5.
17. See for example Duktur Fakhr Mikha'il Faraj, *Taqrir 'an Intishar al-Bigha' wa al-Amrad al-Tanassuliyyah bi-l- Qutr al Masri wa ba'd al-Turuq al-Mumkin Ittiba'iha li-Muharibatihima* (Cairo: al-Matba'ah al-'Asriyyah, 1924); Muhammad Farid Junaydi, *al-Bigha', Bahth 'ilmi 'amali* (Cairo: Matba'at al-Nasr, 1934); Mahmud Abu al-'Uyun, *Mushkilah al-Bigha' al- Rasmi* (Cairo: Matba'at al-Hilal, 1933); Burtuqalis Bay, *al-Bigha' aw Kathir al-'ahara fi-l-Qutr al-Masri* (Cairo: Matba'ah Hindiyyah, 1907).
18. Thornton, *With the Anzacs*, p. 59. As a prominent evangelist and puritan abolitionist, Thornton could have had reasons to exaggerate the numbers in order to create panic and alarmism.
19. Frank Young, 'The cheapest thing in Egypt', *Egyptian Gazette*, 7 October 1913.
20. WL, 4/IBS/6/024, The International Bureau for the Suppression of Traffic in Women and Children, *The Case for the Abolition of the Government Regulation of Prostitution* (Cairo: Nile Mission Press, 1939).
21. Ibid.
22. WL, 4/IBS/6/025, Personal communication of Russell Pasha to Mr Sempkins, Secretary of the National Vigilance Association (hereafter NVA), 23 February 1931. Russell Pasha's judgment certainly sounds as profoundly classist and moralistic, and his claim about the number of Cairene middle-class men patronising clandestine prostitution is hyperbolic and doesn't have any statistical value. As a consequence, Russell Pasha was in favour of the closing down of the licensed quarter in the city centre, and the transfer of the brothel area to the outskirts of the city. The same point of view had been advocated in his Cairo City Police Report for the year 1926: 'I would maintain a purely native licensed prostitution quarter on the outskirts to meet the demand of the

native population until what time that education and civilization made it possible to do away with licensed prostitution altogether.' WL, 4/IBS/5/2/40, Cairo City Police Report, 1926.

23. Data for the years 1921–1927 were taken from *Taqrir Sanawi 'an A'mal Taftish Sahhat al-Qahirah li-sanawat* 1922, 1925, 1927, al-Matba'ah al-Amiriyyah bi-l-Qahirah. Data for the period 1928–1946 were taken from Wizarat al-Dakhiliyyah-Bulis Madinat al-Qahirah, *Taqrir Sanawi-al-'am 1930*, al-Matba'ah al-Amiriyyah bi-Bulaq, 1931; Wizarat al-Dakhiliyyah – Bulis Madinat al-Qahirah, *Taqrir Sanawi al-'am 1933*, al-Matba'ah al-Amiriyyah bi-Bulaq, 1934; Wizarat al-Dakhiliyya-Bulis Madinat al-Qahirah, *Taqrir Sanawi al-'am 1935*, al-Matba'ah al-Amiriyyah bi-Bulaq, 1936; Wizarat al-Dakhaliyyah-Bulis Madinat al-Qahirah, *Taqrir Sanawi al-'am 1937*, al-Matba'ah al-Amiriyyah bi-Bulaq, 1938; Wizarat al-Sahhah al- 'Umumiyyah, *Taqrir Sanawi 'an A'mal Taftish Sahhat- al-Qahirah li-'am 1936*, al-Matba'ah al-Amiriyyah bi-Bulaq, 1939; Wizarat al-Sahhah al-'Umumiyyah- *Taqrir Sanawi 'an sanat-1937*, Dar al-Tiba'ah al-Fayyada, al-Qahirah, 1939; Wizarat al-Dakhiliyyah – Bulis Madinat al-Qahirah, *Taqrir Sanawi li-sanatay 1942–1943*, al-Matb'ah al-Amiriyyah bi-l-Qahirah, 1944; Wizarat al-Dakhaliyyah – Bulis Madinat al-Qahirah, *Taqrir Sanawi li-sanat- 1944*, Matba'ah al-Amiriyyah bi-Bulaq bi-l-Qahirah, 1944; Wizarat al-Sahhah al-'Umumiyyah, *Taqrīr Sanawi li-sanat 1946*, Matba'ah al-Amiriyyah bi-Bulaq bi-l-Qahirah; Wizarat al-Sahhah al-'Umumiyyah, *al-Taqrir al-Sanawi al-'amm li-sanat 1943*, Matba'ah al-Amiriyyah bi-Bulaq bi-l-Qahirah.

24. Willis, *Anti-Christ*, p. 40.

25. Fakhr Mikhail Faraj, *Taqrir 'an Intishar al-Bigha' wa al-Amrad al-Tanassuliyyah bi-l-Qutr al-Masri wa ba'd al-Turuq al-Mumkin Ittiba'iha li-Muharibah* (Cairo: al-Matba'ah al-'Asriyyah, 1924), pp. 40–1.

26. WL, IBS/6/033.

27. See also LaVerne Kuhnke, *Lives at Risk: Public Health in Nineteenth Century Egypt* (Berkeley: University of California Press, 1990), pp. 3–4, p. 334; Amira el-Azhary Sonbol, *The Creation of a Medical Profession in Egypt* (Syracuse, NY: Syracuse University Press, 1991), p. x and pp. 27–35; Serge Jagailloux, *La Médicalization de l'Egypte au XIXe siècle, 1798–1918* (Paris: Editions Recherches sur les Civilizations, 1986); Nancy E. Gallagher, *Egypt's Other Wars: Epidemics and the Politics of Public Health* (Syracuse, NY: Syracuse University Press, 1990). On similar dynamics in other Middle Eastern contexts see Nancy E. Gallagher, *Medicine and Power in Tunisia, 1790–1900* (Cambridge: Cambridge University Press, 1983); Ellen J. Amster, *Medicine and the Saints. Science, Islam, and the Colonial Encounter in Morocco, 1877–1956* (Austin: University of Texas Press, 2014); Cyrus Schayegh, *Who is Knowledgeable is Strong: Science, Class, and the Formation of Modern Iranian Society, 1900–1950* (Berkeley: California University Press, 2004).

28. el-Azhary Sonbol, *Creation*, p. 114.

29. Ibid., p. 112.

30. Liat Kozma, "'We, the sexologists ...'": Arabic medical writing on sexuality', *Journal of the History of Sexuality* 22/3 (2013), p. 431.

31. Faraj, *Taqrir 'an Intishar*, p. 46. In the 'Abbasiyyah bureau, 65 women were inspected each day, while in the Sayyidah Zaynab bureau the number of checked women on a single day was 55.

32. Burtuqalis Bey, *al-Bigha' aw Khatar 'aharah fi-l- Qutr al-Misri*, tarjamah Dawwud Barakat (Cairo: Matba'ah Hindiyyah 1907), p. 26.

33. Ibid., p. 33.

34. Muhammad Shahin, *Taqrir min-Mukafahat-al-Amrad al-Zahriyyah bi-l-Qutr al-Masri* (Cairo: n.p., 1933), Table 1. Muhammad Shahin was the representative of the Ministry of Interior for Health Affairs.

35. Ibid., p. 2.

36. Ibid., p. 9.

37. Faraj, *Taqrir 'an Intishar*, pp. 60–1.

38. Corbain, *Women for Hire*, p. 11.

39. Yunan Labib Rizq. 'Safety first', *al-Ahram Weekly Online*, 6–12 December 2001, no. 563. Available at http://weekly.ahram.org.eg/2001/563/chrncls.htm (accessed 1 May 2017).

40. *Al-Taqrir al-Sanawi li-Bulis Madinat-al-Qahirah 'an-Sanat*, 1933, p. 6.

41. From 1875 to 1947, the Egyptian judicial system was a dual one, meaning that foreign consular courts in which foreigners were judged according to the laws of their respective countries existed alongside Egyptian National Courts for Egyptian subjects. The summary way in which law was enacted in consular courts explains why foreign citizens in Egypt were virtually free to engage in whatever sort of illicit activity. For a good overview see Mark Hoyle, *Mixed Courts of Egypt* (London: Graham and Trotman, 1968).

42. Russell Pasha, *Egyptian Service*, p. 179.

43. Sladen, *Oriental Cairo*, p. 60.

44. Ibid., *Oriental Cairo*, p. 109.

45. Muhammad al-Muwaylihi, *What 'Isa Ibn Hisham Told Us or A Period of Time*, translated by Roger Allen (New York: New York Univeristy Press, 2018), p. 322.

Chapter 4   Sex Work Beyond Prostitution

1. M. Fredolin, *John Bull Sur Le Nil* (Paris: Jules Lévi Editeur, first edition, 1886), pp. 170–1. M. Fredolin is acknowledged as the author of a scathing critique of British colonial rule in Egypt, which he based on his firsthand observation during an eight-month stay in Cairo. See W. Fraser Rae, *Egypt to-day* (London: Bentley and Sons, 1892), p. 246.

2. Michel Foucault, 'The subject and power', *Critical Inquiry* 8/4 (1982), pp. 777–95, p. 781.

3. Ibid.

4. Kharakhanah means 'brothel'. The origin of this name is quite interesting. In the Levant the *karakhanah* identified both the workshop and the brothel. According to Jens Hanssen, in Beirut the majority of prostitutes were unmarried village girls who had formerly worked as silk weavers (*banat al karakhanah*) in the outskirts of Beirut: They 'were initially sent to earn money in the factories to sustain their families by subsidizing their agricultural revenue in adverse economic conditions. Yet, as the Maronite clergy and the patriarchal system considered female labour immoral in a factory where they would come into contact with men, these women suffered social stigmatization'. See Jens Hanssen, 'Public morality and marginality in fin-de-siècle Beirut', in Rogan, *Outside In*, p. 197.

5. Wizarat-al-Dakhiliyyah, *Nizam al-Bulis wa al-Idarah- Lay'hah bi-sha'an buyut al-'ahirat*, 1936. The decree confirms a previous one by the same name, issued on 15 July 1896.

6. Ibid., Art. 1.

7. Ibid., Art. 2.

8. WL, 4/IBS/6/040.

9. Labib Rizq, 'Safety first'.

10. WL, 4/IBS/6/040.

11. The Azbakiyyah had the second highest population density in Cairo after the nearby area of Bab-al-Sha'riyyah, with 36,323 inhabitants per sq. km in 1926. See Abu Bakr 'Abd al-Wahhab, *Mujtama'*, p. 28.

12. NA, FO/841/62.

13. Mahfouz, *Cairo Trilogy*, p. 913.

14. The term *taqtuqah* (pl. *taqatiq*, 'light ditties') identifies popular songs especially composed for commercial recording on 78 rpm records since the 1920s. A notable medium for social commentary, they 'addressed such serious themes as the reconstitution of family around the nuclear model, the dangers of polygamy, the right to get acquainted to the bride or the groom before marriage, the dangers of girls' autonomy for a family's wealth, the minimum age of marriage, the way spouses should deal with their husbands' misconducts, working women and women in the police and the army'. They constitute an interesting source for the study of social change and debates between modernists and traditionalists in interwar Egypt. See Frédéric Lagrange, 'Women in the singing business, women in songs', *History Compass* 7/1 (2009), pp. 226–50, p. 229. About the origins of the form, language and recurrent themes and characters – the coquette, the debauched heir, the corrupt jurisprudent – see Frédéric Lagrange, 'Une Egypte libertine?', in F. Sanaugustin (ed.), *Parole, Signes, Mythes, Mélange offerts à Jamel Eddine Bencheikh* (Damas: IFEAD, 2001), pp. 257–300. See also its extended version 'Quand l'Egypt se chantat, taqatiq et chansons légerès au début du XX siècle'. Available at http://mapage.noos. fr/fredlag/taqatiq.pdf (accessed 1 May 2017).

15. Al-Bannà excelled in interpreting the coquettish girl, 'therefore enhancing any comic material already contained in the lyrics'. Endowed with a high-pitched

voice of almost feminine quality, he was the only male vocalist of his time who did not wear a moustache, in order to divert attention from his masculinity. See Lagrange, 'Women in the singing business', p. 229; p. 233.

16. Ibid., p. 12. On the relationship between spatial practices, subjectivities and the national imagination see Booth, 'Between harem and houseboat', pp. 342–73.

17. I am using Corbain's term to define a private house tenants made available to third parties for commercial sexual encounters. Women were not living on the premises, but frequented the house for the purpose of prostitution. Clients could be either procured by the keeper or by the women themselves. See Corbain, *Women for Hire*, pp. 174–5.

18. Russell Pasha, *Egyptian Service*, p. 178.

19. WL, 4/IBS/6/024.

20. WL, 4/IBS/6/031.

21. See 'White slave traffic in Egypt. Revolting allegations', *Morning Post*, 24 October 1923; 'White slave arrests, Egyptian gang's GHQ raided', *Daily Express*, 23 October 1923; 'White slaves raid, 100 arrests in Cairo', *Daily Mail*, 24 October 1923. It is remarkable that, although the newspapers talked about 'White Slave Traffic', no European woman was in fact involved in the case. The term was probably chosen for sheer sensationalistic reasons, at a time when metropolitan concerns about juvenile sexuality and consent were assumed to be universally valid.

22. The National Vigilance Association (NVA) was founded in Britain in 1885. As a purity association, it campaigned against prostitution, homosexuality, obscene publications and vice.

23. WL, 4/IBS/6/031, Letter of G.W. Hughes, Chief Inspector of Cairo's Native Court of Appeal to Miss Baker, Director of the National Vigilance Association, 3 March 1924.

24. WL, 4/IBS/6/031, Note by Sister Margaret Clare to Miss Baker, 15 November 1924.

25. WL, 4/IBS/6/031, Note by Sister Margaret Clare, 26 May 1924.

26. Russell Pasha, *Egyptian Service* or op. cit., p. 181.

27. Corbain, *Women for Hire*, p. 181.

28. Alfred Cunningham, *To-Day in Egypt, Its Administration, People and Politics* (London: Hurst and Blackett Limited, 1912), p. 41.

29. Ibid., pp. 42–3.

30. See 'Egypt's morals, prominent author interviewed. A scathing indictment. Laws that help the devil', *Egyptian Gazette*, 13 August 1913.

31. See the Historical Archive of the Ministry of Foreign Affairs (hereafter ASMAE), Italian Consular Courts Penal Cases, 1932/99; Report of the Commercial Agent, Italian Embassy of Egypt, 23 April 1932.

32. ASMAE, Italian Consular Courts Penal Cases, 1932, folder 3/96–140.

33. Cunningham, *To-Day*, p. 115.

34. Ibid. On the status of morals within the protected domestic space see Booth, *Harem Histories*, p. 315.

35. ASMAE, Italian Consular Courts Penal Cases, 1932, folder 4/141–95.

36. Many information on the nightlife scene in Cairo until the Revolution can be derived from local publications devoted to the arts and showbusiness in the 1920s and the 1930s, such as *Alf Sinf*, *Dunia-al-Fann*, *al-Kawakib, Majallat-al-Funun*, *al-Malahi-al-Musawwarah* and *Ruz al-Yusuf*. These newspapers used to devote regular columns to the programmes performed in the various venues and commented extensively on the quality of the establishments and performers. It seems that the main entrepreneurs bribed journalists to obtain positive reviews. For the description of Cairene commercial entertainment scene, I draw on Karin van Nieuwkerk, *"A Trade like any Other": Singers and Dancers in Egypt* (Austin: University of Texas Press, 1995), pp. 43–9.

37. In 1940, the Head of Police in the Azbakiyyah area found 459 *garsunat* without a license. After they underwent a compulsory medical check-up, it was found that 97 of them were actually infected with venereal diseases. See Hilal, *al-Baghayya*, p. 66.

38. In some venues, performers had to refrain from sitting with customers by contract, in order to avoid any association being made between the establishment and prostitution. A very famous performer at the beginning of the twentieth century, Tawhidah, wanted to have stated in her contract that she wouldn't drink more than five glasses of cognac in one evening and that she couldn't be compelled to sit with customers.

39. Van Nieuwkerk, *A Trade like any Other*, p. 198, note 8.

40. Ibid., p. 44.

41. Muhammad al-Muwaylihi, *What 'Isa Ibn Hisham told us or a Period of Time*, translated by Roger Allen (New York: New York University Press, 2018), p. 322.

42. Ibid.

43. Ibid., p. 341.

44. Ibid., p. 339.

45. Ibid., p. 342.

46. Ibid., p. 343.

47. Sarah Graham Brown, *Images of Women: The Portrayal of Women in Photography in the Middle East* (New York: Columbia University Press, 1988), p. 171. According to a Gramophone sound engineer in the late 1920s, 'the amount of raw spirits, cocaine and other drugs absorbed by artistes and their entourage throughout sessions lasting from early evening till two and three in the morning [...] rather alarmed me until I got used to it [...] I remember one obese lady consuming the best part of a bottle (full-sized) of Martell's Three Star Brandy at a single session, neat, mind you'. See Lagrange, 'Women in the singing business', p. 236.

48. WL, 4/IBS/6/041.

49. WL, 4/IBS/6/025, Communication of the British Head of the Passport and Permit Office to Miss Saunders, IBS.

50. Van Nieuwkerk, *A Trade like any Other*, p. 45.

51. Ibid.
52. *Salah* was the Arabic name for 'music hall'. Unlike the term *kabarê*, it did not carry a negative connotation. See Van Nieuwkerk, *A Trade like any Other*, p. 43.
53. Fundamental references about these performers include Tawhidah, *Taqatiq al Sitt Tawhidah, al-Mughanniyah al-Shahirah fi Alf Layla wa Layla* (Cairo: Dal al Ma'rusah, 1924), and Ratibah Hifni, *Munira al Mahdiyya* (Cairo: Dal al-Shurouk, 2001); on Badi'ah Masabni see Nazik Basilah, *Mudhakkirat Badi'ah Masabni* (Beirut: Dar Maktabat al-Hayat, 1960), and Roberta L. Dougherty, 'Badi'a Masabni, artist and modernist, the Egyptian print media carnival of national identity', in W. Armbrust (ed.), *Mass Mediations, New Approaches to Popular Culture in the Middle East and Beyond* (Berkeley: University of California Press, 2000), pp. 243–69.
54. Jacques Berque, *L'Égypte, Impérialisme et Révolution* (Paris: Gallimard, 1967), pp. 363–4.
55. See Van Nieuwkerk, *A Trade like any Other*, p. 47.
56. Artemis Cooper, *Cairo in the War, 1939–1945* (London: Hamish Hamilton, 1989), p. 112.
57. See Pennethorne Hughes, *While Shepheard's Watched* (London: Chatto and Windus, 1949), pp. 51–2.
58. WL, 4/IBS/5/2/040.
59. For a description of a 'awamah-brothel see Marilyn Booth, 'Unsafely at home: Narratives of sexual coercion in 1920s Egypt', *Gender & History* 16/3 (2004), pp. 744–68.
60. See Liat Kozma, *Policing Egyptian Women*, pp. 216–17.
61. Ibid.
62. WL, 4/IBS/5/2/040.
63. Naguib Mahfouz, *Midaq Alley* (London: Heinemann, 1966), p. 34.
64. Ibid., p. 35. On contacts between the sexes in public space, specifically big, *khawagah*-owned department stores and moral danger, see Nancy Reynolds, 'Salesclerks, sexual danger, and national identity in Egypt in the 1920s and 1940s', *Journal of Women's History* 23/3 (Fall 2011), pp. 63–88.
65. NA, FO 841/146, Rex versus Giuseppe Mifsud for living on the earnings of prostitution.
66. WL, 4/IBS/6/038.
67. WL, 4/IBS/6/034, Egypt. Messageries Maritimes, folder 1, 1925–30.
68. Ibid.
69. Ibid.
70. Ibid.
71. Ibid.
72. Russell Pasha pointed out in various instances the need for a new scheme for police officers in order to discourage corruption and collusion in illicit activities. Although he was mainly referring to native policemen, it seems that his remarks may apply to British ones as well: 'I fear however that the standard of pecuniary honesty which in the past has been high among the city police, is

being undermined by the inadequacy of the pay. It is today quite impossible for a married policeman to exist on the pay he receives.' He pressed for the introduction of a pension system, free housing in Government cantonments (such as Shubrah, Old Cairo, Sayyidah Zaynab, al-Khalifah and 'Abbasiyyah) and free medical and educational facilities for police families. Russell Pasha, *Egyptian Service* or op. cit., p. 161. In 1927 a major press campaign on *al-Ahram* addressed the issue of reform in law enforcement, public security and police corps' professional standards. See Labib Rizq, 'Safety first'.

73. NA, FO 841/205, Rex versus Gordon Ainslie Ness for living wholly or in part on proceeds of prostitution.

74. Ibid. See the testimony of Eric Leslie Desmond Lees, Head Constable of Cairo Secret Police: 'I know Sophie. She works at the Café Guindi, she sits with clients of the café and if she can come to terms with them, she will go home with them. I have seen Sophie leaving the café with one man and I have seen her go to bed with another man at Villa Napoli, 13 Sharia Qantarat al-Dekkah'. Ibid.

75. NA, FO 841/205, Rex versus John Chas. {Charles?} Shalders for living on proceeds of prostitution.

76. WL, 4/IBS/6/034, Egypt, Messageries Maritimes, 1925–1930.

77. WL, 4/IBS/6/034, Augusta Pellissier's testimony to police, 15 April 1929 (my translation). On the *vol à l'entôlage* see in the same file also the testimony of André Guillet, a French minor brought over by a certain Sachelli, who first seduced her and then forced her to go to Egypt by threatening her with a revolver: 'about 7 months ago, I asked Gros Loui to go to the house of Jeanne Maury, 2 Sikket al-Manakh where I met a young man called Tonnin, whom I found later to be the nephew of Jeanne Maury and I was trained by them in the *vol à l'entôlage*, from the clients, and then I was arrested with the others and detained in the ELU [sic.] awaiting trial. I then was sentenced by the French Consular Court to one year's imprisonment with the first offender's benefit.' See Francesca Biancani, 'International migration and sex work', in L. Kozma, C. Schayegh and A. Wishnitzer (eds), *A Global Middle East Mobility, Materiality and Culture in the Modern Age, 1880–1940* (London: I.B.Tauris, 2014), pp. 123–4.

78. WL, 4/IBS/6/037. In a speech delivered on 7 June 1932 at the meeting of the first committee on prostitution, H.E. Mahmud Shahin Pasha, Ministry of Interior and Public Health, estimated that licensed prostitutes received between eight and 16 customers per day. According to him, clandestine prostitutes received only two customers per day.

79. Clerget, *Le Caire*, p. 156.

80. NA, FO 841/205, Testimony of a landlady, Katina Cephalas. The rent in brothels is taken from WL,4/IBS/6/025. It is possible that in Cairo the segregation associated with regulationism was never adopted in full. A closer study of arrangements between prostitutes and brothel owners will probably support the view that Cairo's brothels were mostly closer to 'open houses', a sort of lodging house inhabited by public women, than thr *maison fermée* of the

continental type. This also explains the fact that many women, although formally prohibited to do so by the law, actually attracted clients in the streets, standing in front of the buildings or under the arches of the Wagh-al-Birkah.

81. WL, 4/IBS/6/ 034.
82. NA, FO 841/146, Rex versus Giuseppe Vassallo for living wholly or in part on the proceedings of prostitution. See Biancani, 'International migration', p. 125.
83. NA, FO 841/164, Rex versus Pasquale Magri for living wholly or in part on the proceedings of prostitution.
84. NA, FO/841/120.
85. It is not possible to derive any information about the baby's father from the trial's minutes. The child was nursed by an old neighbour, Giovannina Valestra, from whom Pasquale Magri managed to steal 15 Egyptian pounds. It seems the baby was entrusted to the 'Abbasiyyah Orphanage at some point.
86. NA, FO 841/186, Rex Versus James Kelly Alias James Hughes for living wholly or in part on proceeds of prostitution.
87. ASMAE, Italian Consular Courts Penal Cases, 1932, folder 2, cases 41–95.
88. 'Attempted murder at Cairo', Egyptian Gazette, 20 August 1913.
89. ASMAE, Italian Consular Courts Penal Cases, 1926, cases 1–65. See Biancani, 'International migration', pp. 125–8.
90. Ibid. My translation.
91. Ibid.
92. WL, 4/IBS/6/044, Report of the IBS Cairo Branch, January 1928.
93. Ibid.
94. NA, FO 841/146.
95. NA, FO 841/186.
96. On subaltern strategic use of nationality and the notion of 'vulgar cosmopolitism' see Hanley, Identifying with Nationality.

Chapter 5   Imperial War, Venereal Disease and Sex Work

1. Howell, Geographies of Regulation, p. 12.
2. Chacko Jacob Wilson, Working Out Egypt: Effendi Masculinity and Subject Formation in Colonial Modernity, 1870–1940 (Durham, NC: Duke Univesity Press, 2010), p. 28.
3. On degeneration see Daniel Pick, Faces of Degeneration: A European Disorder, c.1848–1918 (New York: Cambridge University Press, 1989).
4. The acronym ANZAC stands for Australian and New Zealanders Army Corps. It was part of the Mediterranean Expeditionary Force during World War I, formed in Cairo in 1915. They gave their contribution to the Gallipoli battle, before being dismantled as a consequence of the Allied evacuation of Gallipoli in 1916.
5. See Mario M. Ruiz, 'Manly spectacles and imperial soldiers in wartime Egypt, 1914–1919', Middle Eastern Studies 43/3 (2009), pp. 351–71, p. 357.

6. Available at http://www.mudgeeguardian.com.au/story/3020538/the-road-to-gallipoli-the-anzacs-in-egypt/ (accessed 1 May 2017).

7. Ibid.

8. Harold Roy Williams, *An ANZAC on the Western Front: the Personal Recollections of an Australian Infantryman* (Barnsley: Pen and Sword Military, 2012), n.p.

9. Ibid.

10. Charles Benjamin Purdom, *Everyman at War: Sixty Personal Narratives of the War* (London and Toronto: J.M. Dent, 1930), p. 311.

11. 'Hariq fi-l-Azbakiyyah' (Fire in the Azbakiyyah), *al-Ahram*, 3 April 1915. Kevin Fewster, 'The Wazza Riots 1915', *Journal of the Australian War Memorial* 4 (1984), pp. 47–53.

12. Australian War Memorial (hereafter AWM), C00183.

13. Suzanne Brugger, *Australians and Egyptians* (Melbourne: Melbourne University Press, 1980).

14. See Ruiz, 'Manly spectacles', p. 551, and Frank Chung, 'Underbelly dance: How a brush with the white slave trade sparked the first battle of the Anzacs', 2 April 2015. Available at http://www.news.com.au/national/anzac-day/underbellydance-how-a-brush-with-the-white-slave-trade-sparked-the-first-battle-of-the-anzacs/news-story/123d51fb53067b95ce11650fe43faf33 (accessed 1 May 2017).

15. Alistair Thomson, *Anzac Memories: Living with the Legend* (Melbourne: Oxford University Press, 1994), p. 31; C.E.W. Bean, *Gallipoli Correspondent: the Frontline Diary of C.E.W. Bean*, selected and annotated by Kevin Fester (Sidney: George Allen and Unwin, 1983), pp. 38–9.

16. Lieutenant-Colonel Percy Elgood, *Egypt and the Army* (Oxford: Oxford University Press, 1924), p. 258. Before World War I the percentage of venereal soldiers was nonetheless very high: the rate of hospital admissions for VDs in Egypt was 110.8 per 1,000 men, compared to 55.5 in India and 56.4 at home. See Mark Harrison, 'The British Army and the problem of venereal disease in France and Egypt during the 1st World War', *Medical History* 39/2 (1995), pp. 133–58, p. 150.

17. Dunne, *Sexuality and the Civilizing Process*, p. 212.

18. Philippa Levine, 'Battle colors: Race, sex, and colonial soldiery in War I', *Journal of Women's History* 9/4 (1998), pp. 104–30, p. 106. I would add that it also remained bourgeois.

19. For a thorough review-article on Muscular Christianity as rooted in both domestic social unrest and imperial concerns, see Nick J. Watson, Stuart Weir and Stephen Friend, 'The development of Muscular Christianity in Victorian Britain and beyond', *Journal of Religion and Society* 7 (2005), pp. 1–21; Donald E. Hall (ed.), *Muscular Christianity: Embodying the Victorian Age* (New York: Cambridge University Press, 1994).

20. Mark Harrison, 'The British Army', p. 137.

21. Thornton, *With the Anzacs*, p. 12.

22. Ibid., p. 22.

23. Ibid., p. 24.

24. Ibid., p. 74.
25. Ibid., pp. 86–7.
26. The committee included the Bishop of Jerusalem in exile, Rennie MacInnes, Major-General W.A. Watson, Lieutenant-Colonel T.W. Gibbard, Colonel Harvey Pasha, head of Cairo City Police at the time, Dr H.P. Keating and Dr Ferguson Lees.
27. WL, 4/IBS/6/033; Sir James W. Barrett, 'Management of venereal diseases in Egypt during the War', *The British Medical Journal* (1919), pp. 125–7.
28. 'Purification of Cairo. The question of the artistes', *Egyptian Gazette*, 16 May 1916.
29. Ibid.
30. 'Purification of Cairo. Harvey Pasha and the "danse du ventre"', *Egyptian Gazette*, 2 June 1916.
31. 'Corrupt males of Cairo', *Egyptian Gazette*, 10 June 2016.
32. Thornton quoted in his book a report published in the *Egyptian Gazette*, according to which 37 per cent of the alcohol sold in Cairo was adulterated: 'one thing is certain, banish the liquor and before 6 months 9/10 of the women would have to seek an honest means of procuring a livelihood.' Thornton, *With the Anzacs*, pp. 65–6.
33. 'Britannia and Kursaal artistes assembled at Metro Café, while those of the Aziz Id troupe went to the Café de Ramses in Faggalah. Where actresses now spend their leisure time we don't know'. 'Actresses and Cairo cafés', *Egyptian Gazette*, 15 June 1916.
34. See Philippa Levine, *Prostitution, Race and Politics: Policing Venereal Disease in the British Empire* (New York and London: Routledge, 2003), p. 153. See also *Ettie: a Life of Ettie Rout* (Auckland: Penguin, 1992) and *Ettie Rout: New Zealand's safe sex pioneer* (Auckland: Penguin, 2015), both by Jane Tolerton.
35. Levine, *Prostitution*, p. 148.
36. National Archives of Australia (hereafter NAA), A11803 – 1917/89/252, Prostitution in Egypt. Control of Immorality.
37. WL, 3/AMSH/B/07/05.
38. Ibid.
39. WL, 3/AMSH/B/07/05.
40. Ibid.
41. Ibid.
42. Ibid., By special dressing room is meant venereal wards for the treatment of diseased soldiers.

Chapter 6   Policing 'Suspect' Femininities: The Work of British Purity Movements in Cairo

1. See Philippa Levine, '"A multitude of unchaste women": Prostitution in the British Empire', *Journal of Women's History* 15/4 (2004), pp. 159–63; Levine, *Prostitution*.

2. Anne McClintock, *Imperial Leather: Race, Gender and Sexuality in the Colonial Context* (New York, London: Routledge, 1995), pp. 43–4.

3. Ibid., 48.

4. In order to understand the central role that discourse about white slavery played in the construction of the metropolitan and colonial orders, beyond the materialty of the transnational sex trade, see Jo Dozema, 'Loose women or lost women? The re-emergence of the myth of white slavery in contemporary dicourses of trafficking women', *Gender Issues* (2000), pp. 23–50; Rachel Attwood, 'Vice beyond the pale: Representing white slavery in Britain, 1880–1912' (Unpublished Ph.D. Thesis, UCL, 2013); Rachel Attwood, 'Looking beyond "White Slavery": Trafficking, the Jewish Association, and the dangerous politics of migration control in England, 1890–1910', *Anti-Trafficking Review* 7 (2016), pp. 115–38; Mary Ann Irwin, 'White slavery as a metaphor: Anatomy of a moral panic', *Ex Post Facto: The History Journal*, Vol. V (1996). Available at http://www.walnet.org/csis/papers/irwin-wslavery.html (accessed 1 May 2017); Judith Walkowitz, *City of Dreadful Delight, Narratives of Sexual Danger in Late Victorian London* (Chicago: Chicago University Press, 1992), pp. 81–121; Philippa Levine, 'The white slave trade and the British Empire: Crime, gender, and sexuality in criminal persecution', *Criminal Justice History* 17 (2002), pp. 133–46.

5. Alfred S. Dyer, *The European Slave Trade in English Girls, a Narrative of Facts* (London: Dyer Brothers, 1880). Here the terms 'purity' and 'puritan' are used with the meaning they have in Victorian historiography, that is, referring to a number of civil society movements calling for reform of morals in Britain since the second half of the nineteenth century. Originating in earlier reformist currents such as radical utopianism, slavery abolitionism and the temperance movement, purity organisations started campaigning against the regulation of prostitution in order to cover other issues such as pornography, age of consent, alcohol consumption and contraception at a later stage. See Edward J. Bristow, *Vice and Vigilance: Purity Movements in Britain since 1700* (Dublin: Gill and McMillan, 1977).

6. For a history of the term 'white slavery', its relation to radical labour struggles in the UK and in the USA, and the shifting role of race and gender within subsequent ideological formations, see Gunther W. Peck, 'White slavery and whiteness: A transnational view of the sources of working-class radicalism and racism', *Labor: Studies in Working-Class History of the Americas* 1/2 (2004), pp. 41–63.

7. Victor Hugo to Josephin Butler, 20 March 1870, in Josephine E. Butler, *Personal Reminescences of a Great Crusade* (London: Horace Marshall and Son, 1911), p. 13.

8. See W.T. Stead, *'The Maiden Tribute of Modern Babylon.' The Report of the Secret Commission by W.T. Stead*, edited and with annotations and an introductory essay by Antony E. Simpson (Lambertville: True Bill Press, 2007).

9. Ibid., pp. 109–10.

10. For a thorough discussion of the NVA and how its specific outlook impacted the operations of the Bureau, see Rachel Attwood, 'Stopping the traffic: The National Vigilance Association and the international fight against the "white slave" trade', *Women's History Review* 24/3 (2015), pp. 325–50. Other critical takes on the NVA can be found in Julia Laite, *Common Prostitutes and Ordinary Citizens: Commercial Sex in London 1885–1960* (London: Palgrave McMillan, 2011), pp. 100–15 and Paula Bartley, *Prostitution Prevention and reform in England, 1860–1914* (London: Routledge, 1999), pp. 170–3.

11. Bristow, *Vice and Vigilance*, p. 177.

12. Stephanie Limoncelli, *The Politics of Trafficking: The First International Movement to Combat the Sexual Exploitation of Women* (Stanford: Stanford University Press, 2011) and Jessica Pliley, 'Claims to protection: The rise and fall of feminist abolitionism in the League of Nations. Committee on the Traffic in Women and Children, 1919–1937', *Journal of Women's History* 22/4 (Winter 2010), pp. 90–113.

13. See Julia Laite, 'The Association of moral and social hygiene: Abolitionism and prostitution law in Britain (1915–1959)', *Women's History Review* 17/2 (2008), pp. 209–10.

14. Margot Badran, *Feminists, Islam and the Nation: Gender and the Making of Modern Egypt* (Princeton, NJ: Princeton University Press, 1995), p. 200.

15. See *Blessed Be Egypt*, January 1915, no. 61, Vol. XV, p. 9. Starting in 1905, *Blessed Be Egypt* was the bi-monthly publication of the Nile Mission Press, an independent mission aiming at publishing tracts, books and magazines spreading the Gospel Message. A.T. P. Upson, its First Publishing Superintendent, strictly collaborated with the activists of the AMSH in campaigns for the armies' moralisation. For more on American missionaries in Egypt, see Heather J. Sharkey, *American Evangelicals in Egypt: Missionaries Encounters in an Age of Empire.* (Princeton, NJ: Princeton University Press, 2008).

16. WL, 4/IBS/6/024, Letter of Miss McCall to Mr F. Sempkins, 10 March 1930.

17. WL, 4/IBS/6/025, Mr Sempkins, NVA, to Judge McBarnett, Villa Rowlatt, Bulkeley, Cairo, 29 May, 1930. Letter of Mr Sepkin, NVA, to Judge Booth, Cairo, 28 November 1930. Here he says that it would be better to focus on stopping the traffic than on abolitionism: 'You cannot go to people who are by training and early influence regulationists and expect them to do any good by the simple process of telling them that they are nasty minded people and that they must agree with you.'

18. See Levine, 'A multitude of unchaste women'.

19. WL, 4/IBS/6/023, Miss Cicely McCall application letter, 16 October 1927.

20. WL, 4/IBS/6/044.

21. WL, 4/IBS/6/025, Miss Cicely McCall to Mr Sempkin, 8 October 1930.

22. WL,4/IBS/6/025.

23. WL,4/IBS/6/041.

24. WL,4/IBS/6/041.

25. See for examples the IBS Report of Cases, December 1928, case no. 1050: 'French, 36 years old. This woman turned to us willing to leave the public houses and entering the Refuge. The Police has been informed and agreed on the woman staying with us for a period of 3 months. After that period, if her conduct is satisfying, we'll find her a job.' IBS Report of Cases, January 1929, case no. 1056: 'Italian, 40 years old. She has been working as prostitute and brothel keeper for the past 9 years. She is willing to find a job. She will stay in the refuge for 3 months. After that, if her conduct is satisfying, her name will be struck out the registration lists.' IBS Report of Cases, February 1929, case no. 1063: 'Rumanian Jew, 31 years old. Prostitute in the past 4 years. Now she desires to work and leave the Ezbekiyyah. With the police authorization she can leave the segregated area and go to Helouan for three weeks with her sister. Once back, she will enter the Refuge.'
26. IBS Report of Cases, February 1928, no. 1017.
27. WL, 4/IBS/6/024, 'Vigilance record', March-April 1929, Egyptian National Committee.
28. Ibid.
29. IBS, Monthly Report, April 1924, case no. 748
30. IBS, Monthly Report, April 1924, case no. 750.
31. IBS, Monthly Report, April 1924, case no. 747.
32. IBS, Monthly Report, February 1929, case no. 1061.
33. IBS, Monthly Report, May 1925, case no. 838.
34. IBS, Monthly Report, May 1925, case no. 189.
35. IBS, Monthly Report, June 1925, case nos. 842–3.
36. IBS, Monthly Report, January 1928, case no. 104.
37. IBS, Monthly Report, April 1924, case nos. 743–4.
38. IBS, Monthly Report, April 1924, case no. 746.
39. IBS, Monthly Report, February 1928, without number.
40. IBS, Report of Cases, February 1929, case no. 1059.
41. IBS, Report of Cases, March 1929, case no. 1067.
42. IBS, Report of Cases, February 1929, without number.
43. IBS, Monthly Report, April 1924, case no. 751.
44. IBS, Report of Work, June 1925, case no. 846.
45. WL, 4/IBS/6/024, Letter from Miss Cicely McCall to Mr Sempkins, 17 May 1929.
46. IBS, Report of Cases, May 1925, case no. 736.
47. IBS, Report of Cases, March 1929, case nos. 1065 and 1066.
48. IBS, Report of Cases, February 1928, case no. 1020.
49. IBS, Report of Cases, January 1928, case no. 967. In the same report is also cited a case no. 996, resident in the hostel from September 1927, of whom is said: 'She has been a good worker so far but she always has to be kept under strict control. She takes advantage of whatever circumstance to approach the men living nearby the Refuge and after her friend's Iren Death she threatens to follow her example. She also went up to the terrace, threatening to turn her plan into action. We don't

believe she really wanted to do so, but in order to avoid further tragedy we decided to entrust the case to the Greek Consulate, with the hope that they will able to find a place for her at the Bonne Pasteur. Meanwhile, our Consul informed us that she has been entrusted to a Greek family. We hope for the best.'

50. Levine, *Prostitution*, p. 136.
51. Laite, 'The Association of moral and social hygiene', p. 208.
52. WL, 4/IBS/6/033 containing a leaflet by Louise Dorothy Potter, *Egypt Awakening! Is it True?* (n.p.), p. 5.
53. Ibid., p. 6
54. Ibid., p. 8.
55. See Dunne, *Sexuality and the Civilizing Process*, p. 288.
56. WL, 4/IBS/6/038.
57. Ibid.
58. Margot Badran, 'Dual liberation: Feminism and nationalism in Egypt, 1870s–1925', *Feminist Issues* 8/1 (1988), pp. 15–34, pp. 27–8.
59. Badran, *Feminists*, p. 199.
60. WL, 4/IBS/6/024, Miss Higson's Address to the Central Committee of the International Bureau for the Suppression of the Traffic of Women and Children of Egypt, 25 February 1930.
61. Ibid.
62. Women marrying a foreigner had to give up their citizenship and take their husbands' nationality. Feminists claimed that women had the right to choose, and this was prejudicial to their individual rights.
63. Badran, *Feminists*, p. 203.
64. WL, 4/IBS/6/041, Letter from Lady M. Nunburnholme to Mr Sempkins, 20 July 1939.

Chapter 7   Abolitionism on the Political Agenda

1. Yunan Labib Rizq, 'Backroads', *al-Ahram Weekly Online*, 7–13 June 2001, no. 537. Available at http://weekly.ahram.org.eg/2001/537/chrncls.htm (accessed 1 May 2017).
2. I use the term 'eugenic' in the broad sense, that is as a discourse on the production of a healthy and prosperous human race, the optimisation of the species (*tahsin al-nasl* in Arabic) which entailed primarily the development of scientific theories about birth-control (*tahdid al nasl*) and reproduction, sanitation, hygiene and puericulture. In its negative form, eugenics has to do with the prevention of mentally or physically 'inferior', tainted individuals from reproducing themselves. See Omnia el-Shakry, *The Great Social Laboratory: Subjects of Knowledge in Colonial and Postcolonial Egypt* (Stanford: Stanford University Press, 2007).
3. See Deana Heath, *Purifying Empire: Obscenity and Politics of Moral Regulation in Britain, India and Australia* (Cambridge: Cambridge University Press, 2010), p. 7.

4. James Whidden, 'The Generation of 1919', in A. Goldschmidt, A. Johnson and B.A. Salmoni (eds), *Re-Envisioning Egypt 1919–1952* (Cairo and New York: The American University in Cairo Press, 2005), p. 20.

5. Benedict Anderson, *Imagined Communities: Reflections on the Origins and Spreading of Nationalism* (London: Verso, 1991), p. 52. 'saw the novel and the newspaper as the typical medium for the creation and circulation of the concept of Nation, for the peculiar treatment of time, both individual and collective, they featured.

6. Raya Bint 'Ali Hamam and Sakinah Bint 'Ali Hamam migrated with their husbands from the Sa'id, to Kafr al-Zayyat in the Delta and Alexandria, in search of fortune. They had been active as prostitutes before, and in Alexandria they decided to open a drinking den-cum-brothel in the Laban area. In 1920 they killed, with the help of their husbands, 17 women, some of them prostitutes, some others occasional acquaintances they enticed to the brothel, suffocated, robbed of any valuables they carried, and buried in the basement. They were arrested, tried and executed in 1921. See Shaun T. Lopez, 'Madams, murders and the media: Akhbar al Hawadith and the emergence of a mass culture in 1920s Egypt', in A. Goldschmidt, A. Johnson and B.A. Salmoni (eds), *Re-Envisioning Egypt*, pp. 371–98. See also Salah 'Isà, *Rigal Raya wa Sakinah, sirah siyyasiyyah wa ijtima'iyyah* (al-Qahirah: Dar al-Ahmadi li-l-Nashr, 2002) and Yunan Labib Rizq, 'The women killers', *Al-Ahram Weekly Online*, 17–23 June 1999, no. 343. Available at http://weekly.ahram.org.eg/1999/434/chrncls.htm (accessed 1 May 2017).

7. Lopez, 'Madams', p. 372.

8. Fundamental works on gender, modernity, nationalism and citizenship in Egypt include Beth Baron's *Egypt as a Woman: Nationalism, Gender and Politics* (Berkeley: University of California Press, 2004) and *The Women's Awakening in Egypt: Culture, Society, and the Press* (New Haven, CT: Yale University Press, 1994); Badran, *Feminists*; Selma Botman, *Engendering Citizenship in Egypt* (New York: Columbia University Press, 1999); Lisa Pollard, *Nurturing the Nation: The Family Politics of Modernizing, Colonizing and Liberating Egypt, 1805–1923* (Berkeley: University of California Press, 2005); Hanan Kholoussy, *For Better, for Worse: The Marriage Crisis that Made Modern Egypt* (Stanford, CA: Stanford University Press, 2010); *Leila Ahmad, Women and Gender in Islam* (New Haven, CT: Yale University Press, 1992); See el-Shakry, *The Great Social Laboratory*; Mona Russell, *Creating the New Egyptian Woman: Consumerism, Educaton, and National Identity, 1863–1922* (New York: Palgrave McMillan, 2004).

9. Botman, *Engendering Citizenship*, p. 23.

10. See Baron, *Egypt as a Woman*, especially pp. 40–57.

11. Shaykh Mahmud Abu-al-'Uyun, 'al-Marahid al-'Umumiyyah' ('public toilets'), *al-Ahram*, 15 December 1923.

12. To reconstruct patterns of social interaction among popular classes, sources such as literature and folklore can be useful. Naguib Mahfouz's trilogy characters Zubaydah and Zannubah, for instance, show us how loose women were more integrated than marginalised in neighbourhood life. Social stigma was more a

hegemonic construction than a lived social reality for many sex workers, who, in fact, left the trade upon marriage without this resulting in their husbands' stigmatisation. On the 'imagined' quality of a virtuous and homogeneous national community created by hegemonic groups, see also Hanan Hammad, 'Between Egyptian "national purity" and "local flexibility": Prostitution in al-Mahallah al-Kubra in the frst half of the 20th century', *Journal of Social History* 44/2 (2011), pp. 251–83.

13. Shaykh Mahmud Abu-l-'Uyun, 'al-'afaf yantahib', *al-Ahram*, 8 December 1923.

14. Abdallah al-Nadim, *al-A'dad al Kamilah li-Majallat al-Ustadh* (Cairo: al-Hay'ah al Misriyyah al-'Ammah li-l-Kitab, 1998), pp. 132–40; pp. 395–99.

15. Muhammad Farid, a nationalist leader, writer and lawyer, was the main supporter of Mustafa Kamil, the founder of the Egyptian Nationalist Party. After his death in 1908, he took the lead of the party until his own death 1918.

16. Hammad, 'Between Egyptian "national purity"', p. 772.

17. Shaykh Mahmud Abu-al-'Uyun, 'Min Agil Qublah' ('because of a kiss'), *al-Ahram*, 19 November 1923.

18. Fikri Abaza (1896–1979), journalist and politician, member of the Nationalist Party, *al-Hizb al-Watani*. He seated in the Administrative Committee in 1921 and was MP in 1926. As a journalist, he worked for several major periodicals, among which *al-Ahram* and *al-Musawwar*.

19. Eventually the government passed a law about the establishment of sex-segregated beaches for women. See Walter Armbrust, *Mass Culture and Modernism in Egypt* (Cambridge: Cambridge University Press, 1996), pp. 75–86.

20. Shaykh Mahmud Abu-al-'Uyun, 'Ala Mar'ah min al-Hukumah wa Misma', ('under the eyes and the ears of the government'), *al-Ahram*, 20 November 1923.

21. See Yunan Labib Rizq, 'Back roads', *al-Ahram Weekly Online*, 7–13 June 2001, no. 537. Available at http://weekly.ahram.org.eg/2001/537/chrncls.htm (accessed 1 May 2017).

22. Mahmud Abu al-'Uyun, 'Fada'ih La Hadd Laha', *al-Ahram*, 12 December 1923.

23. Ibid.

24. Mahmud Abu al-'Uyun, 'Kitab Min Shaykh Haram', *al-Ahram*, 28 November 1923.

25. Mahmud Abu al-'Uyun, 'Chastity screams!', *al-Ahram*, 8 December 1923. See also Chapter 3.

26. Ara' al-Wuzarat, *al-Ahram*, 26 August 1926.

27. Lopez, 'Madams', p. 81.

28. On the Raya and Sakina's case see Takla, 'Murder in Alexandria'.

29. On 27 November 1917, Filippidis was sentenced by the Court of First Instance of Cairo Governorate for taking bribes from subordinates, prisoners and politicians, between 1913 and 1916, for a total amount of 784 Egyptian pounds. On the following 30 November, Cairo criminal court sentenced him to

a five-year prison sentence with forced labour. His wife Asma', who also played an active role in the affair, was sentenced to one year imprisonment.

30. Willis, *Anti-Christ*, p. 32. The demonisation of non-normative sexualities, more pointedly homosexuality, and the use of sexual themes to express political criticism, has been studied by Ehud Toledano with reference to Khedive 'Abbas (1849–54) whose alleged homosexuality was used by Egyptian nationalists to call into question the Turco-Circassian leadership's ability to rule the country. See Ehud Toledano, *State and Society in Mid-Nineteenth Century* (Cambridge: Cambridge University Press, 2003), p. 114.

31. 'Qadiyat-al-Raqiq al-Abyad', *al-Ahram*, 4 December 1923.

32. *Al-Ahram*, 27 December 1923.

33. WL, 4/IBS/6/031.

34. Hanan Kholoussy, 'The nationalization of marriage in monarchical Egypt', in A. Goldschmidt, A. Johnson and B.A. Salmoni (eds), *Re-Envisioning Egypt*, pp. 317–50.

35. Hanan Kholoussy, 'Talking about a revolution: Gender and the politics of marriage in early twentieth century Egypt'. Available at http://www.grconsorti um.org/pdf/V.1-2PDF/v12_knoloussy.pdf (accessed 1 May 2017). See also Kholoussy's monographic work, *For Better, for Worse*.

36. Marriage of minors, polygamy and divorce were all extensively debated issues. Since the beginning of the twentieth century, a number of laws and proposals were formulated in order to reform the Islamic personal law in relation with marriage and divorce (*talaq*). As evidence of the important place of marriage in the nationalist agenda, politicians passed major pieces of legislation in 1920, 1923, 1929 and 1931. These laws were preceded by a proposal for the reform of marital law dating back to 1914. In March 1914, in fact, deputy member Zakariyyah Bey Namiq submitted a bill on marital issues, among which a proposal to set the legal female age for marriage at 16 (*tahdid sinn-al-zawaj*). This triggered a heated debate in the press, opposing modernist reformers to conservative Muslim authorities who were against any change to religiously sanctioned practices. For some instances of press articles on the legal marriage age controversy, see the series of articles entitled 'Tahdid Sinn-al-Zawaj', published in *al-Ahram* on 11 December 1923, 17 December 1923, 19 December 1923, 22 December 1923, 26 December 1923, 27 December 1923 and 28 December 1923.

37. Muhammad al-Bardisi, 'A'rad al-Shaban 'an al-Zawaj', Letter to the Editor, *al-Ahram*, 15 December 1913.

38. Ibid. '[M]ost young men earn no more than 5 pounds a month, and it takes an extremely long time for them to set aside from this paltry sum sufficient funds for a dowry and the costs of a wedding, let alone the expenses necessary for the upbringing of their children.'

39. Ibrahim Ahmad Fathi, 'A'rad al-Shaban 'an al-Zawaj', Letter to the Editor, *al-Ahram*, 19 December 1913.

40. 'Ta'adil La'ihat- al -'ahirat', *al-Ahram*, 13 April 1926. A previous report had been issued also by Chief of Cairo City Police Russell Pasha, to the attention of the Ministry of Interior, on the harmful effects of licensed prostitution and the impossibility to guarantee public security under the existing conditions, due to the Capitulary privileges protecting foreigner entrepreneurs of commercial sex and sex workers.

41. Ibid.

42. Report of the Commission of Enquiry into the Problem of Licensed Prostitution in Egypt (Cairo: Government Press, 1935).

43. Ibid., p. 7.

44. Ibid., p. 38.

45. Cooper, *Cairo in the War*, p. 115.

46. Ibid. Artemis Cooper thus describes the Wagh-al-Birkah during World War II: 'the prostitutes sat fanning themselves on the hundreds of little balconies that overlooked the long narrow street, and called down to the man below; while, at ground level, there were little booths, screened by a single curtain. One of these bore the legend "Esperanto spoken here". The booths spilled into alleyways running off the Berka, with peep-shows and pornographic cabaret.'

47. Figures in Cooper, *Cairo in the War*, p. 136; p. 162.

48. Hughes, *While Shepheard's Watched*, p. 53.

49. Ibid., p.54.

50. Lisa Pollard, 'From husbands and housewives to suckers and whores: Marital-political anxieties in the 'House of Egypt', 1919–1948', *Gender & History* 21/3 (2009), pp. 647–69.

51. Ibid., p. 647.

52. Ibid., pp. 663–4.

53. Scott Long, Human Rights Watch Report, *In a Time of Torture: the Assault on Justice in Egypt's Crackdown on Homosexual Conduct* (New York: Human Right Watch, 2004), pp. 133–4. Available at https://www.hrw.org/report/2004/02/29/time-torture/assault-justice-egypts-crackdown-homosexual-conduct (accessed 1 May 2017).

54. See Kholoussy, 'Monitoring', p. 682.

Conclusion

1. Timothy Mitchell, *Colonizing Egypt* (Berkeley: University of California Press, 1991), p. ix.

BIBLIOGRAPHY

Archives, Libraries and Special Collections

The Australian War Memorial (AWM), Canberra.

The Historical Archive of the Ministry of Foreign Affairs (ASMAE, Archivio Storico del Ministero degli Affari Esteri), Rome: Italian Consular Courts Penal Cases (Casi Penali Tribunali Consolari del Cairo), 1916–1932.

Dar al-Kutub, National Library, Cairo.

Dar al-Watha'iq, National Egyptian Archives, Cairo.

The Italian National Archives (ACS, Archivio Centrale dello Stato), Rome: Ministero dell'Interno, Direzione Generale di Pubblica Sicurezza, Centro Nazionale di Coordinamento delle Operazioni di Polizia Criminale, INTERPOL, 1923–1961, 13.180.3.

The National Archives (NA), London: Cairo Consular Courts, 1830–1965, FO 841.

The Rare Books and Special Collections Library, American University in Cairo.

The Women's Library (WL), London School of Economics: International Bureau for the Protection of Women and Children – National Vigilance Association (NVA); International Bureau Country Files, 1905–1939, 4/IBS/6/020-051; Association for Moral and Social Hygiene (AMSH): Armed Forces, 1903–1945, 4/AMSH02-065.

Unpublished Papers

Attwood, Rachel, 'Vice beyond the pale: Representing white slavery in Britain, 1880–1912' (Unpublished Ph.D. Thesis, UCL, 2013).

Bier, Laura, 'Prostitution and the marriage crisis: Bachelors and competing masculinities in 1930s Egypt', paper presented at the annual meeting of the Middle Eastern Studies Association, San Francisco, CA, 20 November 2001.

Dunne, Bruce W., 'Sexuality and the civilizing process in modern Egypt' (Unpublished Ph.D. Thesis, Georgetown University, 1996).

Kalkan, Ibrahim Khalil, 'Prostitution in the Ottoman Empire', paper presented at the annual meeting of the Middle Eastern Studies Association, Montreal, Canada, November 2007.

Takla, Nefertiti, 'Murder in Alexandria: The gender, sexual and class politics of criminality in Egypt, 1914–1921' (Unpublished Ph.D. thesis, UCLA, 2016).

Government Publications

Census of Egypt, 1917, 1927 and 1937.

Nizarah al-Dakhiliyyah, Idarah 'Umum al-Sahhah, Dikritat wa Lawa'ih Sahhiyyah (al-Matba'ah al-Amiryyah bi-Bulaq: al-Qahirah, 1895).

Nizarah al-Dakhiliyyah, al-Qawanin al-Idariyyah wa al-Gina'iyyah, al-Juz' al-Rabi' al-Qawanin al-Khususiyyah (al-Matba'ah al-Amiriyyah bi-Bulaq: al-Qahirah, n.d.).

al-Qarrarat wa al Manshurat al-Sadirah sanat-1885 (al-Matba'ah al-Amiriyyah bi-Bulaq, 1886).

Taqrir Sanawi 'an A'mal Taftish Sahhat al-Qahirah li-sanawat 1922, 1925, 1927 (al-Matba'ah al-Amiriyyah bi-l-Qahira, n.d.).

Wizarat al-Dakhiliyyah, Nidam al-Bulis wa al-Idarah- Lai'hah bi-sha'an buyut al-'ahirat, 1936.

Wizarat al-Dakhiliyyah. Bulis Madinat-al-Qahirah, Taqrir Sanawi-al-'am 1930 (al-Matb'ah al-Amiriyyah bi-Bulaq, 1931).

Wizarat al-Dakhiliyyah. Bulis Madinat-al-Qahirah, Taqrir Sanawi al-'am 1933 (al-Matba'ah al-Amiriyyah bi-Bulaq, 1934).

Wizarat-al-Dakhiliyyah. Bulis Madinat-al-Qahirah, Taqrir Sanawi al-'am 1935 (al-Matba'ah al-Amiriyyah bi-Bulaq, 1936).

Wizarat-al-Dakhiliyyah. Bulis Madinat-al-Qahirah, Taqrir Sanawi al-'am 1937 (al-Matba'ah al-Amiriyyah bi-Bulaq, 1938).

Wizarat al-Dakhiliyyah. Bulis Madinat-al-Qahirah, Taqrir Sanawi li-sanatay 1942–1943 (al-Matba'ah al-Amiriyyah bi-l-Qahira, 1944).

Wizarat al-Dakhiliyyah. Bulis Madinat-al-Qahirah, Taqrir Sanawi li-sanat- 1944 (al-Matba'ah al-Amiriyyah bi-Bulaq bi-l-Qahira, 1944).

Wizarat al-Sahha al-'Umumiyyah, Taqrir Sanawi 'an A'mal Taftish Sahhat-al-Qahirah li-'am 1936 (al-Matba'ah al-Amiriyyah bi-Bulaq, 1939).

Wizarat al-Sahhah al-'Umumiyyah, Taqrir Sanawi 'an sanat-1937 (Dar al-Tiba'ah al-Fayyada: al-Qahirah, 1939).

Wizarat-al-Sahhah al-'Umumiyyah, Taqrir Sanawi li-sanat 1943 (Matba'ah al-Amiriyyah bi-Bulaq bi-l-Qahirah).

Wizarat-al-Sahhah al-'Umumiyyah, al-Taqrir al-Sanawi al-'amm li-sanat 1946 (Matba'ah al-Amiriyyah bi-Bulaq bi-l-Qahirah).

Books and Articles

Abu Bakr, 'Abd al-Wahhab, Mujtama' al-Qahirah al-Sirri, 1900–1951 (Cairo: Maktabah Madbuli, 1987).

Abu al-'Uyun, Mahmud, Mushkilah al-Bigha' al-Rasmi (al-Qahirah: Matba'at al-Hilal, 1933).

Abu Lughod, Janet, Cairo: 1001 Years of the City Victorious (Princeton, NJ: Princeton University Press, 1971).

Abugideiri, Hibba, Gender and the Making of Modern Medicine in Colonial Egypt (Farnham: Ashgate, 2010).

———— 'The scientisation of culture: Colonial medicine's construction of Egyptian womanhood, 1893–1929', *Gender & History*, 16/1 (2004), pp. 83–98.

Abu Lughod, Lila, 'The romance of resistance: Tracing transformations of power through Bedouin women', *American Ethnologist* 17/1 (1990), pp. 41–55.

Aldridge, James, *Cairo* (London: McMillan, 1969).

Alloula, Malek, *The Colonial Harem*. Translation by Myrna Godzich and Wlad Godzich; introduction by Barbara Harlow (Minneapolis: University of Minnesota Press, 1987).

Amster, Ellen J., *Medicine and the Saints. Science, Islam, and the Colonial Encounter in Marocco, 1877–1956* (Austin: University of Texas Press, 2014).

Anderson, Benedict, *Imagined Communities: Reflections on the Origins and Spreading of Nationalism* (London: Verso, 1991).

A Non-Military Journal or Observations Made in Egypt, by an Officer upon the Staff of the British Army (London: T. Cadell and W. Davies, 1803).

Appadurai, Arjun, *Modernity at Large: Global Dimensions of Globalization* (Minneapolis: University of Minnesota Press, 1998).

Armbrust, Walter, *Mass Culture and Modernism in Egypt* (Cambridge: Cambridge University Press, 1996).

Arnaud, Jean Luc, *Le Caire: Mise en Place d'une Ville Moderne* (Arles: Sindbad Acted Sud, 1998).

Attwood, Rachel, 'Looking beyond "White Slavery": Trafficking, the Jewish Association, and the dangerous politics of migration control in England, 1890–1910', *Anti-Trafficking Review* 7 (2016), pp. 115–38.

———— 'Stopping the traffic: The National Vigilance Association and the international fight against the "white slave" trade', *Women's History Review* 24/3 (2015), pp. 325–50.

Auriant (pseudo), *Koutchouk-Hanem, l'almée de Flaubert* (Paris: Mercure de France, 1949).

Awad, Louis, *The Literature of Ideas in Egypt* (Atlanta, GA: Scholar Press, 1986).

el-Azhary Sonbol, Amira, *The Creation of a Medical Profession in Egypt* (Syracuse, NY: Syracuse University Press, 1991).

Badran, Margot, *Feminists, Islam, and Nation: Gender and the Making of Modern Egypt* (Princeton, NJ: Princeton University Press, 1995).

———— 'Dual liberation: Feminism and nationalism in Egypt, 1870s–1925', *Feminist Issues* 8/1 (1988), pp. 15–34.

Baer, Gabriel, 'Slavery in nineteenth century Egypt', *Journal of African History* 8/3 (1967), pp. 417–41.

Banerjee, Sumanta, *Dangerous Outcasts: Prostitutes in Nineteenth Century Bengal* (New York: Monthly Review Press, 1998).

Baron, Beth, *Egypt as a Woman: Nationalism, Gender, and Politics* (Berkeley: University of California Press, 2004).

———— *The Women's Awakening in Egypt: Culture, Society, and the Press* (New Haven, CT: Yale University Press, 1994).

Barrett, James W., 'Management of venereal diseases in Egypt during the War', *The British Medical Journal* (1919), pp. 125–7.

Bartley, Paula. *Prostitution Prevention and reform in England, 1860–1914* (London: Routledge, 2000).

Basilah, Nazik, *Mudhakkirat Badi'ah Masabni* (Beirut: Dar Maktabat al-Hayat, 1960).

Bean, C.E.W., *Gallipoli Correspondent. The Frontline Diary of C.E.W. Bean*. Selected and annotated by Kevin Fewster (Sydney: Allen & Unwin, 1983).

Beherens-Abouseif, Doris, *Azbakiyya and its Environs from Azbak to Isma'il, 1476–1879* (Cairo: Institut Français d'Archéologie Orientale, 1985).

Bernstein, Laurie, *Sonia's Daughters: Prostitutes and their Regulation in Imperial Russia* (Berkeley: University of California Press, 1991).

Berque, Jacques, *Égypte: Impérialisme et Révolution* (Paris: Gallimard, 1967).

Biancani, Francesca, 'International migration and sex work', in L. Kozma, C. Schayegh and A. Wishnitzer (eds), *A Global Middle East Mobility, Materiality and Culture in the Modern Age, 1880–1940* (London: I.B.Tauris, 2014), pp. 123–4.

Booth, Marylin, 'Between harem and houseboat, fallenness, gendered spaces and the female national subject in 1920s Egypt', in M. Booth (ed.), *Harem Histories, Envisioning Places and Living Spaces* (Durham, NC and London: Duke University Press, 2010).

———— 'From the horse's rump and the whorehouse keyhole: Ventriloquized memoirs as political voice in 1920s Egypt', *Maghreb Review* 32 (2007), pp. 233–61.

———— 'Unsafely at home: Narratives of sexual coercion in 1920s Egypt', *Gender & History* 16/3 (2004), pp. 744–68.

Botman, Selma, *Engendering Citizenship in Egypt* (New York: Columbia University Press, 1999).

Bristow, Edward J., *Vice and Vigilance: Purity Movements in Britain Since 1700* (Dublin: Gill and McMillan, 1977).

Brugger, Suzanne, *Australians and Egypt, 1914–1919* (Melbourne: Melbourne, University Press, 1980).

Burckhardt, John Lewis, *Arabic Proverbs: Or the Manners and Customs of the Modern Egyptians Illustrated From Their Proverbial Sayings Current at Cairo* (London: Curzon Press, 1984).

Bey, Burtuqalis, *al-Bigha' aw Khatar al-'Aharah fi-Qutr al Misri*, translated by Dawud Effendi Barakat (Cairo: Matba'ah Hindiyyah, 1907).

Butler, Josephine E., *Personal Reminescences of a Great Crusade* (London: Horace Marshall and Son, 1911).

Chakrabarty, Dipesh, *Provincializing Europe: Postcolonial Thought and Historical Difference* (Princeton, NJ: Princeton University Press, 2007).

Chalcraft, John T., *The Striking Cabbies of Cairo and Other Stories: Crafts and Guilds in Egypt, 1860–1914* (Albany: State University of New York, 2004).

Chaturvedi, Vinayak (ed.), *Mapping Subaltern Studies and the Postcolonial* (London: Verso, 2000).

Chaumont, Jean-Michel, Rodriguez Garcia, Magaly and Paul Servais (eds), *Trafficking in Women 1924–1926, The Paul Kinsie Report for the League of Nations* (Geneva: UN, 2017).

Chiffoleau, Sylvia, *Médecines et Médecins en Égypte. Construction d'une Identité Professionnelle et Projet Medical* (Paris-Lyon: l'Harmattan/Maison de l'Orient Méditerranéen, 1997).

Clancy-Smith, Julia A., *Mediterraneans: North Africa and Europe in an Age of Migration, c.1800–1900* (Berkeley: University of California Press, 2011).

Clerget, Marcel, *Le Caire: Etudes de Géographie Urbaine et d'Histoire Économique* (Paris: Librairie Orientaliste Paul Geuthner, 1934).

Cooper, Artemis, *Cairo in the War, 1939–1945* (London: Hamish Hamilton, 1989).

Cooper, Elizabeth, *The Women of Egypt* (London: Hurst and Blackett, 1914).

Cooper, Frederick and Ann Laura Stoler, *Tensions of Empire: Colonial Cultures in a Bourgeois World* (Berkeley: University of California Press, 1997).

Corbain, Alain, *Women for Hire: Prostitution and Sexuality in France after 1850* (Cambridge: Cambridge University Press, 1990).

Cunningham, Alfred, *To-Day in Egypt, Its Administration, People and Politics* (London: Hurst and Blackett Limited, 1912).

Cuno, Kenneth, *The Pasha's Peasants: Lands, Society, and the Economy in Lower Egypt, 1740–1858* (Cambridge: Cambridge University Press, 1992).

Danielson, Virginia, *A Voice like Egypt: Umm Kulthum, Arab Song, and Egyptian Society in the Twentieth Century* (Chicago: Chicago University Press, 1987).

De Guerville, Amédée B., *New Egypt* (London: William Heinemann, 1906).

D'Erlanger, Henry, *The Last Plague of Egypt. A Survey of the Drug Traffic. With Plates* (London: Lovat, Dickson & Thompson, 1936).

Dozema, Jo, 'Loose women or lost women? The re-emergence of the myth of white slavery in contemporary dicourses of trafficking women', *Gender Issues* (2000), pp. 23–50.

Denon, Dominique Vivant, *Travels in Upper and Lower Egypt, in company with several divisions of the French Amy, during the campaigns of General Bonaparte in that country and published under his immediate patronage by Vivant Denon. Embellished with numerous engravings. Translated by Arthur Atkin in 3 vols* (London: Longman & Rees, 1803).

Dougherty, Roberta L., 'Badi'a Masabni, artist and modernist, the Egyptian print media carnival of national identity', in W. Armbrust (ed.), *Mass Mediations, New Approaches to Popular Culture in the Middle East and Beyond* (Berkeley: University of California Press, 2000).

Dyer, Alfred S., *The European Slave Trade in English Girls, a Narrative of Facts* (London: Dyer Brothers, 1880).

Elgood, Percy, *Egypt and the Army* (Oxford: Oxford University Press, 1924).

el-Shakry, Omnia, *The Great Social Laboratory: Subjects of Knowledge in Colonial and Postcolonial Egypt* (Stanford: Stanford University Press, 2007).

Fahmy, Khaled, 'Modernizing Cairo: A revisionist account', in N. al Sayyad, I.A. Bierman and N. Rabbat (eds), *Making Cairo Medieval* (Lanham, MD: Lexington Books, 2005).

—— *All the Pasha's Men: Mehmet Ali, His Army and the Making of Modern Egypt* (Cairo: American University in Cairo Press, 2002).

—— 'Prostitution in Egypt in the Nineteenth Century', in E. Rogan (ed.), *Outside In: On the Margins of the Modern Middle East* (London: I.B.Tauris, 2002).

—— 'The police and the people in nineteenth century Egypt', *Die Welt des Islams* 39/9 (1999), pp. 340–77.

—— 'Law, medicine and society in nineteenth century Egypt', *Égypte-Monde Arabe* 34 (1998), pp. 17–52.

—— 'Women, medicine and power in nineteenth century Egypt', in L. Abu-Lughod (ed.), *Remaking Women: Feminism and Modernity in the Middle East* (Princeton, NJ: Princeton University Press, 1998).

Faraj, Fakhr Mikha'il, *Taqrir 'an Intishar al-Bigha' wa al-Amrad al-Tanassuliyyah bi-l-Qutr al-Masri wa ba'd al-Turuq al-Mumkin Ittiba'iha li-Muharibah* (al-Qahirah: al-Matba'ah al-'Asriyyah, 1924).

Ferhati, Barkahoum, 'Le danseuse prostituée dite "Ouled Naïl", entre mythe et réalitè (1830–1962). Des rapports sociaux et des pratiques concretes', *Clio. Femme, Genre, Histoire* 17 (2003), pp. 101–13.

Ferraro, Joanne M., 'Making a living: The sex trade in early modern Venice', *American Historical Review* 123/1 (2018), pp. 30–59.

Fewster, Kevin, 'The Wazza Riots, 1915', *Journal of the Australian War Memorial* 4 (1984), pp. 47–53.

Flaubert, Gustave, *Flaubert in Egypt: A Sensibility on Tour.* A Narrative Drawn from Gustave Flaubert's Travel Notes and Letters, translated from the French and edited by Francis Steegmuller (London: Bodley Head, 1972).

Flexner, Abraham, *Prostitution in Europe* (London: Richards, 1914).

Foucault, Michel, *The Birth of Biopolitics: Lectures at the Collège de France 1978–1979.* Edited by Michel Sennelert (Basingstoke: Palgrave Macmillan, 2008).

—— *Society Must be Defended. Lectures at the Collège de France, 1975–76.* Edited by Mauro Bertani and Alessandro Fontana, translated by David Macey (New York: Picador, 2003).

—— *Aesthetics, Method and Epistemology.* Edited by James Faubion (Harmondsworth: Penguin Books, 2000).

—— *Discipline and Punish, the Birth of the Prison.* Translated from the French by Alan Sheridan (New York: Vintage Books, 1995).

—— 'The subject and power', *Critical Inquiry* 8/4 (1982), pp. 777–95.

—— *The History of Sexuality, Vol. I. The Will to Knowledge,* translated from the French by Robert Hurley (New York: Vintage Books, 1980).

—— *The Birth of the Clinic: An Archaeology of Medical Perception* (London: Tavistock Publications, 1973).

—— *The Order of Things. An Archaeology of Human Sciences* (New York: Vintage Books, 1970).

—— *Madness and Civilization: A History of Insanity in the Age of Reason* (London: Tavistock Publications, 1967).

Fraser Rae, W., *Egypt To-Day* (London: Bentley and Sons, 1892).

Fredolin, M., *John Bull sur le Nil.* Introduction by Henri Le Verdier (Whitefish: Kessinger Publishing, 2010).

Gallagher, Nancy E., *Egypt's Other Wars: Epidemics and the Politics of Public Health* (Syracuse, NY: Syracuse University Press, 1990).

—— *Medicine and Power in Tunisia, 1790–1900* (Cambridge: Cambridge University Press, 1983).

Gasper, Mark. E., *The Power of Representation: Public, Peasants, and Islam* (Stanford, CA: Stanford University Press, 2009).

Gibson, Mary, *Prostitution and the State in Italy, 1860–1915* (Columbus: Ohio State University, 1999).

Gilfoyle, Timothy J., 'Prostitutes in history: From parables of pornography to metaphors of modernity', *The American Historical Review* 104/1 (1999), pp. 117–41.

—— 'Prostitutes in the archives: Problems and possibilities in documenting the history of sexuality', *American Archivist* 57/2 (1994), pp. 514–27.

Goldschmidt, Arthur, Amy J. Johnson and Barak A. Salmoni (eds), *Re-Envisioning Egypt, 1919–1952* (Cairo and New York: the American University in Cairo Press, 2005).

Grafftey-Smith, Laurence, *Bright Levant* (London: J. Murray, 1970).

Graham-Brown, Sarah, *Images of Women: The Portrayal of Women in Photography in the Middle East* (New York: Columbia University Press, 1988).

Gregory, Derek, 'Scripting Egypt, Orientalism and the cultures of travel', in J. Duncan and D. Gregory (eds), *Writes of Passage, Reading Travel Writing* (London: Routledge 1999).

Guy, Donna J., *Sex and Danger in Buenos Aires: Prostitution, Family and Nation in Argentina* (Lincoln and London: University of Nebraska Press, 1990).

Hall, Donald E. (ed.), *Muscular Christianity: Embodying the Victorian Age* (New York: Cambridge University Press, 1994).

Hammad, Hanan, *Industrial Sexuality. Gender, Urbanization, and Social Trasformation in Egypt* (Austin: University of Texas Press, 2016).

———— 'Between Egyptian "national purity" and "local flexibility": Prostitution in al-Mahallah al-Kubra in the frst half of the 20th century', *Journal of Social History* 44/2 (2011), pp. 251–83.

Hanna, Nelly, 'The urban history of Cairo around 1900', in J. Edwards (ed.), *Historians in Cairo: Essays in Honor of George Scanlon* (Cairo: Cairo University Press, 2000).

Hanssen, Jens, 'Public Morality and Marginality in Fin-de-Siècle Beyrut', in E. Rogan (ed.), *Outside In: On the Margins of the Middle East* (London: I.B.Tauris, 2002).

Harrison, Mark, 'The British Army and the problem of venereal disease in France and Egypt during the 1st World War', *Medical History* 39/2 (1995), pp. 133–58.

Harrison, Thomas S., *The Homely Diary of a Diplomat in the East* (Boston: Houghton Miffin Co., 1917).

Harsin, Jill, *Policing Prostitution in 19th Century Paris* (Princeton, NJ: Princeton University Press, 1985).

Harvey, David, *The Condition of Postmodernity: An Enquiry into the Origins of Cultural Change* (New York: Blackwell, 1990).

Hatem, Mervat, 'The Professionalization of Health and the Control of Women's Bodies as Modern Governmentalities in Nineteenth-century Egypt', in M.C. Zilfi (ed.), *Women in the Ottoman Empire: Middle Eastern Women in the Early Modern Era* (New York: Brill, 1997).

Hazbun, Waleed. 'The East as an Exhibit: Thomas Cook & Son and the Origins of the International Tourism Industry in Egypt', in P. Scranton and J.F. Davidson (eds), *The Business of Tourism: Place, Faith and History* (Philadelphia: University of Philadelphia Press, 2007).

Heath, Deana, *Purifying Empire: Obscenity and Politics of Moral Regulation in Britain, India and Australia* (Cambridge: Cambridge University Press, 2010).

Henriot, Christian, *Prostitution and Sexuality in Shanghai: A Social History, 1849–1949* (Cambridge: Cambridge University Press, 2001).

Hershatter, Gail, *Dangerous Pleasures: Prostitution and Modernity in Twentieth Century* (Berkeley: University of California Press, 1997).

———— 'Courtesans and streetwalkers: The changing discourses on Shanghai Prostitution, 1890–1949', *Journal of the History of Sexuality* 3/2 (1992), pp. 245–69.

Hifni, Ratibah, *Munira al Mahdiyya* (Cairo: Dal al-Shurouk, 2001).

Hilal, 'Imad, *al-Baghaya fi Misr. Dirasah Tarikhiyyah wa Igtima'iyyah, 1834–1949* (al-Qahirah: al-'Arabi, 2001).

———— *al-Raqiq fi Misr fi-l-Qarn al-Tasi' 'Ashar* (Cairo: al-'Arabi, 1999).

Howell, Philip, *Geographies of Regulation, Policing Prostitution in Nineteenth-Century Britain and the Empire* (Cambridge: Cambridge University Press, 2009).

———— 'Race, space and the regulation of prostitution in colonial Hong Kong', *Urban History* 31/2 (2004), pp. 229–48.

Hoyle, Mark, *Mixed Courts of Egypt* (London: Graham and Trotman, 1968).

Hubbard, Phil, *Sex and the City: Geography of Prostitution in the Urban West* (London: Ashgate, 1999).

Hughes, Pennethorne, *While Shepheard's Watched* (London: Chatto and Windus, 1949).

Humphreys, Andrew, *Grand Hotels of Egypt* (Cairo: American University in Cairo Press, 2012).

Hunwick, John, 'The same but different: Africans in slavery in the Mediterranean Muslim world', in J. Hunwick and E. Troutt Powell (eds), *The African Diaspora in the Mediterranean Muslim World* (Princeton, NJ: Princeton University Press, 2002).

Hyam, Ronald, *Empire and Sexuality: The British Experience* (Manchester: Manchester University Press, 1990).

Hunter, Mark, 'The materiality of eveyday sex: Thinking beyond "Prostitution"', *African Studies* 61/1 (2002), pp. 99–120.

Hunter, Robert F., 'Tourism and Empire: The Thomas Cook & Son Enterprise on the Nile, 1868–1914', *Middle Eastern Studies* 40/5 (2004), pp. 28–54.

———— 'Egypt's High Official in transition from a Turkish to a modern administrative elite, 1849–1879', *Middle Eastern Studies* 19/3 (1983), pp. 277–300.

'Isà, Salah, *Rigal Rayya wa Sakinah, sirah siyyasiyyah wa igtima'iyyah* (al-Qahirah: Dar-al-Ahmadi-li-l-Nashr, 2002).

al-Jabarti, *Napoleon in Egyp: al Jabarti's chronicles of the French Occupation, 1798*, edited and translated by Shmuel More (Princeton, NJ: Markus Wiener Press, 2003).

Jacob, Wilson Chacko, *Working Out Egypt: Effendi Masculinity and Subject Formation in Colonial Modernity, 1870–1940* (Durham, NC: Duke University Press, 2011).

Jagailloux, Serge, *La médicalization de l'Egypte au XIXe siècle, 1798–1918* (Paris: Editions Recherches sur les Civilizations, 1986).

Jallad, Fillib, *Qamus al-Qada' wa al-Idarah*, 3 vols (Alexandria: Lagoudakis, 1906).

Junaydi, Muhammad Farid, *al-Bigha', Bahth 'ilmi 'alami* (al-Qahirah: Matba'at al-Nasr, 1934).

Kholoussy, Hanan, *For Better, for Worse: The Marriage Crisis that Made Modern Egypt* (Stanford, CA: Stanford University Press, 2010).

———— 'Monitoring and medicalising male sexuality in semi-colonial Egypt', *Gender & History* 22/3 (2010), pp. 677–91.

Kitroeff, Alexander, *The Greeks in Egypt, 1919–1937: Ethnicity and Class* (London: Ithaca University Press, 1989).

Koprivec, Dasa, 'Aleksandrinke: življenje v Egiptu in doma', *Etnolog* 16/67 (2006), pp. 97–115.

Kozma, Liat. *Global Women, Colonial Ports. Prostitution in the Interwar Middle East* (Albany, NY: SUNY Press, 2017).

———— '"We, the sexologists ...": Arabic medical writing on sexuality', *Journal of the History of Sexuality* 22/3 (2013), pp. 426–45.

────── *Policing Egyptian Women: Sex, Law, and Medicine in Khedivial Egypt* (Syracuse, NY: Syracuse University Press, 2011).

────── 'Negotiating virginity: Narratives of defloration from late nineteenth-century Egypt', *Comparative Studies of South Asia, Africa and the Middle East* 24/1 (2004), pp. 55–65.

Kuhnke, LaVerne, *Lives at Risk: Public Health in Nineteenth Century Egypt* (Berkeley: University of California Press, 1990).

Lagrange, Frédéric, 'Women in the singing business, women in songs', *History Compass* 7/1 (2009), pp. 226–50.

────── 'Une Egypte libertine?', in F. Sanaugustin (ed.), *Parole, Signes, Mythes, Mélange offerts à Jamel Eddine Bencheikh* (Damas: IFEAD, 2001).

Laite, Julia. *Common Prostitutes and Ordinary Citizens: Commercial Sex in London 1885–1960* (London: Palgrave Macmillan 2011).

────── 'The Association of moral and social hygiene: Abolitionism and prostitution law in Britain (1915–1959)', *Women's History Review* 17/2 (2008), pp. 207–23.

Lane, Edward William, *An Account of the Manners and Customs of Modern Egyptian. The Definitive 1860 Edition Introduced by Jason Thompson* (Cairo: The American University in Cairo Press, 2006).

Lanver, Mak, British in Egypt: Community, Crime, and Crisis, 1882–1922 (London: I.B.Tauris, 2012).

Legg, Stephen, *Prostitution and the Ends of Empire. Scales, Governmentality, and Interwar India* (Durham, NC and London: Duke University Press, 2014).

────── 'Beyond the European province: Foucault and postcolonialism', in J.W. Crampton and S. Elden (eds), *Space, knowledge and power: Foucault and geography* (Aldershot: Ashgate, 2007).

Levine, Philippa, '"A multitude of unchaste women": Prostitution in the British Empire', *Journal of Women's History* 15/4 (2004), pp. 159–63.

────── *Prostitution, Race and Politics: Policing Imperial Disease in the British Empire* (London: Routledge, 2003).

────── 'The white slave trade and the British Empire: Crime, gender, and sexuality in criminal persecution', *Criminal Justice History* 17 (2002), pp. 133–46.

────── 'Battle colors: Race, sex, and colonial soldiery in War I', *Journal of Women's History* 9/4 (1998), pp. 104–30.

Limoncelli, Stephanie A., *The Politics of Trafficking, the First International Movement to Combat the Sexual Exploitation of Women* (Stanford, CA: Stanford University Press, 2010).

Lopez, Shaun T., Madams, murders and the media: Akhbar al Hawadith and the emergence of a mass culture in 1920s Egypt', in A. Goldschmidt, A.J. Johnson and B.A. Salmoni (eds), *Re-Envisioning Egypt, 1919–1952* (Cairo and New York: the American University in Cairo Press, 2005).

Mahfouz, Naguib, *The Cairo Trilogy* (New York, Toronto, London: Everyman's Library 2001).

────── *The Beginning and the End* (London: Anchor, 1989).

────── *Midaq Alley*, translated from Arabic by Trevor Le Gassick (London: Heinemann, 1966).

McClintock, Anne, *Imperial Leather: Race, Gender and Sexuality in the Colonial Context* (New York, London: Routledge, 1995).

McKeown, Adam, 'Global migration, 1846–1940', *Journal of World History* 15 (2004), pp. 155–89.

Mostyn, Trevor, *Egypt's Belle Epoque Cairo*, 1869–1952 (London: Quartet Book, 1989).

Mitchell, Timothy, *Rule of Experts: Egypt, Techno-politics, Modernity* (Berkeley: University of California Press, 2002).

——— *Questions of Modernity* (Minneapolis: University of Minnesota Press, 2000).

——— *Colonising Egypt* (Berkeley: University of California Press, 1991).

al-Muwaylihi, Muhammad, *What 'Isa Ibn Hisham Told or a Period of Time*. Translated by Roger Allen, foreword by Maria Golia, volume editor Philip F. Kennedy (New York: New York University Press, 2018).

Mynti, Cynthia. *Paris along the Nile, Architecture in Cairo from the Belle Epoque* (Cairo: American University in Cairo Press, 2015).

al-Nadim, *al-A'dad al Kamilah li-Majallat al-Ustadh* (Cairo: al- Hay'ah al Misriyyah al-'Ammah li-l-Kitab, 1998).

Olcott, Jocelyn, 'Public in a domestic sense: Sex work, nation-building, and class identification in modern Europe', *American Historical Review* 123/1 (2018), pp. 124–31.

Owen, Roger, *The Middle East in the World Economy, 1800–1914* (London and New York: Methuen, 1981).

Parent-Duchatelet, Alexandre J.B., *De la Prostitution dans la Ville de Paris* (Paris: J.B. Baillière, 1836).

Peck, Gunther W., 'White slavery and whiteness: A transnational view of the sources of working-class radicalism and racism', *Labor: Studies in Working-Class History of the Americas* 1/2 (2004), pp. 41–63.

Petricioli, Marta, *Oltre il mito: L'Egitto degli Italiani, 1919–1947* (Milan: Mondadori, 2007).

Pick, Daniel, *Faces of Degeneration: A European Disorder, c.1848–1918* (New York: Cambridge University Press, 1989).

Pliley, Jessica. 'Claims to protection: The rise and fall of feminist abolitionism in the League of Nations. Committee on the Traffic in Women and Children, 1919–1937', *Journal of Women's History* 22/4 (Winter 2010), pp. 90–113.

Pollard, Lisa, 'From husbands and housewives to suckers and whores: Marital-political anxieties in the 'House of Egypt', 1919–1948', *Gender & History* 21/3 (2009), pp. 647–69.

——— *Nurturing the Nation: The Family Politics of Modernizing, Colonizing, and Liberating Egypt, 1805–1923* (Berkeley: University of California Press, 2005).

Prestel, Joseph Ben, *Emotional Cities: Debates on Urban Change in Berlin and Cairo, 1860–1910* (Oxford: Oxford University Press, 2017).

Purdom, Charles Benjamin, *Everyman at War: Sixty Personal Narratives of the War* (London and Toronto: J.M. Dent, 1930).

Raymond, André, *Cairo* (Cambridge: Harvard University Press, 2000).

Reynolds, Nancy Y., *A City Consumed: Urban Commerce, the Cairo Fire, and the Politics of Decolonization in Egypt* (Stanford, CA: Stanford University Press, 2012).

——— 'Salesclerks, sexual danger, and national identity in Egypt in the 1920s and 1940s', *Journal of Women's History* 23/3 (Fall 2011), pp. 63–88.

Robinson Dunne, Diane, *The Harem Slavery and British Imperial Culture: Anglo-Muslim Relations in the Late Nineteenth Century* (Manchester: Manchester University Press, 2006).

Rodenbeck, John, 'Awalim, or the persistence of error', in J. Edwards (ed.), *Historians in Cairo. Essays in Honour of John Scallon* (Cairo: American University in Cairo Press, 2002).

Rogan, Eugene (ed.), *Outside In: On the Margins of the Modern Middle East* (London: I.B.Tauris, 2002).

Rosen, Ruth, *The Lost Sisterhood, Prostitution in America, 1900–1918* (Baltimore, MD: Johns Hopkins University, 1982).

Ruiz, Mario M., 'Manly spectacles and imperial soldiers in wartime Egypt, 1914–1919', *Middle Eastern Studies* 43/3 (2009), pp. 351–71.

Russell, Mona L., *Creating the New Egyptian Woman: Consumerism, Education, and National Identity, 1836–1922* (New York: Palgrave Macmillan, 2004).

Russell Pasha, Thomas, *Egyptian Service: 1902–1946* (London: J. Murray, 1949).

Ryzova, Lucie, *The Age of the Efendiyya, Passages to Modernity in National-Colonial Egypt* (Oxford: Oxford University Press, 2014).

Schayegh, Cyrus, *Who is Knowledgeable is Strong: Science, Class, and the Formation of Modern Iranian Society, 1900–1950* (Berkeley: California University Press, 2004).

Semerdijan, Elyse, *Off the Straight Path: Illicit Sex, Law and Community in Ottoman Aleppo* (New York: Syracuse University Press, 2008).

Shahin, Muhammad, *Taqrir min-Mukafahat-al-Amrad al-Zahriyyah bi-l-Qutr al-Masri* (Cairo: n.p., 1933).

Sharkey, Heather J., *American Evangelicals in Egypt: Missionaries Encounters in an Age of Empire* (Princeton, NJ: Princeton University Press, 2008).

Sladen, Douglas, *Oriental Cairo, the City of the Arabian Nights* (London: Hurst and Blackett, 1911).

Srebernič, J., 'Die Wanderbegung in der Unmbegung von Görz', *Jahresbericht der Mädchenlyzeums der armen Schulchwestern de Notre Dame in Görz* (1914), pp. 5–17.

Stead, W.T., *'The Maiden Tribute of Modern Babylon.' The Report of the Secret Commission by W.T. Stead*, edited and with annotations and an introductory essay by Antony E. Simpson (Lambertville: True Bill Press, 2007).

St. John, Bayle, *Village life in Egypt*, 2 vols (New York: Arno Press, 1973).

Stoler, Ann Laura, *Carnal Knowledge and Imperial Power: Race and the Intimate in Colonial Rule* (Berkeley: University of California Press, 2002).

——— *Race and the Education of Desire* (Durham, London: Duke University Press, 1995).

——— 'Making Empire respectable: The politics of race and sexual morality in the 20th century colonial culture', *American Ethnologist* 16/4 (1989), pp. 643–60.

Tarrot, Charles, *The Maiden Tribute, a Study of the White Slave Traffic of the Nineteenth Century* (London: Frederick Muller Limited, 1959).

Tawhidah, *Taqatiq al Sitt Tawhidah, al-Mughanniyah al-Shahirah fi Alf Layla wa Layla* (Cairo: Dal al Ma'rusah, 1924).

Thomson, Alistair, *Anzac Memories: Living with the Legend* (Melbourne: Oxford University Press, 1994).

Thornton, Guy, *With the Anzacs in Cairo: the Tale of a Great Fight* (London: Allenson, 1916).

Toledano, Ehud, *Slavery and Abolition in the Ottoman Middle East* (Seattle: University of Washington Press, 1998).

——— *State and Society in Mid-Nineteenth Century Egypt* (Cambridge: Cambridge University Press, 1990).

Tolerton, Jane, *Ettie: a Life of Ettie Rout* (Auckland: Penguin, 1992).

——— *Ettie Rout: New Zealand's Safe Sex Pioneer* (Auckland: Penguin, 2015).

Troutt Powell, Eve M., *Tell This in My Memory: Stories of Enslavement from Egypt, Sudan, and the Ottoman Empire* (Stanford, CA: Stanford University Press, 2012).

──────── 'Will that subaltern ever speak? Finding African slaves in the historiography of the Middle East', in I. Gershoni, A. Singer and Y. Hakan Erdem (eds), *Middle East Historiography: Narrating the Twentieth Century* (Seattle: University of Washington Press, 2006).

Tucker, Judith, *Women in Nineteenth Century Egypt* (Cambridge: Cambridge University Press, 1985).

Van Nieuwkerk, Karin, *"A Trade like any Other": Singers and Dancers in Egypt* (Austin: University of Texas Press, 1995).

Vitalis, Robert, *When Capitalists Collide. Business Conflict and the End of Empire in Egypt* (Berkeley: University of California Press, 1995).

Walkowitz, Judith R., *City of Dreadful Delights: Narratives of Sexual Danger in Late Victorian London* (Chicago: Chicago University Press, 1992).

──────── *Prostitution and Victorian Society: Women, Class and the State* (Cambridge: Cambridge University Press, 1982).

Walz, Terence and Kenneth M. Cuno, *Race and Slavery in the Middle East: Histories of Trans-Saharan Africans in 19th Century Egypt, Sudan, and the Ottoman Mediterranean* (Cairo: American University in Cairo Press, 2010).

Walz, Terence, 'Black slavery in Egypt', in J.R. Willies (ed.), *Slaves and Slavery in Muslim Africa* (London: Frank Cass, 1985).

Watson, Nick J., Stuart Weir and Stephen Friend, 'The development of Muscular Christianity in Victorian Britain and beyond', *Journal of Religion and Society* 7 (2005), pp. 1–21.

White, Luise, *Comforts of Home: Prostitution in Colonial Nairobi* (Chicago: University of Chicago Press, 1990).

Williams, H.R., *An ANZAC on the Western Front: the Personal Recollections of an Australian Infantryman from 1916 to 1918* (Barnsley: Pen and Sword Military, 2012).

Willis, N.W., *Anti-Christ in Egypt* (London: Anglo-Eastern Publishing Company Co., 1914).

Young, Elise G., *Gender and the Nation Building in the Middle East: the Political Economy of Health from the Mandate Palestine to Refugee Camps in Jordan* (London: I.B.Tauris, 2011).

Ze'evi, Dror, *Producing Desire. Changing Sexual Discourse in the Ottoman Middle East, 1500–1900* (Los Angeles and Berkeley: University of California Press, 2006).

Websites

Chung, Frank, 'Underbellydance: How a brush with the white slave trade sparked the first battle of the Anzacs', 2 April 2015. Available at http://www.news.com.au/national/anzac-day/underbellydance-how-a-brush-with-the-white-slave-trade-sparked-the-first-battle-of-the-anzacs/news-story/123d51fb53067b95ce11650fe43faf33 (accessed 1 May 2017).

Howell, Philip, 'Historical geographies of the regulation of prostitution in Britain and the British Empire'. Available at http://www.geog.cam.ac.uk/research/projects/prostitutionregulation/ (accessed 1 May 2017).

Irwin, Mary Ann, 'White Slavery as a Metaphor: Anatomy of a Moral Panic', *Ex Post Facto: the History Journal*, Vol. V (1996). Available at http://www.walnet.org/csis/papers/irwin-wslavery.html (accessed 1 May 2017).

Kholoussy, Hanan, 'Talking about a revolution: Gender and the politics of marriage in early twentieth century Egypt'. Available at http://www.grconsortium.org/pdf/V.1-2PDF/v12_knoloussy.pdf (accessed 1 May 2017).

Labib Rizq, Yunan, 'Safety first', *al-Ahram Weekly Online*, 6–12 December 2001, no. 563. Available at http://weekly.ahram.org.eg/2001/563/chrncls.htm (accessed 1 May 2017).

——— 'Backroads', *al-Ahram Weekly Online*, 7–13 June 2001, no. 537. Available at http://weekly.ahram.org.eg/2001/537/chrncls.htm (accessed 1 May 2017).

——— 'The women killers', *Al-Ahram Weekly Online*, 17–23 June 1999, no. 343. Available at http://weekly.ahram.org.eg/1999/434/chrncls.htm (accessed 1 May 2017).

Lagrange, Frédéric, 'Quand l'Egypt se chantat, taqatiq et chansons légerès au début du XX siècle'. Available at www.mapagenoos.fr/fredlag (accessed 1 May 2017).

Long, Scott, Human Rights Watch Report, *In a Time of Torture: the Assault on Justice in Egypt's Crackdown on Homosexual Conduct* (New York: Human Right Watch, 2004), pp. 133–4. Available at https://www.hrw.org/report/2004/02/29/time-torture/assault-justice-egypts-crackdown-homosexual-conduct (accessed 1 May 2017).

Ryzova, Lucie, 'Strolling in enemy territory', proceedings of the conference *Divercities. Contested Space and Urban Identities in Beirut, Cairo and Tehran* (2013). Available at http://www.perspectivia.net/publikationen/orient-institut-studies/3-2015/ryzova_strolling (accessed 1 January 2018).

N.a., 'The road to Gallipoli: the Anzacs in Cairo', *Mudgee Guardian*, 20 April 2015. Available at http://www.mudgeeguardian.com.au/story/3020538/the-road-to-gallipoli-the-anzacs-in-egypt/ (accessed 1 May 2017).

Newspapers

al-Ahram [The Pyramids], 1913–1926
Blessed Be Egypt, 1915
Egyptian Gazette, 1913–1925
Morning Post, 1923
Soča, 1890; 1910

INDEX